BY RONALD C. WHITE

Lincoln in Private: What His Most Personal Reflections Tell Us About Our Greatest President

American Ulysses: A Life of Ulysses S. Grant

A. Lincoln: A Biography

The Eloquent President: A Portrait of Lincoln Through His Words

Lincoln's Greatest Speech: The Second Inaugural

Liberty and Justice for All: Racial Reform and the Social Gospel

An Unsettled Arena: Religion and the Bill of Rights (editor, with Albright G. Zimmerman)

Partners in Peace and Education (editor, with Eugene J. Fisher)

American Christianity: A Case Approach (with Garth Rosell and Louis B. Weeks)

The Social Gospel: Religion and Reform in Changing America (with C. Howard Hopkins)

LINCOLN IN PRIVATE

All this is not the result of accident– It

a philosophical cause– Without the

tution and the Union, we could not

attained the result; but even these, a

the primary cau great prosperity

There is som these, entw

itself mor human

That so ple of

to all"– clears th

for al and, by

quence all.

than a –

The asse le, at th

was the " which

proved an to us– The

and the Constitution, are the picture

ver, subsequently framed around it–

The picture was made, not to conceal

destroy the apple; but to adorn, a

preserve it– The picture was made fo

apple– not the apple for the picture–

So let us act, that neither picture, or

shall ever be blurred, or bruised or broken–

That we may so act, we must study,

Lincoln IN PRIVATE

What His Most Personal Reflections Tell Us About Our Greatest President

RONALD C. WHITE

RANDOM HOUSE
NEW YORK

Published in the United States by Random House, an imprint and division
of Penguin Random House LLC, New York.

Random House and the House colophon are registered trademarks
of Penguin Random House LLC.

Hardback ISBN 9781984855091
Ebook ISBN 9781984855107

Printed in the United States of America on acid-free paper

randomhousebooks.com

2 4 6 8 9 7 5 3 1

First Edition

Book design by Victoria Wong

For my wife, Cynthia Conger White

Contents

Author's Note

Spelling in the nineteenth century was far from regular or consistent. On a few occasions, I have modernized spelling for the sake of clarity. In the appendix, I have retained all of Lincoln's spelling.

Prologue

It was the spring of 1863, and President Abraham Lincoln faced a chorus of critics after two grueling years of civil war. While Union and Confederate forces fought, the Northern public was becoming increasingly restless. If the North, with a larger army and greater industrial resources, had believed in 1861 they would win the war quickly, by 1863, what was becoming known as "Mr. Lincoln's war," struggled on with no end in sight.

Within the North, a movement arose that wanted to preserve the Union "as it was"—that is, with slavery. A faction of the Democratic Party, known as Peace Democrats or Copperheads, advocated a restoration of the Union through a negotiated settlement with the South. In their protests, they fulminated against Lincoln, charging that he was a tyrannical despot, and the war a means to enlarge presidential power.[1]

That spring, rallies in Northern cities complained of Lincoln's handling of the arrest and trial of Clement Vallandigham, a prominent Ohio Copperhead leader. Shortly after a rowdy protest meeting on May 16 in Albany, New York, Lincoln received the "Albany Resolves," ten resolutions demanding the president "maintain the rights of States and the liberties of the citizen."[2]

As Lincoln began to compose a reply to the protesters, Iowa

congressman James F. Wilson entered the president's office. Observing Lincoln writing at his desk, Wilson expressed his admiration that the president could compose yet another of his eloquent letters from scratch, especially at this moment of heightened anxiety.

Lincoln demurred. "I had it nearly all there," he said, pointing to an open desk drawer.

"It was in disconnected thoughts, which I had jotted down from time to time on separate scraps of paper." The president explained this was the way he saved "my best thoughts on the subject." He told Wilson, "I never let one of those ideas escape me."[3]

LINCOLN DID NOT want his "best thoughts" to escape him, but, across the years, they have escaped us. Over his lifetime, Lincoln wrote countless private notes for his eyes only—scribbled words to capture ideas and insights about the myriad problems and issues he faced. Never expecting anyone else to read them, he left them undated, untitled, and unsigned. While questions remain as to the dates of some of the notes, the identity of their author was never in doubt. We know they all came from Lincoln because of his easily identifiable penmanship: clear and angular in his younger years, then over time gradually smaller and more rounded.[4]

We also know that he himself thought these notes were important. On August 6, 1860, in the midst of that year's presidential campaign, Republican candidate Lincoln sent David Davis, his campaign manager, a fragment he had written thirteen years earlier. In 1847, while preparing to take his seat as a Whig in the 30th Congress, Lincoln had set down his thoughts on tariffs and protections on eleven foolscap half sheets of paper. Now, with economic protectionism a plank in the 1860 Republican platform, he stuffed the pages in a large envelope and mailed it to Davis, with instructions to share them only with Pennsylvania senator Simon Cameron. The first Republican candidate for president, John C.

Frémont, had lost Pennsylvania in 1856, and Lincoln was determined to win the Keystone State in 1860. In this action, we can see how valuable these notes must have been to Lincoln: They served as repositories for his most important insights.[5]

Despite this, his private reflections have been mostly overlooked by scholars and general readers alike. Perhaps this is due to their scattershot configuration; in print, they are spread across massive, multivolume collections of Lincoln's writings. To see them in person is to visit university libraries, the Abraham Lincoln Library in Springfield, Illinois, and an historical collection in the library of a private home.

Engaging with these notes is like entering a world even most history buffs do not know exists. While generations of historians and biographers have written about Lincoln's formal speeches and letters, this book is the first to gather and examine these highly personal scraps of writing and, in doing so, to ask: Is there anything new they can tell us about the notoriously private president?

LINCOLN'S LAW PARTNER William H. Herndon described his senior law partner in Springfield, Illinois, as "the most shut-mouthed man who ever lived."[6] David Davis, a judge Lincoln first met on the Eighth Judicial Circuit in central Illinois, observed of him, "I knew the man so well; he was the most reticent, secretive man I ever saw or expect to see."[7] Lincoln often seemed a closed book even to his intimates. But in these notes, Lincoln articulates not only his ideas and opinions, but also his feelings and fears in a manner he did not allow in public. Looking at these notes in their entirety presents a fresh perspective on Lincoln just when we believed there was nothing new to say about this monumental leader.

These remarkable notes survived thanks to the efforts of those closest to Lincoln. Only five hours after his death, at 7:22 A.M. on April 15, 1865, his eldest son, Robert Todd Lincoln, who was in Chicago overseeing a federal circuit court, wired Davis, now an associate justice of the Supreme Court: "Please come to Washington at once to take charge of my father's affairs."[8]

As Davis hurried to Washington, Lincoln's two secretaries, John Nicolay and John Hay, worked intensely to collect the president's papers.[9] Nicolay and Hay, whom Lincoln affectionately called "the boys," were young men from the president's home state of Illinois, and deeply dedicated to their boss.[10]

While the nation mourned, Davis arranged for the president's

Lincoln sits between his private secretaries, John G. Nicolay, seated, and John Hay, standing, in Alexander Gardner's Washington studio on November 8, 1863.

papers to be shipped to his hometown of Bloomington, Illinois, where they were deposited in a vault at the town's National Bank.[11]

Within weeks of his father's death, twenty-one-year-old Robert began receiving requests from writers and publishers eager to use the papers to write books on Lincoln. He turned down all of them, and the papers remained under lock and key in the Bloomington bank vault for the next decade.

Robert knew his father's loyal secretaries had talked about writing a biography as early as Lincoln's first term in office, and promised them use of the papers, but Nicolay and Hay would have to wait nearly a decade to actually receive them. When the boxes finally made their way back to Washington in 1874, the two men began their mammoth project.

Serialized in the *Century* magazine between 1886 and 1890, *Abraham Lincoln: A History,* was published in 1890. It stretched to ten volumes and lionizes Lincoln—the authors mindful of Robert Lincoln, who had given them access to the papers.[12] The biography was both acclaimed and criticized at the time of its publication—disparaged by some for what critics said was its biased perspective of Lincoln and the Republican Party.[13] Nicolay and Hay included Lincoln's private notes to himself in the *History,* and also in their *Complete Works of Abraham Lincoln,* published fifteen years later in 1905. They labeled the notes "fragments" and recognized their deeply personal nature, observing of one, "It was not written to be seen by men."[14]

A half century later, in 1953, Roy P. Basler, a college English professor who subsequently served as executive secretary of the Abraham Lincoln Association, edited the nine-volume *Collected Works of Abraham Lincoln,* with a further two supplemental volumes published in 1974. Basler and his editors included Lincoln's notes to himself in the *Works* and retained Nicolay and Hay's term "fragments" when discussing them.

Why "fragments"? Many of these notes are fragmentary—incomplete—beginning or ending in midsentence. Thus, a fragment on slavery written in 1854 begins: "dent truth. Made so plain by our good Father in Heaven," and ends, "in its aggregate grandeur, of extent of country, and numbers of population—of ship, and steamboat, and rail[.]" This gives one the sensation of being in the room with Lincoln himself.

I imagine Lincoln, in the midst of working through a particularly knotty question on, say, how to respond to the charge that the new Republican Party was a sectional party, writing a note to himself only to be interrupted by someone like Congressman Wilson. Ever the attentive listener, Lincoln puts his pencil or pen down and does not return to that particular note. But he does save it—in a desk drawer, a letter box, a coat pocket, or even his top hat. He saves it because, like his letter in response to the "Albany Resolves," he wants these notes at the ready as he tackles thorny issues over and over again in the weeks and years to come.

A new editorial venture, *The Papers of Abraham Lincoln* in Springfield, Illinois, begun in 2001, uses the term "notes" in addition to "fragments" for their online project. Dr. Daniel Worthington, the project's director, and Kelley Clausing, assistant editor, generously offered their cooperation for this book. They have provided their list of 111 of Lincoln's surviving fragments and notes. For the first time, the transcripts of all 111 of these fragments and notes are published in the appendix here, starting on page 168. In what follows, I will call all of them notes except where editors have specifically labeled them fragments.

While writing my 2009 biography of Lincoln, *A. Lincoln,* I often wished he had kept a diary or journal. Perhaps he did. Maybe it is out there, waiting to be unearthed in some dusty attic. But for now, the closest thing we have are these 111 private notes.

I've lived with Lincoln for three decades, writing four books on him in that time, and I continue to be intrigued by this question: How did a person with only one year of formal education become such an eloquent writer and speaker? I have come to believe these notes are building blocks that can help us reconstruct

Lincoln's thought processes as he approached history-altering decisions. Although a few of the notes appear to be part of a first draft or preparation for a more polished public speech, the large majority are reflections and analyses that did not reappear anywhere else.

I invite you to look over Lincoln's shoulder as he thinks about how best to encourage young lawyers when the profession of law is under attack; as he wrestles with contentious topics like the birth of the Republican Party and, above all, the issue of slavery, at one point unleashing his fury on prominent pro-slavery authors with triple exclamation points; as he engages in a notable rumination about the presence of God in the Civil War. Knowing Lincoln prized reason and seldom spoke about his feelings, you may join me in surprise to see Lincoln express his deep feeling of failure at a critical juncture in his political career.

Beyond their revelatory content, these notes are a testament to Lincoln's nimble mind. One surviving note is lyrical, a style not usually associated with Lincoln. A famed orator, Lincoln was known for delivering powerful speeches with a central theme, but in these notes, we consistently see him considering an issue from many angles, often turning to more philosophical language than he tended to in public speaking. Many are deductive in reasoning, using logic to ask, challenge, probe, and analyze. He often begins by outlining an opponent's argument before articulating his own, differing point of view. Even in these brief notes, Lincoln often concludes with a resolution of the problem under investigation or suggests some future course of action.

Since they can be, at times, fragmentary and lacking context, I have written this book as a guidebook for the curious reader. I have chosen twelve notes that I believe reveal new and interesting aspects about Lincoln—they did for me. Each chapter focuses on one note or, in two chapters, two notes. You may want to turn to the color inserts to see the original images, which will help bring Lincoln's words to even greater life. In each chapter, I place the note in its historical context and then offer analysis of its meaning in Lincoln's life and thought.

I encourage readers to embark on their own personal journey, using these notes to discover sides of Lincoln that may be different from the Lincoln they have seen before. In the appendix, where the 111 fragments and notes appear together for the first time, more adventurous readers can go even deeper, including: an 1848 note in which Lincoln imagines what Whig candidate General Zachary Taylor ought to say, writing three times, "were I President," something Lincoln would never have spoken in public; an 1857 note speculating on the ramifications of the as yet undecided Dred Scott case; and an 1864 note in which, convinced that he could not be reelected, Lincoln wrote a statement to that effect, folded it so the text was not visible, and asked each member of his cabinet to sign his name on the back of the document.

After studying Lincoln these many years, I sometimes feel I know his voice as well as those of dear friends. And yet, when I immersed myself in the hidden world of his notes to himself, I found myself encountering, in many ways, an entirely new man. I invite you to meet the private Abraham Lincoln.

philosophical cause— Without t
tion and the Union, we could no
tained the result; but even these
primary cause of our great prosp
here is something back of these,

PART ONE

LAWYER

ned an "apple of gold" to us—
nd the Constitution, are the pict
, subsequently framed around i
he picture was made, not to co
stroy the apple; but to adorn,
serve it— The picture was made
ple— not the apple for the picture.

Of the 111 Lincoln fragments and notes that have survived until today, only one is from the 1830s and six are from the 1840s. I say "survived" because I believe that Lincoln wrote many more, probably hundreds more, adopting early in his life a habit of writing notes to himself that he never expected anyone else to see.

How do we explain the absence of these early notes?

One possibility is that, after Lincoln's death, his son Robert Todd Lincoln may have discarded some of them during his long custodianship of his father's papers. To Robert, these fragments may have seemed less important than his father's formal public writing.

But, more important, let's consider Lincoln's itinerant lifestyle as a young adult, especially compared with his presidential predecessors. The earliest presidents lived on large Virginia estates that had mostly belonged to their respective families for generations. Lincoln's immediate predecessor, James Buchanan, lived at Wheatland, a sprawling twenty-two-acre estate just outside Lancaster, Pennsylvania.

By stark contrast, when Lincoln struck out on his own as a young adult after arriving in Illinois from Indiana with his father and stepmother, he took up residence in the small village of New Salem, sleeping first among the crates and barrels in the back room of Denton Offutt's store. In these New Salem years, from 1831 to 1837, he followed the practice of single men of his day, sleeping where he worked or boarding with various families, usually staying weeks or months at a time.[1] Even when he was first elected to the lower house of the Illinois legislature in 1834, Lincoln had still not yet settled into a permanent home, so it was unlikely he would have been able to preserve or keep any notes.

On April 15, 1837, Lincoln saddled a borrowed horse to ride from New Salem to Springfield to take up residence there. On that spring day, he entered Abner Ellis's general store on the west side of the town square. Short of money, he readily accepted the offer of the store's young clerk, Joshua F. Speed, who invited him to share a bed in the room above the first floor.[2]

Lincoln's single lifestyle did not change until he met Mary Todd in the summer of 1839. After a sometimes tumultuous courtship, they married in 1842. One week after the wedding, Lincoln wrote to his friend Sam Marshall, "Nothing new here, except my marrying, which to me, is a matter of profound wonder."[3]

Abraham and Mary began their married life together in a rented eight-by-fourteen-foot room at Springfield's Globe Tavern. After the 1843 birth of their first child, Robert, they rented a small frame cottage at 214 South 4th Street; it would not be until 1844 that Lincoln finally purchased a house, at the corner of 8th and Jackson streets.

Though he now owned a home, within four years Lincoln would resume his peripatetic lifestyle when he left for Washington in November 1847 to serve in the 30th Congress. He spent much

In 1837, Lincoln moved to Springfield, where he would live until 1861. He spent much of his life in the law offices, courts, and stores on this town square.

The first photograph of Mary Lincoln showcases the twenty-eight-year-old's taste in fashion; she wears a silk dress with a large pin at her neck and ruffles at her wrists.

of the next two years in the nation's capital, where he rented rooms at a boardinghouse operated by Ann Sprigg—again not affording him space advantageous to keeping notes to himself.[4]

THE TWO FRAGMENTS selected for Part One offer quite different subjects and styles of writing.

The first fragment, his reflections on a trip to Niagara Falls in 1848, reveals a lyrical, almost poetic dimension to the thirty-nine-year-old Lincoln. In his response to the then preeminent wonder of nature in nineteenth-century America, we are given insight into an expressive, emotional side of Lincoln not usually seen.

The second fragment selected, Notes for a Lecture to Lawyers, was penned at some point after Lincoln resumed his full-time practice of law in 1849 following his single term in Congress. While his purpose was to write notes for a lecture he intended to give to lawyers, there is no record that he ever delivered such a lecture. We turn to this note because it reveals a self-portrait of Lincoln's legal thinking better than any of the public documents related to his long vocation as a lawyer do.

In this photograph, made by Nicholas H. Shepherd in his daguerreotype studio on the Springfield town square, Lincoln's powerful hands, magnified by a flaw in the daguerreotype process, reveal his rugged past, but his formal dress points to his future as a congressman.

CHAPTER I

The Lyrical Lincoln: The Transcendence of Niagara Falls

September 25–30, 1848

Niagara-Falls! By what mysterious power is it that millions and millions, are drawn from all parts of the world, to gaze upon Niagara Falls? There is no mystery about the thing itself. Every effect is just such as any intelligent man knowing the causes, would anticipate, without [seeing] it. If the water moving onward in a great river, reaches a point where there is a perpendicular jog, of a hundred feet in descent, in the bottom of the river,—it is plain the water will have a violent and continuous plunge at that point. It is also plain the water, thus plunging, will foam, and roar, and send up a mist, continuously, in which last, during sunshine, there will be perpetual rain-bows. The mere physical of Niagara Falls is only this. Yet this is really a very small part of that world's wonder. Its power to excite reflection, and emotion, is its great charm. The geologist will demonstrate that the plunge, or fall, was once at Lake Ontario, and has worn its way back to its present position; he will ascertain how *fast* it is wearing now, and so get a basis for determining how *long* it has been wearing back from Lake Ontario, and finally demonstrate by it that this world is at least fourteen thousand years old. A philosopher of a slightly different turn will say Niagara Falls is only the lip of the basin out of which pours all the surplus water which rains down on two or three hundred thousand square miles of the earth's surface. He will estimate [with] approximate accuracy, that five hundred thousand [to]ns of water, falls with its full weight, a distance of a hundred feet each minute—thus exerting a force equal to the lifting of the same weight, through the same space, in the same time. And then the further reflection comes that this vast amount of water, constantly pouring *down,* is supplied by an equal amount constantly *lifted up,* by the sun; and still he says, "If this much is lifted up for *this one* space of two or three hundred thousand square miles, an equal amount must be lifted for every other equal space, and he is overwhelmed in the contemplation of the vast power the sun is constantly exerting in quiet, noiseless operation of lifting water *up* to be rained *down* again.

But still there is more. It calls up the indefinite past. When Columbus first sought this continent—when Christ suffered on the cross—when Moses led Israel through the Red-Sea—nay, even, when Adam first came from the hand of his Maker—then as now, Niagara was roaring here. The eyes of that species of extinct giants, whose bones fill the mounds of America, have gazed on Niagara, as ours do now. Co[n]temporary with the whole race of men, and older than the first man, Niagara is strong, and fresh to-day as ten thousand years ago. The Mammoth and Mastodon—now so long dead, that fragments of their monstrous bones, alone testify, that they ever lived, have gazed on Niagara. In that long—long time, never still for a single moment. Never dried, never froze, never slept, never rested,

The train carrying the Lincoln family from Buffalo to Niagara Falls passed close enough to the river for them to glimpse its white-peaked rapids and hear its roar as it surged to the falls. Arriving at the small village on the American side of the falls in late September 1848, Lincoln, then one year into his congressional term as a representative for Illinois, his wife, Mary, and their two small sons, Robert and Eddy, checked into a tourist hotel.

Like many nineteenth-century tourists, Lincoln probably purchased Oliver G. Steele's popular pocket-sized guidebook, *Steele's Book of Niagara Falls,* then in its tenth edition.[1] Steele, a successful Buffalo businessman, was serving as that city's first superintendent of public schools.[2]

Sometime in the afternoon, they boarded a carriage and crossed the three-hundred-foot bridge to Bath Island to register at the tollbooth, where Lincoln paid the price of admission of twenty-five cents for full access to the falls area for up to a year.[3]

The young family probably then strolled along a gravel path under the yellow and scarlet fall foliage of elm, ash, and maple trees, heading toward the thunderous roar of the waters of the Great Lakes as they plummeted 167 feet into a deep, surging pool.

Suddenly, there it was: Niagara Falls.

Lincoln's visit to Niagara Falls prompted him to write his most lyrical surviving fragment. Captivated by America's preeminent natural wonder of his day, his intellectual curiosity shines through in this private piece of writing. This reflection expresses a rhapsodic, imaginative spirit with a Thoreau-like admiration for nature.[4]

The note, at over five hundred words long, was designated as a fragment by Nicolay and Hay, Lincoln's first biographers, because it ends abruptly with an incomplete sentence.[5]

What drew Lincoln to Niagara Falls?

Congressman Lincoln, having just completed the first of two

sessions of the 30th Congress, decided to spend part of the summer and fall recess campaigning in New England for the Whig presidential candidate, General Zachary Taylor. Months earlier, when he came out in favor of Taylor, Lincoln had made no bones about the pragmatism of his decision to support the slaveholding war hero, whose military bravery at the Battle of Buena Vista in America's War with Mexico made him a popular figure. "I am in favor of Gen. Taylor as the whig candidate for the Presidency," Lincoln wrote earlier that year to a fellow Whig, "because I am satisfied we can elect him, and that he would give us a whig administration, and that we cannot elect any other whig."[6]

Two months later, as the contest for the presidential nominee ramped up before the Whig convention would meet in June, Lincoln admitted that no one really knew where Taylor stood on many issues, but "I go for him, not because I think he would make a better president than [Henry] Clay, but because I think he would make a better one than [James] Polk, or [Lewis] Cass, or [James] Buchanan, or any such creatures, one of whom is sure to be elected, if he is not."[7] Lincoln had long idolized Clay, the Whig candidate who unsuccessfully ran for president in 1824, 1832, and 1844—but in 1848 realism trumped idealism. Lincoln opposed the candidacies of Lewis Cass, the Democrat, and Martin Van Buren, running on a Free Soil ticket.

Lincoln and his family arrived in Massachusetts on September 12, 1848. He immediately set out on a speaking tour across the Bay State.

After the freshman congressman gave a speech in Taunton, Massachusetts, the *Old Colony Republican,* a Whig newspaper, captured the dynamism of his speaking style. "It was an altogether new show for us—a western stump speaker." The newspaper reporter described Lincoln: "Leaning himself up against the wall, as he commenced, and talking in the plainest manner, and in the most indifferent tone, yet gradually fixing his footing, and getting command of his limbs, loosening his tongue, and firing up his thoughts, until he had got possession of himself and of his audience."[8]

The content of Lincoln's stump speech also fascinated the reporter. "Argument and anecdote, wit and wisdom, hymns and prophecies, platforms and syllogisms, came flying before the audience like wild game before the fierce hunter of the prairie."[9]

The western congressman won his way in speeches in Worcester, Lowell, Dorchester, Chelsea, Dedham, and Cambridge.[10]

Lincoln's speaking tour climaxed at a giant Whig rally at Tremont Temple in Boston, where he shared the platform with the main speaker, former New York governor William H. Seward. The soon-to-be-elected U.S. senator—January 1849—gave such a drawn-out speech that Lincoln was not introduced until 9:30 P.M.[11]

The late hour did not stop Lincoln from giving a one-hour speech of his own, which caught the attention of the *Boston Courier.* Its reporter wrote that Lincoln spoke "in a most forcible and convincing speech, which drew down thunders of applause."[12]

ON SEPTEMBER 23, the Lincoln family began their journey back home to Springfield. On the way, ever the networker, Lincoln stopped in Albany, New York, to meet with Millard Fillmore, the Whig vice-presidential candidate, and Thurlow Weed, the editor of the *Albany Evening Journal* and a political ally of Seward's.[13] Then, in the last week of September, the Lincolns took a detour and traveled by train from Buffalo to view the fabled falls.

Niagara Falls ("Thunder of Waters") is the collective tribal name for three conjoining falls—American Falls, Horseshoe Falls, and Bridal Veil Falls—that span the international border between New York and the Canadian province of Ontario. One hundred forty-eight years before the Lincolns made their visit, a Franciscan missionary, Louis Hennepin, was the first European to visit the falls, although its waters had been flowing from the Great Lakes for an estimated twelve thousand years.[14]

In the first decades following the Revolutionary War, citizens of the fledgling American nation looked for symbols to mark their newfound sovereignty. They quickly lighted on the falls as a natural wonder they could claim as their own. The falls represented a distinctive feature of the new nation that further separated it from Old World Europe: the wild, expansive beauty of the American landscape. Feeling self-conscious about its lack of cultural resources compared with Europe and England, the country began to tout the grandeur of its natural wonders as the embodiment of American distinctiveness.[15]

By the 1820s, the 167-foot falls had emerged as a peerless tourist destination—its popularity fueled by the development of an American middle class that could enjoy the luxury of leisure time and domestic travel. The falls thus occupied a unique space in the popular imagination, inspiring the many painters, novelists, and poets who encountered it.

Young Nathaniel Hawthorne, describing his first visit to Niagara Falls in September 1832, began his account, "Never did a pilgrim approach Niagara with deeper enthusiasm than mine."

Purchasing a walking stick, "using this as my pilgrim's staff," the novelist and poet ventured forth to see the falls. He wrote of the

At the time of Nathaniel Hawthorne's visit to Niagara Falls in 1832, the twenty-eight-year-old's remarkable literary career still lay ahead of him.

Charles Dickens, the greatest novelist of the Victorian era, visited Niagara Falls during his triumphant 1842 tour of America, throughout which he was greeted like a modern rock star.

experience, "Gradually, and after much contemplation, I came to know my own feelings, that Niagara is indeed a wonder of the world, and not less wonderful because time and thought must be employed in comprehending it."[16]

English author Charles Dickens, renowned for his hugely popular novels, visited the falls on his first trip to the United States in 1842.

From the vantage of a ferryboat, Dickens beheld their immense power. In his *American Notes,* he mused, "Then, when I felt how near to my Creator I was standing, the first effect, and the enduring one—instant and lasting—of the tremendous spectacle, was Peace."[17]

By the 1830s and '40s, visitors to the falls had begun to speak of their experience in religious terms. They often described themselves as "pilgrims," paralleling the imagery of pilgrims made famous in John Bunyan's *Pilgrim's Progress,* which continued to appeal to the faith traditions of both children and adults in the early years of the century. The use of such language in this largely Protestant culture gave these natural wonders a sacred quality. Six hundred and fifty miles southwest of Niagara, visitors to Ken-

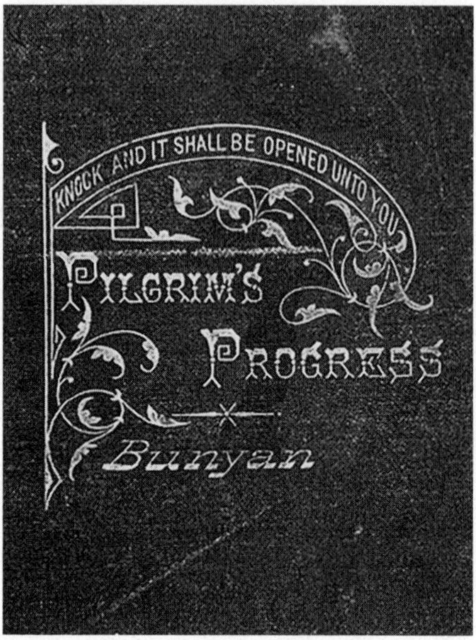

John Bunyan, a seventeenth-century Puritan preacher, wrote this enormously popular Christian allegory, which took its place alongside the Bible in the homes of nineteenth-century American Protestants.

tucky's Mammoth Cave would crawl through the "Valley of Humility," make their way over the "Bottomless Pit," and pass along "Bunyan's Way."[18]

Five years before Lincoln's visit, former president John Quincy Adams used the falls to praise both America's distinctiveness and God's creation: "You have what no other nation on earth has. At your very door there is a mighty cataract—one of the most wonderful works of God."[19]

Alvan Fisher, a father of landscape painting in the new United States, conveyed the allure of the falls in his 1820 oil canvas *A General View of the Falls of Niagara*. The twenty-eight-year-old Fisher's painting combined a distant depiction of the falls with a foreground of tiny human figures on the rim of the cataract gesturing to express their awe, the same awe that Lincoln would experience three decades later.[20]

. . .

Alvan Fisher, a pioneer of American landscape art, conveys the awe of Niagara Falls in his 1820 painting. Tiny figures stand at the rim of the cataract, their gestures expressing their delight at the grandeur of the scene before them.

YET LINCOLN, AN avid newspaper reader, may have been drawn to Niagara Falls for a more specific reason. Six months before his visit, he was sure to have read about a dramatic natural incident at the falls. On the morning of March 29, 1848, people in the quickly growing villages on both the American and Canadian sides of the Niagara River woke up to an unfamiliar silence. For the first time in human memory, the falls had gone dry. After an unusually harsh winter, strong southwesterly winds had swept huge chunks of ice into the tip of Lake Erie, blocking the outlet for water to flow into the river.[21]

At the mills and factories dependent on waterwheels, work halted. The bed of the barren Niagara River lay exposed. Ignoring warnings that the mighty falls could rush again at any moment, residents and tourists dashed down to the riverbed for what was likely a once-in-a-lifetime view. As they walked along in the rocky mud, they scooped up guns, tomahawks, and bayonets dating from the War of 1812.[22]

All through the daylight hours of March 29 an eerie calm persisted.

But that evening, from upriver, a distant rumble began. Within hours, it grew to a deafening roar. The ice had given way. As the moon rose, a white wall of water thundered down the Niagara River and once again cascaded over the falls.

If Niagara Falls was already well known, the remarkable events of March 1848 only served to heighten the public's awareness of nature's power and unpredictability. In the succeeding months, streams of tourists made sure this was the year they would visit, not knowing when or whether nature would decide to stop the falls again.

Lincoln decided to be one of those tourists.

ONCE HE HAD the chance to commit his thoughts to paper, Lincoln's first reaction to the thundering cascades of water is astonishment: "Niagara-Falls!"

But while his initial response was one of wonder, his lively mind quickly moves beyond that sentiment. Long curious about and knowledgeable of feats of engineering from his days of piloting boats on central Illinois's Sangamon River, Lincoln writes that Niagara Falls was actually "no mystery." He believes "any intelligent man" could determine what caused such a "violent and continuous plunge" of water. Yet he goes on to call his geological observations the "mere physical," reminding himself that there were other perspectives.

Its power to excite reflection, and
emotion, is its great charm

He next reflects that the "philosopher, of a slightly different turn," would ask questions more metaphysical. Niagara Falls is only "the lip of the basin" of a much larger story. Upon "further reflection," Lincoln feels "overwhelmed in the contemplation of the vast power the sun is constantly exerting in quiet, noiseless operation of lifting water *up* to be rained *down* again." Typical of many of his writings, Lincoln is drawn to ponder original causation.

"But there is still more." Lincoln's intellectual curiosity leads him beyond the geologist and the philosopher to the historian, to add the dimension of human time to his reflections. His musings call up "the indefinite past."

In the coming years, Lincoln the politician would increasingly call upon the definite past of the founding fathers to support his political ideas—one need only recall the famous opening line of his Gettysburg Address: "Four score and seven years ago our fathers brought forth on this continent, a new nation, conceived in Liberty, and dedicated to the proposition that all men are created equal."

Yet in this note he refers to the "indefinite past." Why "indefinite"?

In this reflective writing, he combines secular and sacred history—Columbus in the New World, with Christ and Moses in the Old World, the latter not lending itself to exact dating. Then he goes back even further—to the dawn of creation: "when Adam first came from the hand of his Maker." Lincoln reflects on the agency of God in the pages of human history. But he does not stop there. Even before God created Adam, mysterious "extinct giants" also "gazed on Niagara."

The unifying theme of the entire note is that everyone—Lincoln in the present, Columbus, Christ, Moses, and the Mammoth in the past—are all connected, having gazed upon the same, thundering Niagara Falls at very different moments in time.

Lincoln's intellectual curiosity about indefinite time may have been prompted by some recent reading. William Herndon recalled

The Scottish journalist Robert Chambers's early interest in geology prompted him to write *Vestiges of Creation,* a controversial work of natural history that created an immediate sensation on both sides of the Atlantic.

that in either 1846 or 1847, "Mr. Lincoln borrowed . . . and thoroughly read and studied, *The Vestiges of Creation*."[23] Robert Chambers, a Scottish journalist, published his *Vestiges of the Natural History of Creation* in England in 1844, with an American edition published in 1845.[24]

Chambers aimed to explain the "natural history of creation." He wrote his book a decade after Scottish geologist Charles Lyell published his three-volume *Principles of Geology*.[25] Lyell argued that the earth's geology was the result of gradual long-term development, not the result of an instantaneous creation. If Lyell's work created enthusiasm in the scientific community, it generated anxiety in religious communities.[26]

Not a geologist, Chambers wanted to present "the true view of the history of nature." He stated that his book was "the first attempt to connect the natural sciences into a history of creation." Thus, he hoped that in his conclusions there would be "as little vexatious collision as possible with existing beliefs, whether philosophical or religious."[27] Yet, following Lyell, Chambers made clear that in his new view, inherent in nature was a "progressive, not instant effect is his [God's] sublime rule."[28] As we will see,

Lincoln's fragmentary reflections were often written in response to his recent reading.

Lincoln concluded this most poetic note with a powerful literary image: "Never dried, never froze, never slept, never rested," With this comma, the fragment is left incomplete.

UPON THE CONGRESSMAN'S return to Springfield, his law partner Herndon asked about his impressions of Niagara Falls. Herndon had recently visited the falls himself and was eager to hear how his friend and colleague remembered the experience. "What," he inquired, "made the deepest impression on you when you stood in the presence of the great natural wonder?"[29]

Recalling this conversation years later, after Lincoln's death, the self-assured Herndon—who believed he knew Lincoln best—recorded the story without sentimental varnish. Herndon wrote, "He had no eye for the magnificence and grandeur of the scene, for the rapids, the mist, the angry waters, and the roar of the whirlpool." This Lincoln, according to Herndon, was "heedless of beauty or awe."[30] Herndon recalled, "I shall never forget his answer, because it in a very characteristic way illustrates how he looked at everything." Lincoln had replied, "The thing that struck me most forcibly when I saw the Falls was where in the world did all that water come from?"[31]

Herndon then offered his own analysis of their exchange. "It was in this light he viewed every question. However great the verbal foliage that concealed the nakedness of a good idea Lincoln stripped it all down till he could see clear the way between cause and effect. If there was any secret in his power this surely was it."[32]

Herndon was mostly wrong—he did not know Lincoln as well as he later professed, but he did get this right: Lincoln was continually fascinated by the mystery of cause and effect.

. . .

This private musing revealed a Lincoln neither understood by his close colleague Herndon, nor often revealed in Lincoln's public speaking.

When Lincoln spoke earlier in Massachusetts, he employed logic to speak on behalf of General Zachary Taylor as the Whig candidate for president. He freely admitted he would have preferred Henry Clay to be the Whig candidate that year, but believed Taylor had the best chance to defeat Lewis Cass, the Democratic candidate, and Martin Van Buren, the Free Soil candidate.

If Lincoln valued logical thought, this fragment demonstrates that he was also capable of great imagination as well as lyrical writing. It also shows his intellectual curiosity. By asking the question, "Where in the world did all that water come from?" Lincoln allows himself, for a brief moment, to become geologist, philosopher, humorist, and historian. He is interested in seeing connections among all things on earth, even as he finally wants to push back to a first cause. He is able to occupy different vantage points in his eagerness to think about America's leading natural wonder from every angle. In response to such awe, Lincoln must commit to writing his appreciation of this transcendent experience.

LINCOLN & HERNDON,

ATTORNEYS AND COUNSELLORS AT LAW—will practice in the Courts of Law and Chancery in this State,—Springfield, Ill. aug5

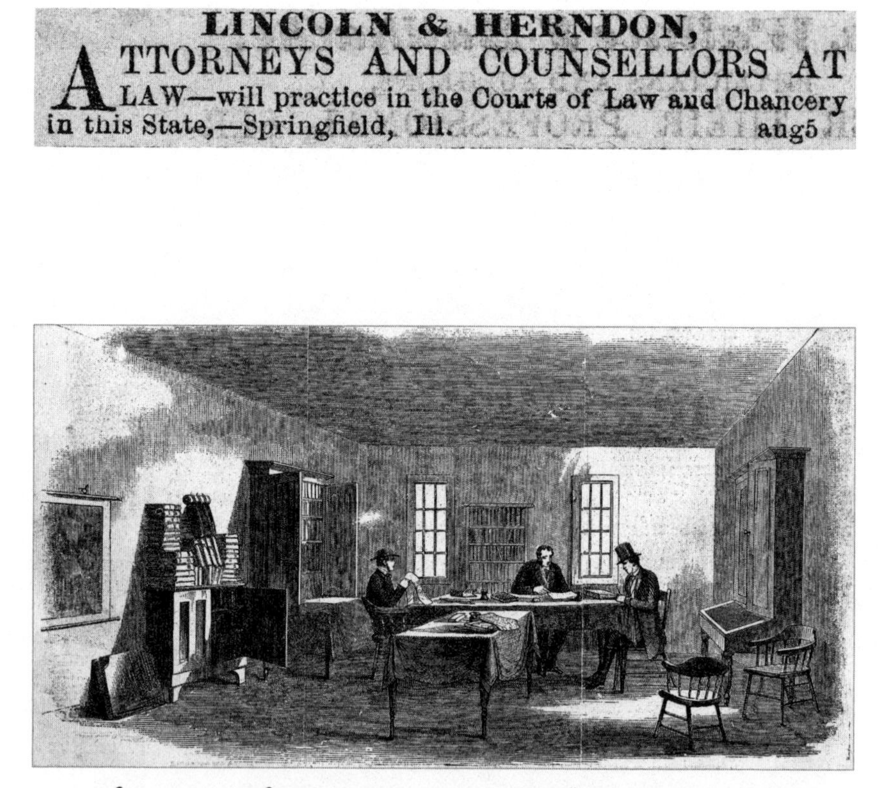

After returning from Congress in 1849, Lincoln spent much of the next decade in these law offices. *Frank Leslie's Illustrated Newspaper* published this illustration in December 1860.

CHAPTER 2

The Humble Lincoln: A Lawyer's Vocation

[July 1, 1850?]

I am not an accomplished lawyer. I find quite as much material for a lecture in those points where I have failed, as in those wherein I have been moderately successful. The leading rule for the lawyer, as for the man of every other calling, is diligence. Leave nothing for tomorrow which can be done today. Never let your correspondence fall behind. Whatever piece of business you have in hand, before stopping, do all the labor pertaining to it which can then be done. When you bring a common-law suit, if you have the facts for doing so, write the declaration at once. If a law point be involved, examine the books, and note the authority you rely on upon the declaration itself, where you are sure to find it when wanted. The same of defenses and pleas. In business not to be litigated,—ordinary collection cases, foreclosures, partitions, and the like,—make all examinations of titles, and note them, and even draft orders and decrees in advance. This course has a triple advantage; it avoids omissions and neglect, saves you labor when once done, performs the labor out of court when you have leisure, rather than in court when you have not. Extemporaneous speaking should be practiced and cultivated. It is the lawyer's avenue to the public. However able and faithful he may be in other respects; people are slow to bring him business if he cannot make a speech.

Discourage litigation. . . . Persuade your neighbors to compromise whenever you can. Point out to them how the nominal winner is often the real loser—in fees, expenses, and waste of time. As a peacemaker the lawyer has a superior opportunity of being a good man. There will still be business enough.

Never stir up litigation. A worse man can scarcely be found than one who does this. Who can be more nearly a fiend than he who habitually overhauls the register of deeds in search of defects in titles, whereon to stir up strife, and put money in his pocket? A moral tone ought to be infused into the profession which should drive such men out of it.

The matter of fees is important, far beyond the mere question of bread and butter involved. Properly attended to, fuller justice is done to both lawyer and client. An exorbitant fee should never be claimed. As a general rule never take your whole fee in advance, nor any more than a small retainer. When fully paid beforehand, you are more than a common mortal if you can feel the same interest in the case, as if something was still in prospect for you, as well as for your client. And when you lack interest in the case the job will very likely lack skill and diligence in the performance. Settle the amount of fee and take a note in advance. Then you will feel that you are working for something, and you are sure to do your work faithfully and well. Never sell a fee note—at least not before the consideration service is performed. It leads to negligence and dishonesty—negligence by losing interest in the case, and dishonesty in refusing to refund when you have allowed the consideration to fail.

There is a vague popular belief that lawyers are necessarily dishonest. I say vague, because when we consider to what extent confidence and honors are reposed in and conferred upon lawyers by the people, it appears improbable that their impression of dishonesty is very distinct and vivid. Yet the impression is common, almost universal. Let no young man choosing the law for a calling for a moment yield to the popular belief—resolve to be honest at all events; and if in your own judgment you cannot be an honest lawyer, resolve to be honest without being a lawyer. Choose some other occupation, rather than one in the choosing of which you do, in advance, consent to be a knave.

THE NOTES BEGIN with a remarkable sentence: "I am not an accomplished lawyer." On the contrary, by the early 1850s Lincoln enjoyed a growing reputation as a leading lawyer in Illinois. His abilities were known throughout the state, and he enjoyed the respect of his peers.

He goes on: "I find quite as much material for a lecture in those points where I have failed, as in those wherein I have been moderately successful." (Imagine a leader today—in law, politics, or business—beginning a lecture so modestly.)

Even with the recent discoveries of Lincoln legal documents, none is as illuminating of Lincoln's self-understanding of the vo-

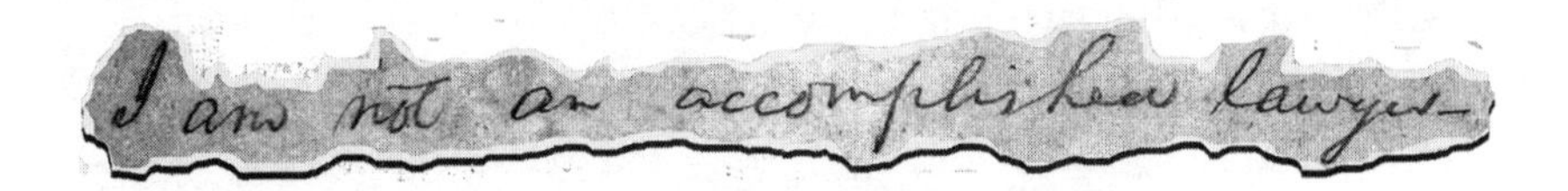
I am not an accomplished lawyer.

cation of a lawyer as this fragment of notes for a lecture to an imagined audience.

What motivated Lincoln to write these notes? When did he actually write them? Who was his intended audience? He doesn't answer any of these questions, but perhaps we can.

LINCOLN WORKED AS a lawyer for nearly a quarter century, from 1836 to 1860, yet historical exploration of his substantive legal career has too often been overlooked in biographies.

A fresh reexamination of Lincoln the lawyer began in the 1980s. The staff of the newly established Lincoln Legal Papers in Springfield, Illinois, searched the 102 county courthouses in Illinois. The searchers found hundreds of documents, many having turned blue with age, most often with Lincoln's signature razor-bladed out. (In the nineteenth century, people regularly collected autographs from celebrities.[1])

Yet these documents, as valuable as they are, do not include anything as revelatory as this fragment. Only 663 words long, it is far from a complete lecture. Nevertheless, it provides an intimate look at how Lincoln understood his vocation as a lawyer.

LINCOLN TOOK PRIDE in being a self-taught lawyer. In the 1830s, very few of his colleagues would have attended a formal law school.[2] Only seven American law schools existed in 1834, and of those, only two were in the West, in Cincinnati, Ohio, and Lexington, Kentucky.[3] Of the forty-four lawyers who received a license to practice law in Chicago between 1831 and 1850, only five had attended law school; the remaining thirty-nine received their professional training in a law office.[4]

Lincoln neither attended law school nor served as a clerk in a law office. In an autobiographical statement provided for a presidential campaign biography in 1860, Lincoln wrote that he "studied with nobody."[5]

His decision to become a lawyer after being elected to political office reversed the usual pattern of his day. Most men became lawyers first, and only later turned to politics. He was initially encouraged to consider a law career by John Todd Stuart, who, like Lincoln, was Kentucky-born. One of Springfield's eminent lawyers, Stuart befriended Lincoln when they were both serving in the Black Hawk War in 1832. Stuart reached out to Lincoln in 1834, when the twenty-five-year-old began his first term in the lower house of the Illinois legislature. Soon Lincoln started traveling the twenty-one miles from New Salem to Springfield to borrow books from Stuart's law office.[6]

In March 1836, Lincoln received his law license from the clerk of the Sangamon County Circuit Court. There was no bar exam.

John Todd Stuart, a fellow Kentuckian and a successful Springfield attorney, encouraged Lincoln to study law.

The clerk certified Lincoln was "a man of good moral character."[7] He was admitted to the practice of law by the Illinois Supreme Court in Vandalia on September 9, 1836. In April 1837, Lincoln moved from New Salem to the much larger Springfield and joined Stuart as a junior partner in his firm.

Twelve years later, in 1849, Lincoln returned to Illinois from Washington after his single two-year term in Congress, believing his political career might be over. He had openly challenged President James K. Polk, a Democrat, on the United States' War with Mexico, disputing Polk's assertion that the Mexicans had fired the first shot in the war. Using the word "spot" again and again in a speech before Congress, he argued that the "spot" of the first shot fired was on Mexican soil, thus making the United States the aggressor. This would become known as Lincoln's "spotty" resolutions.[8]

Many Whigs and anti-slavery Democrats opposed the war, and these debates were part of the larger ongoing power struggle between the Whigs and the Democrats. But numerous constituents in Lincoln's Illinois district believed his words against the president were close to treason. Newspapers across the state jumped in to attack the young politician, one going so far as to call him a modern Benedict Arnold. The *Illinois State Register,* the Democratic newspaper in Springfield, offered this as Lincoln's political epitaph: "Died of Spotted Fever."[9]

So, in 1849, the forty-year-old Lincoln returned to Springfield to resume his law career, picking up his partnership with William Herndon once more.[10]

Each morning for half the year, Lincoln walked seven blocks from his home to his law offices on the third floor of the Tinsley Building, located on the corner of Springfield's capitol square. He practiced law before the Sangamon County Circuit Court, the basic trial court in the Illinois court system; the Illinois Supreme Court, the court for the appeals process from the lower courts; and the U.S. District Court, the court that tried federal cases.

Whereas the President of the United States, in his message of May 11th 1846, has declared that "The Mexican Government not only refused to receive him" (the envoy of the U.S.) "or listen to his propositions, but, after a long continued series of menaces, have at last invaded our territory, and shed the blood of our fellow citizens on our own soil"

And again, in his message of December 8. 1846 that "We had ample cause of war against Mexico, long before the breaking out of hostilities. But even then we forbore to take redress into our own hands, until Mexico herself became the aggressor by invading our soil in hostile array, and shedding the blood of our citizens"

And yet again, in his message of December 7- 1847 that "The Mexican Government refused even to hear the terms of adjustment which he" (our minister of peace) "was authorized to propose; and finally, under wholly unjustifiable pretexts, involved the two countries in war, by invading the territory of the State of Texas, striking the first blow, and shedding the blood of our citizens on our own soil"

And whereas this House desires to obtain a full knowledge of all the facts which go to establish whether the particular spot of soil on which the blood of our citizens was so shed was, or was not, our own soil, at that time; therefore

December 22 1847
A. Lincoln

As a young congressman, Lincoln delivered his "spot" resolutions speech challenging President James Polk's assertion that the Mexicans started the war with the United States.

. . .

BUT LINCOLN TOOK particular pleasure in practicing law on the Eighth Judicial Circuit. Twice a year, for nearly three months, Lincoln would travel this vast circuit—encompassing an area of ever-shifting boundaries in central Illinois, nearly twice the size of Connecticut—offering his services. He traveled by carriage in the fall, and by horseback in the spring, when the dismal country roads were not as good. He brought with him his legal papers, some books, and an extra shirt, all crammed into his carpetbag, along with a large cotton umbrella that he'd purchased for seventy-five cents to defend himself against the unpredictable Illinois weather. His traveling companion was "Old Bob," a horse he acquired in 1849 when he returned from Washington.[11]

LINCOLN WOULD TYPICALLY be on the road from early March to the middle of June, and from early September to the first week of December, riding more than five hundred miles during each cycle as he visited each of the fifteen county seats (when the circuit was its largest). He would stay in each town from several days to a week or more.

Although an early biographer called these Lincoln's "desolate years," in truth he loved his itinerant lifestyle on the circuit.[12] Most Illinois lawyers practiced in only a few counties near their hometowns. But after sixteen months living amid the constant hubbub of the nation's capital, Lincoln relished his travels across the vast

Lincoln carried his few belongings in a carpetbag like this one. Made from used carpets, it was the first mass-produced luggage.

Illinois prairies. The county seats that hosted the courts were often mere hamlets of at most a few hundred people.[13]

The sprawling prairies combined Indian, Canadian white rye, and bluestem grasses. By the time Lincoln would start his early September cycle, these grasses could be a full foot higher than the lanky lawyer's six-foot-four-inch frame. After the heat of an Indian summer, the prairies would often turn from green to yellow-brown, sometimes even vermilion. By October, he had to be ready for thunderstorms, winds, even sleet and snow, which could change the placid paths and roads into rivers of mud. He'd ride with an eye on the skies.

Solitary travel days were interspersed with social days and nights in the county seats. The food was often so bad in local taverns or hotels that he preferred to stay in private homes. Many houses on the circuit displayed a latchstring on their doors, indicating their welcome for traveling lawyers like Lincoln. With housing scarce, the lawyers sometimes slept two to a bed. In the evenings, they gathered in local taverns to share stories and swap humor—with Lincoln usually at the center of the conviviality.

Although he enjoyed the sociability of traveling with other lawyers on the circuit, Lincoln occasionally withdrew to take time for reading, contemplation, and writing (sometimes jotting down notes like this one).

When the sun rose, and it came time to try his cases, Lincoln would saunter to the county's courthouse, perhaps the grand Woodford County Courthouse in Metamora or the two-story brick Greek Revival courthouse in Mount Pulaski, two original courthouses from the Eighth Judicial Circuit still standing today.

Lincoln came prepared to litigate all kinds of cases for all manner of people. As a general-practice lawyer, he worked with and against fellow attorneys on the circuit to resolve or settle broken

The Woodford County Courthouse, built in 1845, is one of two remaining courthouses where Lincoln practiced law when he rode the Eighth Judicial Circuit. The county seat moved to Eureka in 1896. Today the courthouse is called the Metamora Courthouse.

contracts, divorces, partitions of farms and estates, larceny, and murder. He also handled many different kinds of slander cases, all having to do with maintaining or restoring a plaintiff's reputation—everything from defamatory speech to charges of dishonesty to defending a woman's honor. Lincoln understood that all of these cases involved maintaining and caring for community in these small villages and towns. He believed the American system of laws was essential in supporting the sometimes fragile moral sinews undergirding these prairie populations.

The vast majority of Lincoln's cases centered on the collection of debts, for both individuals and businesses. Respected for his honesty and integrity, he received requests from individuals to argue their cases throughout Illinois, and from lawyers to take on appeals of their cases before the Illinois Supreme Court in Springfield.[14]

As much as he loved the challenge of arguing in the various courtrooms, Lincoln also looked forward to seeing his acquaintances in each town, cultivating friendships, and talking shop with his fellow lawyers. He made one such circuit friendship with David Davis, a three-hundred-pound judge who presided at the courts.[15]

The rotund Davis and the long-limbed Lincoln made an odd couple, but their bond grew strong: Davis would become Lincoln's manager in the 1860 presidential political campaign. The judge recalled later, "I think Mr. Lincoln was happy, as happy as *he* could be, when on this circuit. . . . This was his place of Enjoyment."[16] Lincoln would draw upon this and other friendships he made on the circuit in his subsequent political career.

LINCOLN WROTE THESE notes for a law lecture sometime in the 1850s. Nicolay and Hay assigned them the date of July 1, 1850, in their *Complete Works of Abraham Lincoln*. This date was retained by

Lincoln first befriended David Davis when the Bloomington, Illinois, resident served as judge on the Eighth Judicial Circuit.

Roy Basler in his 1953 *Collected Works of Abraham Lincoln* "in the absence of satisfactory evidence to the contrary."[17]

I believe it probable that Lincoln wrote these notes not within the first year of resuming his practice as a lawyer, but some years later, after he had accumulated more experience.[18] To offer a lecture to lawyers within months of returning from Congress would be out of character with Lincoln. The notes themselves are infused with a self-confidence that feels shaped by experience. Later, in a presidential campaign statement, he wrote, "From 1849 to 1854, both inclusive, [I] practiced law more assiduously than ever before," suggesting that it was during this period that he began to reflect seriously on the profession.[19]

As Lincoln's reputation as a lawyer grew, many young men sought to study with him in his law office—but he could not accept their requests. He knew he was away from Springfield too long to take on such responsibility—nearly two hundred days a year in the early 1850s, before the extension of the railroad allowed him to return home more often. Though he could not mentor the young lawyers one by one, he could offer a lecture that would outline his beliefs as a lawyer. To start with, he would compile some notes as the basis of this future lecture.[20]

In these opening lines, Lincoln voices one of his core principles: humility. He had freely admitted to having personal ambition eighteen years earlier in 1832 when he first announced his intention to run for political office at the age of twenty-three: "Every man is said to have his peculiar ambition."[21]

Yet Lincoln did not just have political ambition; he had ambition as a lawyer. Each of three partnerships offered him an opportunity to advance his career. Joining John Todd Stuart allowed Lincoln to partner with a popular lawyer in Springfield; Stuart provided the contacts Lincoln needed for his advancement. But Stuart, who traveled constantly, proved not to be the mentor young Lincoln needed.

In 1841, Lincoln joined Stephen Trigg Logan, who had the rep-

Lincoln started his own law practice in 1844 and invited William Herndon to be his junior partner.

utation as the best lawyer in Springfield; Logan provided Lincoln with the mentorship he sought. When Lincoln tired of being a junior partner three years later, he started his own practice in 1844 and invited the twenty-five-year-old Herndon to join him. Herndon was willing to take second chair to Lincoln, handling all the administrative and financial aspects of the office, leaving Lincoln free to travel the circuit.

Lincoln never shied away from his ambition. Through the years, however, he learned to balance it with humility. In the notes for his lecture, he deemed it important, at the outset, to admit to a new generation of lawyers that he had made—and learned from—mistakes. For Lincoln, humility meant being fully mindful of one's limitations. Even when speaking of his successes in this note, he qualifies them with the word "moderately."

Of course, Lincoln understood that humility wasn't the only quality a lawyer needed. "The leading rule for the lawyer, as for the man of every other calling, is diligence," he wrote. Lincoln greatly admired Benjamin Franklin, seeing in him a model of diligence. He may have read one of the maxims offered by Franklin's pseudonym, Poor Richard, in his yearly almanac, "Let us be up and be doing, and doing to the purpose; so, by diligence we do more with less perplexity."[22]

Ironically, Lincoln has sometimes been portrayed as a less-than-diligent lawyer because of his response to an opportunity he was presented when he returned from Washington to Illinois in 1849: an offer of a partnership in a prestigious Chicago law firm. His close friend Judge Davis recalled Lincoln saying, "If [I] went to Chicago [then I] would have to sit down and Study hard—That would kill [me]."[23] This Davis statement, oft repeated, has led to depictions of Lincoln as far from diligent, crediting his success in the courtroom to his abilities as a speaker and storyteller. I believe that his decision to emphasize "diligence" in the first sentences of these notes refutes this depiction.

HUMILITY AND DILIGENCE are all well and good, but a question lingers: How did Lincoln, with only one year of formal education, rise to such success as a lawyer? These notes offer some clues. "Extemporaneous speaking should be practiced and cultivated," he wrote. He was committed to advancing his abilities as a first-rate public speaker and suggests here that a key to legal success is in developing this skill.

We often make the mistake of believing that "extemporaneous" speaking requires no prior preparation: one need only speak whatever comes into one's mind at the moment. Lincoln, however, knew that extemporaneity was an art to be practiced. In a culture oriented around the spoken word, he planned to tell his audience of lawyers that those who learned the craft of public speaking would be rewarded, with clients and in the courtroom. "However able and faithful he may be in other respects; people are slow to bring him business if he cannot make a speech."

Lincoln himself took a step to improve his public speaking skills when he moved from New Salem to Springfield in 1837. During his first year as a lawyer, he began attending the Young Men's Lyceum, a Springfield organization established to help young men improve their speaking and debating abilities. On a cold, bracing January evening in 1838, Lincoln gave his first public speech at a Lyceum meeting held at Springfield's Second Presbyterian Church. The speech, titled "The Perpetuation of Our Political Institutions," pulsed with drama. In this maiden address, he was responding to what he called "mobocracy," epitomized, he said, by a mob in nearby Alton, Illinois, that attacked Elijah Lovejoy, a young Presbyterian minister. The crowd, seeking to shut down Lovejoy's abolitionist newspaper, the *Observer,* had murdered the young editor in the street in front of his newspaper office.[24]

After evoking the nation's founders, and the blessings they bequeathed of "civil and religious liberty," Lincoln turned quickly from the past to the dangers facing the present generation.[25] That threat would not come from outside, from "some transatlantic military giant," but rather "must spring up amongst us." In words that would be remembered years after he spoke them, the young Lincoln declared, "If destruction be our lot, we must ourselves be its author and finisher. As a nation of freemen, we must live through all time, or die by suicide."[26]

Lincoln was still learning the art of rhetoric, and his early speech betrays the young orator's tendency to be florid and wordy, an ornate manner that echoed the prevailing fashion of the day. Despite the elaborate style, the young Lincoln was beginning to live into the values he set forth in his speech.

HUMILITY, DILIGENCE, AND effective oration were the values Lincoln believed all lawyers needed, ones that would go far in serving a principle he emphasizes to his fellow lawyers: "Discourage litigation."

This was central to Lincoln's core definition of the lawyer's calling. "As a peacemaker the lawyer has a superior opportunity of being a good man," he writes in this note. He knew that residents of the frontier state of Illinois were itching to "go to law" over the least aggravation. Land, the basis of wealth for those who populated early Illinois, was a popular subject of litigation, and it figured in many of the period's most contentious cases: fairness of land sales, disputes over indebtedness, and family members disagreeing over wills.[27] Lincoln's admonition in the midst of the contentiousness that walked into the lawyer's office every day: Be a peacemaker.

Lincoln's second partner, Logan, was known for preferring compromises to lawsuits. Benjamin Edwards, a student of Logan's, described him as a lawyer who "never encouraged litigation, but as a friend and neighbor strove for the peaceful adjustment of all controversies."[28] Lincoln's law practice reflected what he had learned under Logan, as do these notes, which counsel: "Persuade your neighbors to compromise whenever you can. Point out to them how the nominal winner is often the real loser—in fees, expenses, and waste of time."

Lincoln worked for three years as a junior partner with Stephen Trigg Logan, who served as a mentor to the young lawyer.

Although history's focus has understandably been on Lincoln's impressive ability as a courtroom lawyer prosecuting cases, he was also a peacemaker who worked equally hard to prevent hot-tempered clients from going to court unnecessarily. As Noah Webster, whom Lincoln may have read as a young man, observed in his popular *American Spelling Book,* "Somebody is always the worse for lawsuits, and of course society is less happy."[29] Years later, Lincoln would earn a reputation as an astute commander in chief; a war president, he looked forward to a second term where he could be a peacemaker, the very quality he commended to the lawyers.

In Lincoln's cases on the circuit, he dealt with individuals rather than corporations. Later in his career, he would defend and prosecute corporate bodies such as the Illinois Central Railroad. Whether litigating land or hogs, he understood that the people he represented would continue to live in the same communities after both parties had their say in the small county-seat courts. Lincoln wanted to emphasize that a neighbor might win a case but lose a friendship—or secure a verdict in his favor but split a community.

In this note, in strong language, Lincoln points his long finger at the "fiend" who regularly inspects the register of deeds, hoping to find defects in titles for no other purpose than "to stir up strife, and put money in his pocket." Lincoln's ethics discouraged this kind of lawyerly malpractice. "Never stir up litigation," he wrote.

At this point in his notes, Lincoln seems to anticipate a question from his imagined audience: Is not litigation the very source of a lawyer's business and fees? Lincoln answers calmly, "There will still be business enough."

Lincoln ends this note by confronting a widespread popular belief that worried him greatly: "that lawyers are necessarily dishonest." He said that if such accusations of dishonesty were often "vague," nevertheless "the impression is common, almost universal." The charge impelled him to offer a challenge to younger persons thinking of joining the law profession: "Resolve to be honest at all events; and if in your own judgment you cannot be an honest lawyer . . . choose some other occupation."

This final sentence reveals Lincoln's deeply felt protection of the profession of law. He wanted to shepherd persons younger than himself to a brighter, more honest future for the vocation.

LINCOLN WOULD SPEND nearly twenty-four years as a lawyer, nearly double the fourteen years he served in political office. The core values he enunciated here and wished to encourage in others would serve him in the coming decade when he was inaugurated to be the sixteenth president of the United States just as the nation's greatest crisis, the Civil War, broke out. The ethical principles he would bring to the enormous responsibility thrust upon him were surely honed in his four terms in the Illinois legislature, his one term in Congress, and his debates with Stephen Douglas—a story told by biographers and historians of many different generations—but these values were sharpened and refined in his self-understanding as a lawyer. Although he wrote these notes for an imaginary audience of other lawyers, what emerges here is a self-portrait of Lincoln the lawyer.

philosophical cause— Without t

tion and the Union, we could no

tained the result; but even these

primary cause of our great pros

here is something back of these, a

PART TWO

POLITICIAN

ned an "apple of gold" to us—

and the Constitution, are the pict

, subsequently framed around i

he picture was made, not to co

stroy the apple; but to adorn

serve it— The picture was made

ple— not the apple for the picture

"We were thunderstruck and stunned; and we reeled and fell in utter confusion. But we rose each fighting, grasping whatever he could reach—a scythe—a pitchfork—a chopping axe, or a butcher's cleaver. We struck in the direction of the sound; and we are rapidly closing in upon him."[1]

An emotional Lincoln, responding to the passage of the Kansas-Nebraska Act by Congress on May 30, 1854, restarted his political career with a fiery speech expressing his fears about the extension of slavery. By the provisions of this act, white residents of the Kansas and Nebraska territories—which then stretched much farther west than today's states—could decide whether they would allow slavery within their borders.[2]

Steered through the U.S. Senate by Illinois senator Stephen A. Douglas, the act upended the tenuous balance the nation had established over the question of whether the institution of slavery would be extended to newly formed territories and states. More than three decades earlier, in 1819, Missouri's request for admission to the Union as a new slave state touched off a huge political controversy. At the time, the United States comprised twenty-two states, evenly divided between free and slave states. To try to keep the peace, the 16th Congress effected a two-part agreement called the Missouri Compromise. First, it approved Missouri's request, while also admitting Maine as a free state, thus keeping the balance. Second, it established a line between free and slave state regions of the country; slavery would be prohibited north of the 36°30' latitude line.[3]

The Missouri Compromise would be tested over the course of the next few decades, and mounting tensions between the North and South forced Congress to buttress its original tenets with new attempts at diplomacy. In 1850, as a lawyer traveling the Eighth Judicial Circuit in central Illinois, Lincoln followed with keen interest the peacekeeping efforts by Kentucky senator Henry Clay. The seventy-year-old Clay pulled together a disparate eight resolutions to provide "an amicable arrangement of all questions in controversy between free and slave states, growing out of slavery." He hoped these resolutions would encourage "a great national scheme of compromise and harmony."[4]

Among the provisions, California would join the Union as a free state. The slave trade, but not slavery, would be abolished in the District of Columbia. The territories of New Mexico and Utah would be organized without a decision on slavery, leaving that to be decided later by their citizens. In an offering to the South, the Fugitive Slave Act of 1793, granting a slave owner the right to recover an escaped slave, long unpopular in the North, would be amended but essentially retained. In faraway Illinois, Lincoln perceived that what would eventually come to be called the Compromise of 1850 was only a momentary truce.

With the passage of the Kansas-Nebraska Act, 1854 would become a decisive turning point in Lincoln's life. As he wrote six years later for a presidential campaign biographer, his "profession [law] had almost superseded the thought of politics in his mind, when the repeal of the Missouri compromise aroused him as he had never been before."[5]

Lincoln's response to this congressional action in 1854 restarted his political career. He feared that this act, as opposed to Douglas's claim, would not keep the peace. During the summer of 1854, as a new anti-Nebraska movement spread across the North and West, he prepared to add his voice.

THE SEVEN FRAGMENTS examined in the five chapters of part 2 all grew out of Lincoln's reemergence into politics. In these years, Lincoln surely wrote more notes to himself than have survived. His note keeping took on a new urgency during this period because the issues he faced—slavery, the birth of the Republican

Party, the Dred Scott case about to be decided in the Supreme Court—as well as his rivalry and debates with Stephen Douglas, demanded that he think carefully and thoroughly about each issue.

As in his other notes, Lincoln often begins these thoughts with a question, or a series of questions. But even though a note may begin in the same manner as his earlier writing, the content of these notes stands out for how politically risky some of the opinions were, especially in comparison with what Lincoln was willing to voice in public. Here he is willing to consider criticisms—that the new Republican Party is a sectional party, for example—that he fears party loyalists do not want to hear. In this same spirit, he reads and responds thoughtfully to two pro-slavery books, even though he disagrees with their authors' arguments. Lincoln often goes further in his private thinking about the place of African Americans in American society than he is willing to say in public. His concise definition of democracy is a fragment that only sees the light of day when a troubled Mary Lincoln, assigned by a Chicago court to an asylum for the insane, gives it to her rescuers. And in one of the most memorable fragments, Lincoln confesses his deepest feelings of failure less than four years before he would be elected president.

Taken together, Lincoln's fragments and notes from the 1850s allow us to appreciate the breadth of the rising politician thinking about the contentious issues of his day.

This photograph by Polycarpus von Schneidau, taken in Chicago in October 1854—the moment Lincoln reentered politics—highlights the future president's intellect. Lincoln is holding the well-known German Republican newspaper *Staat Zeitung*.

CHAPTER 3

The Fiery Lincoln: Slavery and a Reentry to Politics

[July 1, 1854?]

If A. can prove, however conclusively, that he may, of right, enslave B.—why may not B. snatch the same argument, and prove equally, that he may enslave A?—You say A. is white, and B. is black. It is *color*, then; the lighter, having the right to enslave the darker? Take care. By this rule, you are to be a slave to the first man you meet, with a fairer skin than your own.

You do not mean *color* exactly?—You mean whites are *intellectually* the superiors to blacks, and therefore have the right to enslave them? Take care again. By this rule, you are to be slave to the first man you meet, with an intellect superior to your own.

But say you, it is a question of *interest*; and, if you can make it your *interest*, you have the right to enslave another. Very well. And if he can make it his interest, he has the right to enslave you.[1]

The story of Lincoln's reentry into politics in 1854, fighting against a Kansas-Nebraska Act that would allow slavery to expand, has long been represented as a pivotal moment in his biography, but what is missed is that he did not immediately jump back into the partisan wars. During that sweltering summer, with emotions rising to a fever pitch as the anti-Nebraska movement gathered strength, Lincoln held his fire.

In these silent months, Lincoln followed a pattern that would come to mark his political career: He carefully gathered his thoughts. This was a period of intellectual gestation; he would think deeply about the ramifications of the Kansas-Nebraska Act before he spoke about it.

That summer, he could be seen walking across the street from his law office in the Tinsley Building to the Illinois statehouse, where he'd enter the state library to take down from the shelves books about past political and legal practices related to slavery in the United States.

Springfield's *Illinois State Register* tracked his movements. The Democratic newspaper, a strong supporter of Douglas and no friend of Lincoln, grumbled that Lincoln "had been nosing for weeks in the State Library pumping his brain and his imagination for points and arguments."[2]

Alongside his reading, Lincoln wrote his thoughts and responses in short, fragmented private reflections. Given the intensity of his involvement in the issue of slavery, it is likely he wrote a number of other notes on the subject—now lost.

Successive editors have dated this fragment to the summer of 1854. The proposed date, July 1, is approximately halfway between the congressional passage of the Kansas-Nebraska Act and the start of Lincoln's public campaign against the act.

When Congress adjourned on August 7, Douglas rushed home to defend his bill in a two-month speaking tour up and down Illinois. As he spoke in support of the controversial Kansas-Nebraska Act, a series of opposition speakers trailed him from town to town.

Lincoln was a frequent patron of the state capitol's library as he prepared to speak about slavery in his reentry to politics.

On September 26, in Bloomington, for the first time that opposition speaker was Lincoln. When Douglas concluded his speech, many in the crowd called out, "Lincoln! Lincoln! Lincoln!" Lincoln told the attendees to return in the evening when he would reply: After months of silence, he finally felt ready to speak.[3]

That night, Lincoln—dressed in shirtsleeves and ill-fitting pants—asked Douglas—attired in his usual formal dress—to sit directly in front of him. Lincoln carried with him newspaper clippings of Douglas's previous speeches, having carefully studied the senator's main arguments. The atmosphere was extremely tense, but Lincoln began with conciliation: "I do not propose to question the patriotism, or assail the motives of any man, or class of men; but rather strictly confine myself to the naked merits of the question."[4]

The heart of Douglas's argument, which he called "popular sovereignty," promoted the idea that citizens of a territory should be able to vote on whether they wanted slavery. According to Douglas, "popular sovereignty" advanced the democratic principle.

That evening, Lincoln responded with force: "The doctrine of self-government is right—absolutely and eternally right—but it has no just application, as here attempted." Why? "Such just application depends upon whether a negro is *not* or *is* a man." Lincoln pressed his point. "If the negro *is* a man, is it not to that extent, a total destruction of self-government, to say that he too shall not govern *himself*?" Finally, "When the white man governs himself that is self-government; but when he governs himself, and also governs *another* man, that is *more* than self-government—that is despotism."[5]

This phrase, used by British and American abolitionists, appeared in the 1837 publication of John Greenleaf Whittier's antislavery poem "Our Countrymen in Chains."

Lincoln spoke for three hours and ten minutes. Typical of an outdoor audience, nearly everyone stood the entire time.

In the coming weeks Lincoln delivered virtually the same speech two more times: on October 4 in Springfield, at the opening of the Illinois State Fair, and on October 16 in Peoria, at the time the state's second largest town after Springfield. In Peoria, Lincoln provided a complete copy of his address to the press—the text now used when discussing these several speeches. Lincoln's seventeen-thousand-word speech—the longest he ever delivered—is remembered for its authoritative and eloquent appeal:

> Our republican robe is soiled, and trailed in the dust. Let us repurify it. Let us turn and wash it white, in the spirit, if not the blood, of the Revolution. Let us turn slavery from its claims of "moral right," back upon its existing legal rights, and its arguments of "necessity." Let us return it to the position our fathers gave it, and there let it rest in peace. Let us re-adopt the Declaration of Independence, and with it, the practices, and policy, which harmonize with it.[6]

Going forward, the Declaration of Independence would be at the heart of Lincoln's approach to the crisis.[7]

WRITTEN DURING THOSE quiet months before these speeches, this chapter's first fragment allows us to understand how Lincoln arrived at the famous Bloomington, Springfield, and Peoria speech, and his refreshed antislavery commitment.

Remember that when Lincoln worked as a junior law partner with Logan, the older jurist encouraged him to see each case from his opponent's point of view—both intellectually and emotionally. Stand in your opponent's shoes, Logan urged Lincoln. Make it your intention to genuinely understand his arguments.

In this fragment, one can imagine Lincoln pacing the floor of a

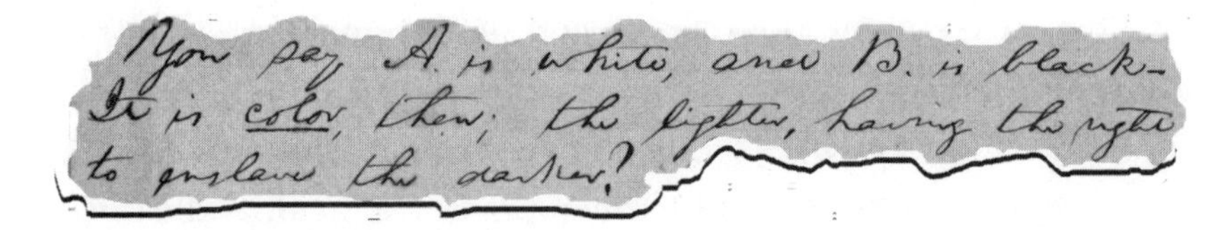

You say A. is white, and B. is black—
It is color, then; the lighter, having the right
to enslave the darker?

courtroom as the prosecuting lawyer. Listening to his imaginary opponent: "You say." Processing his argument: "You mean." Then pushing back: "But say you."

Lincoln envisioned his opponent's first line of argument to be about color. He knew the very term "Negro" was rooted in a fixation with skin color. He recognized that variations of skin color often made a difference in the way slaves were viewed. This was so especially when they were appraised in slave markets.

He deftly turns this definition of color on its head with a brisk "Take care." He argues that if one were to follow "this rule," his opponent could become a slave to the first person met "with a fairer skin than your own."

Having easily overturned this first argument, Lincoln posits that his opponent might next argue that whites were "intellectually the superiors to blacks." He understood that behind this line of reasoning was the nearly universal belief held by whites that black slaves did not possess the intelligence to live on their own, as free people, alongside whites in American society in the nineteenth century.

Lincoln quickly punctures this argument by replying to his imagined opponent, "By this rule, you are to be slave to the first man you meet, with an intellect superior to your own." Underlying Lincoln's response lay his belief that the intellectual capacity of slaves had never been measured because they had never been given the opportunity for real education. Lincoln was convinced that the verdict on their intelligence was thus yet to be rendered.

Fast-forward nine years: President Lincoln issued the Emancipation Proclamation on January 1, 1863. Within the document, barely noticed by most at the time, lay the possibility that African Americans might serve in some capacity in the Union army. But most Americans, including white Union soldiers, asked: Did freed slaves have the capacity to fight?

Encouraged by Secretary of War Edwin M. Stanton and the congressional Republican troika of Benjamin Wade, Zachariah Chandler, and Thaddeus Stevens, Lincoln's answer soon came. He authorized the recruitment of black soldiers, who quickly proved their courage, fighting abilities, and intelligence on the battlefields of the Civil War.[8]

In the logical progression of the fragment, Lincoln next queries the value of economic "interest" as a rationale for slavery. In the Southern political and economic ecology, slaves were property. The owners of slaves argued that they could not be asked to give up the economic value of this property.

Lincoln, the prosecuting lawyer of this fragment, wonders aloud whether, if you could demonstrate your "interest" to be superior to your neighbor's "interest," you would then "have the right to enslave another."

Thus, in three successive justifications for slavery, Lincoln rolls each pro-slavery argument back on itself, showing the fundamental contradiction in each justification—be it color, intellect, or interest—that could easily be turned around to make the owner the slave.

A SECOND FRAGMENT on slavery—also with a suggested date of July 1, 1854—offers a window into Lincoln's reading habits as he geared up for his major speeches of 1854.

> dent truth. Made so plain by our good Father in Heaven, that all *feel* and *understand* it, even down to brutes and

This print shows an idealized depiction of a Southern white family and their contented black slaves.

creeping insects. The ant, who has toiled and dragged a crumb to his nest, will furiously defend the fruit of his labor, against whatever robber assails him. So plain, that the most dumb and stupid slave that ever toiled for a master, does constantly *know* that he is wronged. So plain that no one, high or low, ever does mistake it, except in a plainly *selfish* way; for although volume upon volume is written to prove slavery a very good thing, we never hear of the man who wishes to take the good of it, *by being a slave himself.*

Most governments have been based, practically, on the denial of equal rights of men, as I have, in part, stated them;

ours began, by *affirming* those rights. *They* said, some men are too *ignorant*, and *vicious*, to share in government. Possibly so, said we; and, by your system, you would always keep them ignorant, and vicious. We proposed to give *all* a chance; and we expected the weak to grow stronger, the ignorant, wiser; and all better, and happier together.

We made the experiment; and the fruit is before us. Look at it—think of it. Look at it, in its aggregate grandeur,

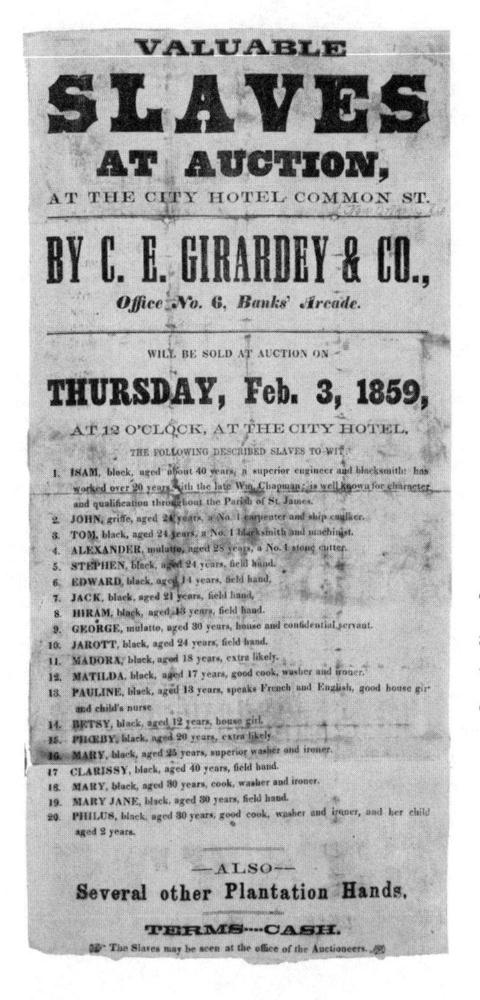

This 1859 poster advertises a slave auction in New Orleans. It states that all forty-eight slaves are from one plantation in "Carolina."

of extent of country, and numbers of population—of ship, and steamboat, and rail-

When Lincoln writes in this fragment about "volume upon volume . . . written to prove slavery a very good thing," he may have been thinking specifically of a book Herndon had recently purchased for their joint reading: George Fitzhugh's *Sociology for the South; or, The Failure of Free Society.*

Fitzhugh, a Virginia polemicist, was one of the most extreme Southern pro-slavery writers. He argued that a slave was "but a grown up child, and must be governed as a child." Furthermore, "The Negro is improvident; will not lay up in summer for the wants of winter." Therefore, he believed a slave "would become an insufferable burden to society. Society has the right to prevent this and can only do so by subjecting him to domestic slavery."[9]

Lincoln read George Fitzhugh's slavery-based social theories in the Virginian's *Sociology for the South,* published in 1854.

We can only imagine Lincoln's emotions as he read Fitzhugh's vitriolic descriptions.

Lincoln would have been aware that Fitzhugh, a self-impressed aristocrat, despised his fellow Virginian Thomas Jefferson. Four and a half years later, after Lincoln had gained national attention for his performance in the seven debates with Douglas, he was invited to a festival in Boston celebrating Jefferson's birthday. Lincoln could not come, but he sent a letter declaring "all honor to Jefferson."[10]

I suggest the missing part of the first word in this fragment—"dent truth"—may be "self-evident truth," for Lincoln is intent on challenging Fitzhugh's criticism of Jefferson and the Declaration of Independence's opening statement: "We hold these truths to be self-evident."

In *Sociology for the South,* after quoting the first paragraph of the declaration, Fitzhugh wrote, "Men are not born physically, morally, or intellectually equal." Actually, "their natural inequalities beget inequalities of rights." The pro-slavery writer could not be more blunt: "Life and liberty are not 'inalienable.' "[11]

Fitzhugh also mocked John Locke, a crucial thinker for Jefferson and others of the nation's founding leaders, calling the English philosopher's ideas on individual rights "heresy," which "must infect all theories built on it." Drawing instead on what he claimed was the authority of the Bible, and what he called sociology, Fitzhugh promoted a Southern society that trumpeted a natural inequality—slave and master—as the best face of America.[12]

In this fragment, Lincoln counters Fitzhugh from multiple directions. He grounds his case in the political declaration of Jefferson, but also in a theological declaration: "Made so plain by our good Father in Heaven."

Lincoln uses Fitzhugh's language in arguing that both the ant and the slave instinctively will defend the fruit of their labor from a robber or a master. Both know they are wronged. When Lincoln refers to the volumes defending slavery, he shows how he has grown tired of reading the paternalistic argument that slavery is good for the slave. Rather, he asserts: "we never hear of the man who wishes to take the good of it, *by being a slave himself*."

If in the first paragraph of this second fragment Lincoln makes his case against slavery by writing in personal terms, in the second paragraph he broadens his thinking to discuss the role of *governments*.

Lincoln, who in these fragments often likes to work with contrasts, draws a distinction here between *most governments* and *ours*. If *most* deny rights, *ours* began by *affirming* rights. When he writes, "*Most governments* have been based, practically, on the denial of equal rights," he is again responding directly to Fitzhugh's arguments.

When, in this dialogue, Lincoln invokes "*They* said," he uses one of Fitzhugh's favorite assertions, that some men are too "*ignorant,* and *vicious*" to participate in government. Lincoln then extends Fitzhugh's logic, and that of all the pro-slavery advocates like him, who would "always keep them ignorant and vicious."

His answer: "give *all* a chance." "All" is a preferred word in Lincoln's lexicon. It is his way, again and again, of writing and speaking in inclusive language. Eleven years later, in his second inaugural address, Lincoln begins his second paragraph with such inclusive language: "On the occasion corresponding to this four years ago, all thoughts were anxiously directed to an impending civil war. All dreaded it—all sought to avert it."[13] In this address, to the surprise of his audience, rather than blaming the South for the Civil War, his rhetorical strategy is to use inclusive language to suggest that no one wanted this war.

In this fragment, Lincoln employs the inclusive "all" to express his conviction that the promise of the Declaration of Independence is for all men, including African American men who are presently slaves. Furthermore, Lincoln, an optimist about the nation's future, counters Fitzhugh's pessimism; he expects "the weak to grow stronger . . . And all better, and happier together," he writes. Once more, the "all" includes African Americans. The function of Lincoln's fragments is for him to write in private what he may not yet be willing to say in public.

Fitzhugh's book deeply troubled Lincoln. Herndon recalled how the book "aroused the ire of Lincoln more than most pro-slavery books."[14] Yet, however much he was appalled by the Virginian's arguments, Lincoln took his time in responding to them with careful thought. He knew that he needed to understand Fitzhugh, and other pro-slavery advocates, in order to take on Douglas in the summer of 1854.

LINCOLN DID NOT use any of the contents of these two small fragments in the sprawling seventeen-thousand-word speech he delivered in Bloomington, Springfield, and Peoria. But that was not the purpose of the fragments. Rather, they served as intellectual primers that allowed Lincoln to think through a most critical issue from many different angles. They show him taking Logan's advice to heart—and mastering it.

Before 1854, although Lincoln had put forth ideas attacking slavery, he had not yet developed a comprehensive antislavery philosophy. This year would be a turning point in his political career. Furious about the idea that one could vote on the morality of slavery, Lincoln's voice was silent for months after the Kansas-Nebraska Act was passed, but these two fragments show that his mind was very much alive.

Lincoln told photographer Alexander Hesler in Chicago on February 28, 1857, that he did not know why people wanted photos of such a homely face. When Hessler insisted on smoothing out Lincoln's hair, he did not like the effect and ran his fingers through his hair before sitting.

CHAPTER 4

The Defeated Lincoln: Failure and Ambition

[December 1856?]

> Twenty-two years ago, Judge Douglas and I first became acquainted. We were both young then; he a trifle younger than I. Even then, we were both ambitious; I, perhaps, quite as much so as he. With *me*, the race of ambition has been a failure—a flat failure; with *him* it has been one of splendid success. His name fills the nation; and is not unknown, even, in foreign lands. I affect no contempt for the high eminence he has reached. So reached, that the oppressed of my species, might have shared with me in the elevation, I would rather stand on that eminence, than wear the richest crown that ever pressed a monarch's brow.

FROM OUR TWENTY-FIRST-CENTURY vantage point, Lincoln is usually recognized as the greatest president in American history. Given the widespread agreement about Lincoln, this expression of failure—written less than four years before being elected president—is remarkable.

The race he refers to here is against Stephen Douglas, the Illinois senator who had championed the Kansas-Nebraska Act in

The "Little Giant" who would become Lincoln's perennial rival in Illinois.

1854. For nearly three decades Lincoln and Douglas fought each other for political power—on village greens, debate stages, and public squares—all across Illinois. For a period of time, it looked like a lopsided race: In the 1850s, while Douglas came close to becoming the Democratic nominee for president twice, Lincoln rode the back roads of the Eighth Judicial Circuit and walked the muddy streets of Springfield. By 1856, when in this brief note Lincoln mulled over his overriding sense of "failure—a flat failure," Douglas had nearly lapped Lincoln in their "race of ambition."[1]

Lincoln and Douglas arrived in Illinois in the early 1830s, only sixteen months apart. Douglas, born and raised in Vermont, was just a teenager when his family moved to Canandaigua in the Finger Lakes region of New York. In June 1833, not quite twenty-one, he set out from New York for what he called the "great west" to make his mark. His mother, expressing her concern that her son was too young for such an adventure, asked when she would next see him. He allegedly replied, "On my way to Congress." After several brief stops, Douglas stepped off a stage in Jacksonville, Illinois, with five dollars in his pocket.[2]

Lincoln first saw Douglas at the second state capital, Vandalia, in December 1834. Lincoln was a first-term Whig member of the state legislature; Douglas an applicant for state's attorney general for the First Judicial District. Douglas began serving on the Illinois Supreme Court when it expanded from four to nine judges in 1841. From that year forward, Lincoln typically called him "Judge Douglas."[3]

Five feet four inches tall, with bushy brown hair and an aggressive jaw, Douglas radiated strength. Although a foot shorter than Lincoln, Douglas nonetheless commanded—and demanded—attention. For the next twenty-two years, Lincoln was consigned to live in the same state as "the Little Giant," as Douglas's admirers called him. While Lincoln labored as a local politician, he watched

Lincoln first met Stephen Douglas in Vandalia in 1836 when both served in the Illinois legislature.

Douglas emerge on the national stage, elected to the U.S. Senate in 1847. Ten years later, in 1856, some Democrats were putting Douglas's name forward as a presidential possibility.

While he watched Douglas's political star rise, Lincoln compared their two careers and recognized much of himself in Douglas. In this private note, Lincoln asserts himself to be ambitious "quite as much so as [Douglas]."

Lincoln first declared his intention to run for political office on March 15, 1832; he was just twenty-three years old. Following the custom of the day, he placed an announcement in the Springfield *Sangamo Journal,* saying he was running for a seat in the Illinois General Assembly. In his concluding paragraph, he acknowledged,

> Every man is said to have his peculiar ambition. Whether it be true or not, I can say for one that I have no other so great as that of being truly esteemed of my fellow men, by rendering myself worthy of their esteem. How far I shall succeed in gratifying this ambition, is yet to be developed.[4]

Lincoln sought the genuine respect of others; his ambition did not come from a narcissistic hunger for power. He embodied the ideal of the "self-constructed" individual, which took on significant meaning in nineteenth-century America. While the "self-made man" would come to be defined in the twentieth century as one who achieved economic advancement, in the nineteenth century the term implied shaping or reshaping one's character by adhering to such values as integrity, truthfulness, and courage.[5] We cannot be sure of the specific factors that motivated Lincoln to pursue a career in politics. His father, Thomas Lincoln, a farmer and carpenter, showed no interest in that realm. In New Salem, some of his new friends, especially Bowling Green, the jovial justice of the peace, and James Rutledge, founder of a local debating society, encouraged him to run for political office just one year after his arrival. They respected young Lincoln, but they also had their own motives: They had been looking to elect a representative in the state legislature who could promote their interests, specifically to advance commercial transportation on the Sangamon River.[6]

Sangamon County was entitled to four representatives in the lower house of the state legislature. When the votes were counted for the 1832 state elections, Lincoln finished eighth among thirteen candidates. Despite the loss, Lincoln's first taste of politics was not all bad; he was heartened that he received 277 of 300 votes in the precinct that included New Salem.[7]

In 1834, Lincoln won election to the Illinois General Assembly. When the poll monitors counted the votes on August 4, he had finished second among thirteen candidates.[8]

Once in office, Lincoln quickly made an impression on his peers. In 1836, although he was the second youngest member of the minority Whigs, the party elected him their leader in the General Assembly. His ambition—and skill—would go on to win him four consecutive two-year terms in the legislature.

Yet Lincoln continued to be extremely sensitive to disappointments and frustrations. Early in his political career, in November and December 1839, he took part in a "tournament"—a public debate in which Whigs and Democrats debated issues of national policy. On the first day, Lincoln faced off with Douglas and did well.

But on the next evening, again debating Douglas, Springfield's *Illinois State Register* reported, "Mr. Lincoln of Wednesday night was not the Mr. Lincoln of Tuesday."[9] The Democratic newspaper opined that Lincoln "left the stump literally whipped off it, even in the estimation of his own friends." Lincoln's longtime friend Joseph Gillespie recalled, "He was conscious of his failure and I never saw any man so much distressed."[10]

It may seem a stretch to call Lincoln's missteps during his early years in political office "failures," for they occurred when he was young and inexperienced, trying to figure out a new and complicated landscape. Yet he continued to struggle with a sense of his shortcomings. He won election to the U.S. Congress in 1846, but served only one term and returned to practice law in Springfield.

In 1851, in a conversation with Herndon, he told his law partner, "Oh how hard it is to die and leave one's Country no better than if one had never lived for it."[11] Lincoln set a high standard for himself, and in his own estimation he was not measuring up.

Not long after he returned to political combat in 1854, his friends persuaded him that he would be better off using his gift of political oratory from the authority of political office. Heeding their counsel, he accepted their nomination to the Illinois General Assembly once again. He won, but ultimately decided that the office would be a step backward or sideways rather than forward. He also knew that he could not be a member of the body that elected U.S. senators—the position to which he ultimately aspired. In the end he declined to accept the seat.

Lincoln aspired to higher office. Toward the end of 1854, he mounted a spirited campaign to win the Illinois U.S. Senate seat then held by James Shields, who political pundits agreed could be defeated by a strong anti-Nebraska candidate. Shields, a Democrat and the state auditor, was no stranger. Lincoln had tangled with the Irish immigrant in 1842 when he attacked Shields via a series of satirical letters from "Rebecca," a country woman who lived in "Lost Townships," published in the *Sangamo Journal*.[12]

Lincoln's invective had enraged Shields. Known for his volatile temper, Shields challenged Lincoln to a duel. Lincoln accepted. On September 22, 1842, two boats carrying the duelers crossed the Mississippi River to Missouri, where dueling was legal. In the end, cooler heads, and the threat of Lincoln's long reach—as the challenged party, Lincoln had opted to duel with lengthy broadswords—prevailed. The duel ended before it even began.[13]

In November 1854, Lincoln sent a flurry of letters to friends and newspaper editors, resourcefully calling in chits or favors he

Lincoln challenged James Shields, the incumbent Democratic U.S. senator, for an Illinois Senate seat in 1855.

had accumulated in both his political and legal vocations. In the nineteenth century, U.S. senators were elected by state legislatures, a system that would not change until 1913 when the Seventeenth Amendment mandated that senators be elected by popular vote.[14]

Writing to Hugh Lemaster, editor of the *Fulton Republican* in Lewistown, Lincoln thanked him for his support and asked him to send "the names, post-offices, and '*political* position' of members round about you." He enclosed a text of his Peoria speech with each letter.[15] Lemaster replied: "We want someone that can stand right up to the little Giant (*excuse me*) it takes a great Blackguard (you know) to do that—and *thou art* (excuse again) *the man*."[16]

In December, an array of friends, including Judge Davis, lawyer Leonard Swett, and Congressman Elihu B. Washburne, traveled the state, canvassing on Lincoln's behalf.

As Lincoln's campaign took shape, he meticulously wrote down the names of all one hundred members of the Illinois Senate and House who would cast votes. On seven pages of lined paper he placed after each name a "W" for Whig, a "D" for Democrat, and an "A.N.D." for Anti-Nebraska Democrat.[17] He made a number of duplicate lists complete with vote tabulations and sent them to his allies across Illinois. On January 6, 1855, he sent one such list to Washburne, writing, "I cannot doubt but I have more committals than any other one man."[18]

Delayed by the severest snowstorm in a quarter century, the Illinois House and Senate finally convened in joint session on February 8, 1855, to begin voting. Many Democrats, believing Shields could not be reelected, put forward two formidable alternative candidates, Joel A. Matteson, the popular tenth governor of Illinois, and Lyman Trumbull, a lifelong Democrat from Alton and the former Illinois secretary of state, just elected to Congress from the Eighth District.[19] Traditional Democrats despised Trumbull for his anti-Nebraska stance, but he was gaining momentum within a group of independent Democrats who had broken with Douglas over the Kansas-Nebraska Act.

On the first ballot, Lincoln led with forty-five votes, followed by Shields with forty-one votes. Trumbull had just five votes, and Matteson and eight other candidates trailed with one vote each. Lincoln's first-round total left him just six votes short of the majority fifty-one votes needed for election.[20]

It was not unusual for an election to last many rounds. The regular Democrats made their move on the seventh ballot. As Lincoln's backers anxiously looked on, the Democrats discarded Shields, who fell from forty-one to one, and gave their votes to Matteson, who went from zero to forty-four. Lincoln trailed Matteson by six votes.

On the eighth ballot Lincoln fell from thirty-eight to twenty-seven, and on the ninth, down to fifteen against Matteson's forty-seven, the highest total any candidate had yet received, but still four votes shy of being elected. Meanwhile, Trumbull, the anti-Nebraska Democrat, climbed up to thirty-five votes on the ninth ballot.[21]

Lyman Trumbull, a Democrat derided by regular Democrats for his anti-Nebraska position, defeated Lincoln in February 1855 for a U.S. Senate seat in a contest voted on by the Illinois legislature.

Lincoln's old legal colleagues Logan and Davis urged him to stay in the fight, but Lincoln expressed concern that the pro-Nebraska Matteson might win by peeling away some of Trumbull's votes.

Ultimately, Lincoln decided he could not let this happen. He instructed his backers to shift their votes to Trumbull, a Democrat but an avowed anti-Nebraska man. Trumbull was elected on the tenth ballot with the necessary fifty-one votes.[22]

Ballots for U.S. Senate[23]

1855

	1st	**2nd**	**3rd**	**4th**	**5th**	**6th**	**7th**	**8th**	**9th**	**10th**
Lincoln	45	43	41	38	34	36	38	27	15	0
Shields	41	41	41	41	42	41	1	0	0	0
Trumbull	5	6	6	11	10	8	9	18	35	51
Matteson	1	1	0	2	1	0	44	46	47	47

At this critical moment, with Lincoln so close to what he then saw as the highest political prize in his life, a seat in the U.S. Senate, he decided that the long-term cause of stopping slavery surpassed his short-term political ambition.

After his defeat, Lincoln was publicly magnanimous. He wrote Congressman Washburne, "I regret my defeat moderately, but I am not nervous about it." He added, "On the whole, it is perhaps as well for our general cause that Trumbull is elected."[24]

Lincoln's family and friends refused to take his defeat so graciously. Mary Lincoln, who had been friends with Julia Jayne Trumbull since they were girls—Julia was a bridesmaid in Mary's wedding—ended the long friendship. Mary, who thought of herself as a political adviser to her husband, was certain Julia could have influenced her husband's vote.[25]

Judge Davis was equally angry. Lincoln might have professed to trust Trumbull, but Davis did not, saying the congressman was "a Democrat all his life—dyed in the wool—as ultra as could be."[26]

Lincoln was more forthright about the bitter sting of defeat with Joseph Gillespie, confiding to his friend he "would never strive for office again."[27] He wrote a long-overdue letter to a New York law firm. "I was dabbling in politics; and, of course, neglecting business. Having since been beaten out, I have gone to work again."[28] Lincoln was a few days short of age forty-six, and defeat tasted even more bitter than it had back in 1832.

But in the following months, with more time to consider all that had taken place, Lincoln began to see things in a different light—at least publicly. He realized that the person who had been defeated was not Matteson, nor Shields, nor even himself, but Douglas. The Little Giant was the personification of the Kansas-Nebraska Act, and, as such, had been rejected by voters. Lincoln told Washburne, "His defeat now gives me more pleasure than my own gives me pain."[29]

This prominent young lawyer treated Lincoln with disrespect after hiring him to do considerable preparatory work for the reaper case.

Lincoln started back out on the legal circuit but interrupted his traditional routine to participate in a patent case that was gaining national attention in 1855. Cyrus McCormick of Virginia had invented a reaper that could mow, gather, tie, and stack wheat. So had John H. Manny of Rockford, Illinois. McCormick was suing Manny for infringement, asking for damages of $400,000.[30]

Both sides hired leading lawyers. The Manny Company's defense team included Edwin M. Stanton, a prominent young lawyer from Pittsburgh.[31] But since the case was to be tried in Chicago, they also needed an Illinois lawyer who could familiarize himself with Manny and his reaper. They invited Lincoln to join the team. Over the course of July, he spent considerable time in Rockford and prepared a brief for the defense.[32]

Shortly before the trial was to begin in September, the case was moved to Cincinnati, Ohio. When Lincoln arrived, the Manny Company legal team informed him that his services were no longer needed. They did not include him in their deliberations, and they told him he could not sit at the defense table with them. They further informed him they did not even intend to use his brief.

Despite this treatment, Lincoln decided to attend all the court sessions. The case lasted a week. Judge John McClean invited the lawyers from both sides to his house for dinner, but Lincoln was not included in the invitation. In the end, the case was decided in favor of the Manny Company.[33]

Stanton, a lawyer with a reputation for an acidic manner, acted with particular discourtesy toward Lincoln. When Lincoln returned to Springfield, he told Herndon he had been "roughly handled by that man Stanton."[34] Yet nearly seven years later, in January 1862, President Lincoln, desperate to find an effective secretary of war, was able to surmount his humiliation at the hands of "that man Stanton," appointing him to a critical cabinet position.

A failed return to politics. Professional humiliation as a lawyer in a high-profile legal case. A lifelong Illinois rival, Douglas, whose rising star was based on a hateful policy. Starker than anything Lincoln had written or said before, in public or to friends like Gillespie or Herndon, this private note gives voice to his rawest feelings. His "race of ambition" is a "failure," indeed "a flat failure." The word "failure" was not typically a part of Lincoln's lexicon. To brood on his failure was his means of focusing on the meaning—or lack of meaning—of his life.

In writing this note, Lincoln fell into the timeless human habit of measuring his worth against that of another: in this case, Douglas, whose ambition had resulted in his "splendid success."

AND YET, IN this brief seven-sentence note, Lincoln did not allow himself to wallow. Take another look at it. It is as if after sentence five, Lincoln looks down at what he has written and recognizes

With me, the race of ambition has been a failure— a flat failure; with him it has been one of splendid success—

how self-pitying it sounds. He then does what he would often do—he changes gears and moves from negative to positive. He magnanimously gives Douglas his due by writing, "I affect no contempt for the high eminence he has reached."

He shifts the tone away from the first six short sentences to conclude with a thirty-four-word sentence in which he moves from self-absorbed introspection to musing about the elevation of all of humanity, or, as he calls it, "the oppressed of my species." In this brief note, Lincoln makes a final, decisive comparison with Douglas. Not only has the slave not joined in Douglas's "elevation," but the Little Giant, through the sham of popular sovereignty, has given encouragement to the oppressors of the slaves. After an initial admission of failure, Lincoln concludes by declaring—to himself—that going forward he wants to be counted as one who stood with the oppressed rather than "wear the richest crown that ever pressed a monarch's brow."

How we wish he would have written more. But he did not. Perhaps some responsibility pulled him away from his thinking and writing before he was finished with this particular note.

LINCOLN MAY HAVE felt doomed to live in the shadow of Douglas in his home state of Illinois. The two could not have been more different, not simply in outward physical appearance, but in inward emotional makeup as well. Lincoln's calm, rational demeanor contrasted with Douglas's aggressive and excitable deportment. Lincoln did not drink or smoke; Douglas enjoyed whiskey and Cuban cigars. Together they fought over the great issues of the day.

Douglas had become the measure of Lincoln's success or failure. What he still did not realize as he wrote this note in 1856 was that whoever challenged Douglas would be given a major stage for his ideas and political career. In less than two years, Lincoln would face Douglas in seven debates that would bring him national attention. In less than four years, Lincoln would be elected the sixteenth president of the United States. One of the three candidates he would defeat would be his longtime rival Douglas.

ON MARCH 4, 1861, on a windy, overcast Inauguration Day, Lincoln stood to speak but fumbled awkwardly with his new stovepipe hat. Sitting nearby, Senator Douglas rose and with a brief "Permit me, sir," stepped forward to take the hat from the president. He held it in his hands during his rival's inaugural address.[35]

This May 27, 1857, photograph was made by Amon T. Joslin in Danville, Illinois, one of Lincoln's favorite places to stop as a traveling lawyer.

CHAPTER 5

The Republican Lincoln: The Birth of a Party

July 23, 1856, and February 28, 1857

It is constantly objected to Fremont & Dayton, that they are supported by a *sectional* party, who, by their *sectionalism*, endanger the National Union. This objection, more than all others, causes men, really opposed to slavery extension, to hesitate. Practically, it is the most difficult objection we have to meet.

For this reason, I now propose to examine it, a little more carefully than I have heretofore done, or seen it done by others.

First, then, what is the question between the parties, respectively represented by Buchanan and Fremont?

Simply this: "*Shall slavery be allowed to extend into U.S. territories, now legally free?*" Buchanan says it *shall*; and Fremont says it shall *not*.

That is the *naked* issue, and the *whole* of it. Lay the respective platforms side by side; and the difference between them, will be found to amount to precisely that.

True, each party charges upon the other, *designs* much beyond what is involved in the issue, as stated; but as these charges can not be fully proved either way, it is probably better to reject them on both sides, and stick to the naked issue, as it is clearly made up on the record.

And now, to restate the question "*Shall slavery be allowed to extend into U.S. territories, now legally free?*" I beg to know *how one* side of that question is more sectional than the other?

But, Fremont and Dayton, are both residents of the free-states; and this fact has been vaunted, in high places, as excessive *sectionalism*.

While interested individuals become *indignant* and *excited*, against this manifestation of *sectionalism*, I am very happy to know, that the Constitution remains calm—keeps cool—upon the subject. It does say that President and Vice President shall be resident of different states; but it does not say one must live in a *slave*, and the other in a *free* state.

It has been a custom to take one from a slave, and the other from a free state; but the custom has not, at all been uniform. In 1828 Gen. Jackson and Mr. Calhoun, both from slave-states, were placed on the same ticket; and Mr. Adams and Dr. Rush both from the free-states, were pitted against them. Gen. Jackson and Mr. Calhoun were elected; and qualified and served under the election; yet the whole thing never suggested the idea of sectionalism. . . .

The Democratic Party, in 1844, elected a Southern president. Since then, they have neither had a Southern candidate for *election*, or *nomination*. Their Conventions of 1848–1852 and 1856, have been struggles exclusively among *Northern* men, each vying to outbid the other for the Southern vote—the South standing calmly by to finally cry going, going, gone, to the highest bidder; and, at the same time, to make its power more distinctly seen, and thereby to secure a still higher bid at the next succeeding struggle.

"Actions speak louder than words" is the maxim; and, if true, the South now distinctly says to the North "Give us the *measures*, and you take the *men*."

LINCOLN STRUGGLED WITH the decision of whether to join the new Republican Party.

As a lifelong Whig, he was not certain which way the political winds were wafting in the 1850s. Today, it seems like we have always had two major parties, but it is important to remember that people living in the 1840s and '50s experienced the largest reallocating of political parties in American history. In those years, you might join a party one year, and watch it disappear in the next few years.

The Liberty Party, composed of abolitionists who rejected abolitionist leader William Lloyd Garrison's nonpolitical stance, won some local and regional victories in the 1840s, especially in New York.[1] James G. Birney, an abolitionist politician, ran as their presidential candidate in 1840 and 1844. Lincoln was upset that Birney's fifteen thousand votes in New York in 1844 cost Whig candidate Henry Clay the presidency in that year. Lincoln complained that extreme antislavery men, whom he called the "righteous," would rather be right than win.[2]

There was also the more moderate Free Soil Party, which attracted both Whigs and Democrats, as well as Liberty Party men with its slogan "Free soil, free speech, free labor, and free men." Active in the North, it nominated former U.S. president Martin Van Buren in the 1848 election and won 10 percent of the vote. In 1852, with John P. Hale as its presidential nominee, its share of the vote slipped to 5 percent. The Free Soil Party was never able to generate widespread support.[3]

In 1852, amid this shifting political landscape, a moderate antislavery movement began to attract disgruntled Whigs, Democrats, Liberty men, and Free Soilers. While the problem of slavery was a primary catalyst for this new movement, its first leaders also expressed long-held economic beliefs about protective tariffs, internal improvements, and the use of public lands in the West. The urgency to organize and form a new party grew in the North and West from their sense that their ideas were being blocked by a Southern oligarchy that had long exercised power in Washington.

This newly formed Republican Party was born out of protests against the 1854 Kansas-Nebraska Act, and the possibility of slavery spreading westward. In that pivotal year, anti-Nebraska protest meetings were held in Wisconsin, Michigan, Iowa, Indiana, Ohio, Vermont, and Maine under many names. The "Republican" label may have been first used by former members of the Whig Party at a protest meeting in Ripon, Wisconsin, in February 1854. As the movement picked up steam, leaders who took on the name "Republican" saw themselves also as successors to Thomas Jefferson's old Democrat-Republicans, the first opposition party in American politics. On July 6, 1854, upward of ten thousand "Republicans," probably the largest mass meeting so far, gathered just outside Jackson, Michigan.[4]

AS LINCOLN WEIGHED the pros and cons of joining the new party, he became alarmed by a nativist spirit gaining traction among both the old Whigs and the new Republicans. In the 1840s and '50s, immigration exploded, as newcomers escaping revolutions in continental Europe and famine in Ireland arrived in America. The biggest group of immigrants, the Irish, along with many Germans, were Catholic. In response, an anti-immigrant, anti-Catholic nativist movement sprang up in the early 1850s, leading to the formation of the American Party. Members of the nativist group were popularly known as Know-Nothings. They earned this moniker because when members were asked about their organization, they professed ignorance of the party, wishing to preserve its secrecy.[5]

Lincoln watched with alarm as Know-Nothings appealed to voters who were for temperance—they were opposed to the stereotype of the hard-drinking Irish and German Catholics—but also against slavery, though their chief impetus was against "foreigners." Dispirited, he observed the Know-Nothings make inroads into the Whig Party. In a letter to his old friend Joshua Speed, he declared, "I am not a Know-Nothing. That is certain. How could I be?" Expanding on his frustration with the anti-immigrant sentiments developing throughout the nation, Lincoln wrote:

> Our progress in degeneracy appears to me to be pretty rapid. As a nation, we began by declaring that "*all men are created equal*." We now practically read it, "all men are created equal,

Lincoln was appalled by nativist inroads into the Republican Party in the 1850s. "The Know Nothing Citizen" portrays a fair-haired young man as the epitome of the native-born citizen.

> For this reason, I now propose to examine it, a little more carefully than I have heretofore done, or seen it done by others—

> *except negroes.*" When the Know-Nothings get control, it will read "all men are created equal, except negroes, *and foreigners, and catholics.*" When it comes to this, I should prefer emigrating to some country where they make no pretense of loving liberty—to Russia, for instance, where despotism can be taken pure, and without the base alloy of hypocracy.[6]

With loyalty baked into his DNA, Lincoln initially hoped for a renewal of the Whig Party, even as enthusiasm for the "Republican" movement grew. He worried that the Republican Party might become a narrow party of abolitionists, rather than an antislavery party embracing a wide platform of reforms. As late as August 1855, Lincoln wrote Speed, "I think I am a whig; but others say there are no whigs, and that I am an abolitionist."[7]

Lincoln ultimately decided to become a Republican in 1856, and from that point on he was publicly upbeat about the fledgling party, but privately, he expressed some concern. Because he would go on to become the first Republican president, his early apprehensions often have been forgotten. This chapter's two fragments reveal the complexity of Lincoln's thinking about the meaning, mission, and challenges facing the new party. In these notes, he worries about criticisms put forward by the party's opponents, and what these objections might mean for its ability to attract new members.

TO APPRECIATE LINCOLN'S concerns, let's turn first to the 1856 fragment in which he seeks to respond to the charge that the Republican Party was a sectional party.

In the weeks following the party's June 1856 convention at Philadelphia's Musical Fund Hall, its candidates for president and vice president, John C. Frémont and William L. Dayton, were confronted by the charge they represented, as Lincoln summarizes it, "a sectional party, who, by their sectionalism endangered the 'National Union' of the country."

By "sectional," critics meant that the new party represented voters only in Northern and western states, and, unlike its Whig predecessor, did not include voters in the South. Democratic Party leaders boasted that they were, by contrast, a national party. Lincoln worried this charge of sectionalism might stop many people who might otherwise throw in their lot with the new Republicans and vote for Frémont and Dayton.

The first national Republican convention was held here in 1856. John C. Frémont was nominated the first Republican candidate for president.

He decided to respond to this charge in a public address. One month after the Republican convention in Philadelphia, he traveled to Galena, Illinois, in the far northwest corner of the state, to speak on July 23. No text of the speech survived, but a reporter for Galena's *Weekly North-Western Gazette,* "reproducing from memory" an account of Lincoln's words, trumpeted, "Hon. Abraham Lincoln hits the nail on the head every time."[8]

In his speech, Lincoln sought to answer the accusation that Republicans, by choosing two candidates from free states—Frémont from California and Dayton from New Jersey—were "Disunionists." Most prominently, Millard Fillmore, the thirteenth president and the last Whig to sit in the White House, now the presidential candidate of the nativist American Party, had recently charged that the election of a Republican president "would dissolve the Union."[9]

Lincoln's public response: "All this talk about the dissolution

In a long note to himself, Lincoln sought to answer the criticism that the Republican Party in 1856 was a sectional party when they nominated John C. Frémont and William L. Dayton.

of the Union is humbug—nothing but folly. *We* won't dissolve the Union, and you *shan't*."

But the first sentences of the surviving 1856 fragment reveal Lincoln's private concern that Republican surrogates campaigning for Frémont and Dayton were not taking the time to hear, understand, and respond to the criticism of sectionalism.

In writing this first note, Lincoln frames what he believed to be the deeper question behind the charge of sectionalism: "Simply this: '*Shall slavery be allowed to extend into U.S. territories, now legally free?*' "

In this 1856 cartoon, Republican candidate John C. Frémont is depicted as the champion of a motley assortment of radicals and reformers. As he stands patiently, he is "called upon" by a temperance advocate, a cigar-smoking suffragette, a ragged socialist, a spinsterish libertarian, a Catholic priest, and a stylish free black man.

He observed that the two leading presidential candidates, Republican Frémont and Democrat James Buchanan, disagreed. Lincoln underlined, "That is the *naked* issue, and the *whole* of it."

In Lincoln's notes to himself, when he examined key issues he often asked: What does the Constitution say? In this instance he underscored that there was no requirement in the Constitution that candidates for president and vice president must live in different states, much less that one must live in a free state and the other in a slave state.

In another characteristic common to his notes, Lincoln delved into the historical record. On this occasion, he started in 1828 when Democrats Andrew Jackson and John C. Calhoun, both from slave states, were elected president and vice president.

Always willing to hear alternatives to his point of view, Lincoln then examined the argument that Frémont, if elected, would do so almost exclusively with votes from free states. He answered that the same would be true if Buchanan, although from Pennsylvania, were elected almost exclusively by Southern slave states. In other words, one could make the charge of sectionalism for both the Republican and Democratic presidential candidates.

Continuing his historical detective work, Lincoln noted that after the election of a Southerner as president in 1844—James K. Polk of Tennessee—the Democratic Party did not have another Southern candidate for president. All future Democratic conventions—1848, 1852, 1856—were contested "exclusively" by "*Northern* men." He pointed to the irony that the parade of Northern candidates became a spectacle of men vying to outdo one another to secure the Southern vote.

What did this mean? Evoking the maxim "Actions speak louder than words," Lincoln concluded that Southern Democrats were willing to support Northern candidates for president if those candidates were willing to turn a blind eye to slavery—which they all did.

Recounting the 1854 discussion in the Democratic-controlled

Illinois legislature of the proposed repeal of the Missouri Compromise, Lincoln remembered that many Democrats admitted that repeal was wrong, but went along with it to support its author, Senator Douglas.

His fragment on sectionalism reveals his understanding of the paradox embedded within the charge that the Republican Party was a sectional party. He believed that Democrat Douglas, despite being the representative of a national party, advocated a local solution to the vexing problem of slavery, whereas in this note to himself he emphasized that the Republican Party, criticized as sectional, actually advocated a national solution.

If in this 1856 note Lincoln honestly addressed the charge of sectionalism, what can we learn from the note he wrote eight months later about the formation of the Republican Party?

> Upon those men who are, in sentiment, opposed to the spread, and nationalization of slavery, rests the task of preventing it. The Republican organization is the embodyment of that sentiment; though, as yet, it by no means embraces all the individuals holding that sentiment. The party is newly formed; and in forming, old party ties had to be broken, and the attractions of party pride, and influential leaders were wholly wanting. In spite of old differences, prejudices, and animosities, [its] members were drawn together by a paramount common danger. They formed and manouvered in the face of the deciplined enemy, and in the teeth of all his persistent misrepresentations. Of course, they fell far short of gathering in all of their own. And yet, a year ago, they stood up, an army over thirteen hundred thousand strong. That army is, to-day, the best hope of the nation, and of the world. Their work is before them; and from which they may not guiltlessly turn away.

Lincoln may have written this second note in preparation for a speech he would deliver in Chicago's Metropolitan Hall on the evening of February 28, 1857, at a meeting to ratify Republican candidates for the city's upcoming election.

Almost every surviving Lincoln fragment begins with a problem or challenge. In this one, the challenge is two-headed: first, the obvious provocation of Senator Douglas's "popular sovereignty," which portended the spread of slavery westward into the new territories and states. But for Lincoln the less obvious but even more dangerous challenge was that slavery might become nationalized.

Two decades earlier, after his travels in the new nation, Alexis de Tocqueville observed in *Democracy in America,* "Race prejudice seems stronger in those states that have abolished slavery than in those states where it still exists."[10]

Lincoln recognized the truth in de Tocqueville's observation. In his home state of Illinois, a free state, the largest number of early settlers came from the South. The initial state constitution of 1818 outlawed slavery, but in the 1830s and '40s there was a sharp rise in anti-black sentiment. At the 1847 Illinois constitutional

Alexis de Tocqueville, the French diplomat and historian, wrote *Democracy in America* about what he had learned in his travels in the United States.

convention, a proposal for black suffrage was defeated 137–7. The next year, a revised constitution directed the state's general assembly to pass a law barring black migration to Illinois.[11]

As Lincoln watched apprehensively, other free states passed a series of anti-black laws. His greatest worry, embodied in this note, was that anti-black laws in the North could transmute into pro-slavery laws, and bring the detestable "peculiar institution" to the rest of the country.

It is clear from this second note that Lincoln believed there was still much work to do in attracting people who shared the anti-slavery "sentiment," despite their "differences, prejudices, and animosities." But alongside that hope is concern that many people holding antislavery views had not yet joined the new party. He hoped he could be an encourager of such holdouts to join.

Why the concern? Lincoln recognizes the strength of the "old party ties" and "party pride" that stopped some people, especially "influential leaders" and anti-Nebraska Democrats, from joining a movement that some feared might be short-lived. In the end, he expresses hope that a "common danger"—the spread of slavery—would overcome these hesitations.

As an astute political observer, Lincoln never underestimated the opposition—what he calls here "the disciplined enemy," although he believed this adversary gained its adherents through "persistent misrepresentations," such as those he'd been seeing in speeches by Douglas. The senator berated Lincoln and the Republicans as a party of radical abolitionists bent on granting African Americans social equality with whites.

LINCOLN CLOSES THIS fragment with a military metaphor to describe the new Republican Party: "army." Having fought twenty-five years earlier in the Black Hawk War, he may have had in mind a disciplined body of men united in purposeful action. Although the Republican Party was actually three years old, he writes that "a year ago, this army stood up" (referring to 1856) the first time Republicans offered up candidates for the president and vice president of the United States. Though admitting that the Republican Party "fell far short" of turning out all the voters it needed to win, he uses a surprisingly specific number, "thirteen hundred thousand strong," to emphasize its strength.

Looking to the future, he portrays this army as "the best hope of the nation, and of the world." This private note anticipates a theme in Lincoln's future public speeches: The struggle against slavery was more than an American struggle; it had implications for the meaning of freedom for the entire world.

In his final sentence, Lincoln issues a warning. Despite his defeat for the Illinois U.S. Senate seat in 1855, and the new Republican Party's national defeat in 1856, this is no time to turn away from the challenge. In fact, it would be impossible to do so "guiltlessly."

TODAY, LINCOLN'S DECISION to become a Republican is sometimes seen through the prism of his election as the first Republican president in 1860. These fragments reveal that his choice was not obvious or simple. He wrestled with his loyalty to Clay and the Whig tradition that for more than two decades had shaped his political life.

It is also easy to forget the complexity of Lincoln's early relationship with his new political party. He wanted the party to be a big tent. Yet he was extremely worried about the anti-immigrant, nativist spirit that seemed to him too prevalent. He also did not want the Republican Party to be perceived as welcoming only to abolitionists.

These two fragments about the birth of the Republican Party show that while Lincoln seldom spoke about problems confronting the new party in public, he wrestled with these challenges in private. At the same time, we see a political leader eager to enlist recruits for the new party. He wrote these fragments as he thought about how best to do so. He acknowledged that the Republican Party was far from perfect, but the center of the party for him was a moral anchor, his own and the party's deep commitment to anti-slavery reform.

On August 26, 1858, William P. Pearson asked Lincoln if he would like to look in a mirror to "fix up" before taking a photo at Macomb, Illinois. Lincoln declined, replying it would not be much of a resemblance if he fixed up.

CHAPTER 6

The Principled Lincoln: A Definition of Democracy

[August 1, 1858?]

As I would not be a *slave*, so I would not be a *master*. This expresses my idea of democracy. Whatever differs from this, to the extent of the difference, is no democracy.

NEARLY ALL OF Lincoln's notes to himself would remain unknown until Nicolay and Hay first serialized their 1890 biography in *Century Magazine* in 1886, but this fragment emerged through unusual circumstances just a decade after Lincoln's death. In September 1875, Mary Lincoln, who had been committed to Bellevue Place, a private sanatorium for disturbed women, expressed her gratitude for her release by giving her deliverers a gift: her husband's succinct note on democracy. The story of how Lincoln's fragment became this unusual present is one of intrigue, controversy, and determination.

Four months earlier, in May 1875, Lincoln's widow found herself charged with insanity in an emotional trial.[1]

Concerns about Mary's mental health stretched back long before 1875. In 1850, Lincoln and Mary's three-and-a-half-year-old son, Eddy, passed away, which was followed by the death of their eleven-year-old son, Willie, in 1862. After Lincoln's assassination on April 14, 1865, Mary mourned intensely and would wear black clothing for the rest of her life. Then, in 1871, heartbreak struck yet again when her fourth son, Tad, died at the age of eighteen. Although we need to be wary of diagnosing a person's illness from historical distance, in these years, mounting signs of her mental instability concerned her family and friends. Her symptoms included depression, mood swings, delusions, and anger.

A particularly disturbing episode occurred in 1867. Believing herself impoverished and abandoned, Mary tried to sell some of her clothes and jewelry in New York under an assumed name. The press dubbed it "the Old Clothes Scandal." Her oldest son, Robert, writing to his future wife, Mary Harlan, worried, "The simple truth, which I cannot tell anyone not personally interested, is that my mother is on one subject not mentally responsible. I have supposed this for some time from various indications and now have no doubt of it."[2]

No longer wearing the elegant dresses she purchased while living in the White House, Mary Lincoln now wore what she called her "widow's weeds."

Mary Lincoln traveled to New York in 1867 determined to sell her old clothing and jewelry. Hoping to hide her identity, she assumed a disguise, but was found out by two merchants. The resulting embarrassing story became known as "the Old Clothes Scandal."

Nearly eight years later, on May 19, 1875, inside the mahogany doors of a courtroom in the massive Cook County Courthouse in Chicago, a stunned Mrs. Lincoln sat for three hours listening to testimony from physicians, personnel from the Grand Pacific Hotel where she lived, and Chicago storekeepers, all charging her with unsoundness of mind. Most painful of all: The chief witness was her only surviving son, Robert. In tears, he argued that for his mother's safety she should be placed in an asylum.

Robert's motivations have been endlessly debated. The 2005 discovery of the "lost" letters of Mary Lincoln from these years—previously assumed to have been burned by Robert—have added a dramatic new angle to this debate. The letters provide new insight into Mary's mental state, the attitudes of her family members, especially Robert, and her own thoughts and feelings during this ordeal.[3]

Robert Todd Lincoln, Mary Lincoln's oldest and only surviving son, testified against his mother at her 1875 insanity trial in Chicago.

Mary Lincoln did not defend herself during the trial. She did not say a word. She couldn't.[4]

On May 19, 1875, after only ten minutes of deliberation, the all-male jury reached its conclusion: "Mary Lincoln is insane."[5]

The next day, Mary walked up the spiral staircase to her newly assigned second-story room at the massive three-story Bellevue Place sanatorium in Batavia, Illinois, thirty-five miles west of Chicago, with no idea how long she would be confined. The Illinois statute simply stated: until "reason was restored."[6]

Bellevue Place was a respected private asylum for well-to-do female patients. The sanatorium's twenty acres of manicured lawns, four thousand square feet of greenhouses, and locally famous rosebushes were meant to convey the image of a quiet, restful setting conducive to recovery from mental illness. Inside the well-lit interior, elegant furniture gave, in the words of a

The Chicago Daily Tribune.

CHICAGO, THURSDAY, MAY 20, 1875.

CLOUDED REASON.

Trial of Mrs. Abraham Lincoln for Insanity.

Why Her Relatives and Friends Were Driven to This Painful Course.

Testimony of Physicians as to Her Mental Unsoundness.

Hearing Strange Voices---Fears of Murder---Sickness of Her Son.

What Was Seen by the Employes of the Hotel.

Tradesmen Testify Concerning Her Purchases of Goods.

She Is Found Insane, and Will Be Sent to Batavia.

Scenes in Court.

The death of President Lincoln was one of

poison. She said she drank it, and took a second cup, that the overdose of poison might cause her to vomit. He did not see any traces of her having taken any poison, and was of opinion that she was insane. On general topics, her conversation was rational.

SAMUEL M. TURNER,

manager of the Grand Pacific Hotel, was the next witness: Mrs. Lincoln arrived at his hotel March 15. The 1st of April she visited him at the hotel office, and had a shawl wrapped about her head. She asked him to go into the reception-room with her, as she had something to say to him. She said something was wrong about the house, as she heard strange sounds in the rooms. He went with her, and, when about to leave her, she said she was afraid to be left alone. He left her in charge of some female help, and told her he would return in a few minutes. He had scarcely reached the office when a messenger told him that Mrs. Lincoln was at the elevator and wanted to see him. She said there had been a strange man in the corridor, and that he was going to molest her. He went up in the elevator and walked with her through the house, but did not see any strange man; She was greatly excited, and desired to go to some of the lady-boarders' rooms that she might be safe. He showed her to Mrs. Dodge's room, who at the time was at dinner, promising that he would return soon. He was again summoned by her, when her appearance was wild and her fears were repeated. He believed her deranged. No one had called to see her since her arrival except her son. He did not regard it as safe to leave her alone.

MRS. ALLEN,

housekeeper at the hotel, testified that Mrs. Lincoln seemed to suffer from nervous excitement. She imagined that a small window in her room boded ill, and used to say that the window disturbed her. She walked her room most of the night. Witness had slept with her two nights at her request. Last Wednesday Mrs. Lincoln was very much excited. She mixed several kinds of medicine together and took the mixture. She had a large closet filled with unopened packages she had purchased. She considered her insane, and that she ought to be placed somewhere for treatment and care.

MAGGIE GAVIN,

employed at the hotel, testified that she had had the care of Mrs. Lincoln's room, and heard her complain frequently that people were speaking to her through the wall. She was most anxious about her son, and sometimes called her attention to voices she heard through the floor. She complained that a man had taken her pocket-book, but witness found it in the bureau drawer. She at times called witness to the window, and

epilepsy, but he did not regard her safe to be left alone. He had visited her professionally years ago, but saw nothing in her to indicate unsoundness of mind. She was eccentric, and suffered from nervousness.

W. H. WOOSTER,

doing business on Wabash avenue, said he knew Mrs. Lincoln. She had called to purchase watches and spectacles of him. She contracted a bill of $300, but the goods were taken to her son before delivering them, and he ordered them returned.

J. B. TOWNSEND,

of a jewelry firm, and E. T. Moulton, of a dry-goods house, testified to having similar dealings with Mrs. Lincoln, and they regarded her as insane.

T. C. MATTOCK,

under THE TRIBUNE Building, testified to a long list of dealings with Mrs. Lincoln, and to selling her several trunks. He regarded her as insane, and her manners were eccentric and excited.

DR. JOHNSON

testified that he knew Mrs. Lincoln, and that from the evidence heard was satisfied that she was deranged. He did not regard her as in condition to be left alone, and thought she ought to be sent to a private asylum.

DR. SMITH

had listened to the evidence, and seeing that her actions had been without proper motives, was of opinion that her mind was not sound. On cross-examination he stated that, if she was not of sound mind, he attributed it to the events in her recent history.

Robert T. Lincoln was recalled, and testified that insanity was not hereditary in her family, and that she was 56 years of age.

Mr. Swett then spoke to the jury of the sadness of the case and the necessity of Mrs. Lincoln being cared for, after which the jury retired.

DURING THE ABSENCE OF THE JURY,

Robert T. Lincoln approached his mother and extended his hand. She grasped it fondly, remarking with a degree of emphasis, "Robert, I did not think you would do this." His response was stifled by the spring of tears, and the conversation ended. She was next approached by Mr. Swett, who tried to persuade her that it was for her good that the action had been taken. She could not be persuaded to believe what was said, however, but replied with promptness that she would try to endure her persecutions.

THE VERDICT.

The jury had been absent but a few minutes, when it returned with the following verdict:

We, the undersigned, jurors in the case of Mary Lincoln, alleged to be insane, having heard the evidence in the case, are satisfied that the said Mary

The trial of Mary Lincoln was the lead story of the *Chicago Daily Tribune* for May 20, 1875.

Bellevue pamphlet, "a bright, cheerful and homelike expression."[7]

Mary was housed in a private suite consisting of two rooms on the second floor, which included a private bath. The door to her room was locked only at night, the key retained by a personal attendant. She was permitted to receive visitors. Daily progress reports show that she got along well with staff and other patients. Still, she was held against her will.

As weeks turned into months, Mary turned to Chicago lawyers and political activists Myra and James Bradwell for help. Six years

Mary Lincoln was held against her will at a private asylum for well-off female patients.

earlier, Myra Colby Bradwell had passed the Illinois bar exam with high marks, but her application for a license to practice law was denied. The Illinois Supreme Court informed her she was turned down "by reason of THE DISABILITY IMPOSED BY YOUR MARRIED CONDITION." As a woman, according to the culture of the day, Myra's primary duty was to attend to her husband and take care of her children; said duties would not allow her adequate time to practice law.[8]

Myra disagreed. Even before the bar exam, she had founded the *Chicago Legal News,* serving as editor as well as publisher and business manager. Living out the paper's motto *Lex Vincit*—"Law Conquers"—she successfully made the *Chicago Legal News* the largest circulating legal newspaper in America.[9] Her husband, James, a transplanted Englishman and a graduate of Knox College in Galesburg, Illinois, was a respected lawyer and judge. By the time Mary Lincoln was committed to the sanatorium in 1875, James was serving in the Illinois state legislature.[10]

The "lost letters" show that the Bradwells were more involved at Bellevue Place, Batavia, Ills. 11

NO.	NAME.	DATE OF ADMISSION.	DATE OF DISCHARGE.	M or S.	AGE.	RESIDENCE.	Condition when Disch'd.	Nativity.	REMARKS.
190	Rawlin, M. M.	May 24 '74	Aug 18 '74	M		Kaneville, Ill.	S		
191	Douglas, Mrs. John	June 6 "	Oct. 15 "	M		Winona, Minn.	S		
192	Sawyer, Mary E.	" "	Jan. 27 '75	S	22	Lake Forest, Ill.	R		
193	Judd, Mary	July 1 "	Sept. 4 "	S	21	Chicago, "	I		2d admis. Orig. No. 171
194	Hoffman, Sophia	" 18 "	July 20 '74	S	16	" "	I		
195	Ford, Lillie E.	Aug 12 "	Oct. 2 "	M	34	[illegible] "	I		
196	Brooks, Louise	" 20 "	Jan. 13 '75			Red Wing, Minn	R		
197	Morris, Mary L.	Sept. 7 "	June 21 '77	S	32	St. Paul, "	S		
198	Harcourt, Helen	" 21 "	Sept. 24 '74	M	28	Chicago, Ill.	D		Exhaustion from mania.
199	Ayres, Sarah Ann	Nov. 11 "	Dec. 2 "	M	55	Keokuk, Iowa	I		
200	Anderson, Lena	Dec. 27 "	Jan. 12 '75	M	30	Batavia, Ill	I		To Elgin
201	Howe, Mrs.	Feb. 11 '75	Apr. 5 "	M		" "	S		
202	LeBrown, Dr.	" 18 "	" 19 "			Geneva, "	S		
203	McCloud, Hattie	Mar. 11 "	" 8 "	M	32	Chicago, "	I		Committed suicide [illegible]
204	Blake, Adela	" 27 "	Oct. 4 "	M	41	Indianapolis, Ind.	I		
205	Haight, Clara F.	Apr. 1 "	July 14 "	M	28	Rockford, Ill.	I		
206	Reinsburg, Rebecca	" 5 "	May 27 "	M		Limerick "	S		
207	Austin, Kate P.	" 12 "	July 10 "	M	40	Chicago, "	R		
208	Lincoln, Mary	May 20 "	Sept. " "	M	56	" "	I	X	
209	Sharp, Carrie	" 21 "	May 15 '76	S	27	" "	R		
210	Hawkinson, Nellie	" 28 "	Sept. 9 '75	M	36	" "	R		Suicided Sept. 14 '75.

This register reported on Mary Lincoln's status at Bellevue Place.

with Mary Lincoln's release than previously understood. The correspondence includes five letters from Mary to the Bradwells in August 1875. With their combined legal experience, Myra and James mounted a publicity campaign that convinced the court to release Mary Lincoln. They argued that she was of sound mind and therefore perfectly capable of handling her own finances, which the court had placed under Robert's supervision. She was set free on September 11, 1875, after four months of confinement.[11]

Enormously grateful, Mary gave Myra and James much more than her verbal thanks; she showered them with gifts and commemorations of her husband, among them an oil painting that hung in their Springfield home and a bloodstone seal given to President Lincoln from the sultan of Turkey. Most important, she gave them the fragment that captured her husband's definition of democracy.[12]

How and why she came to be in possession of this note remains

An able lawyer and publicist, Myra Bradwell worked to free Mary Lincoln from Bellevue Place.

a mystery. Almost all the other fragments were in Robert's possession, so this one must have been particularly special to her.

It is impossible to know when Lincoln wrote it. Untitled, unsigned, and undated, it cannot be connected to any known speech or event. In an annotated footnote, Roy Basler and the editors of *The Collected Works of Abraham Lincoln* admitted that their suggestion of a date—August 1, 1858—was "pure conjecture."[13] The Lincoln signature on the note was clipped at some later date from another document and pasted below the statement.

I believe that Lincoln wrote the fragment sometime in 1858, the year of the Lincoln-Douglas debates, for in that critical year, he wrestled with the idea of slavery in his every waking moment.

"DEMOCRACY" IS A word that can be traced throughout Lincoln's speeches and writings. He referred to democracy specifically 138 times in the writings that appear in Basler's *Collected Works,* and all but 18 occurred before he was president. In virtually every instance, however, he uses it as a proper noun—referring to the Democratic Party, which its followers called the "Democracy." So, when Lincoln used the word, he rarely had something good to say about it.[14]

So why employ the word now, as a political concept?

I imagine Lincoln writing the note as he worked to respond to Douglas, Lincoln's bête noire, across their seven legendary debates. The Democratic senator continually touted "popular sovereignty" as the democratic answer to the problem of slavery. In their first joint debate at Ottawa, Douglas, speaking first, stated, "I hold that each and every State of this Union is a sovereign power, with the right to do as it pleases on this question of slavery."[15] In the conclusion of the debate, when Douglas had the opportunity to answer Lincoln, the Little Giant stated that "democracy is founded—in eternal principles of truth."[16] Lincoln was furious to hear popular sovereignty, which he profoundly disagreed with, touted as a democratic principle.

At their fifth debate at Galesburg, a frustrated Lincoln responded to Douglas's continued defense of popular sovereignty by saying, "the Judge is not in favor of making any difference between slavery and liberty." He went on, "Every sentiment he utters, discards the idea that there is any wrong in slavery."[17]

At first glance, it may appear that Lincoln wishes to craft a positive definition of democracy in this fragment. But a second, longer look reveals that the note's power comes from his use of the negative. In just thirty-three words, he salts his definition with "not," "not," and "no."

Lincoln was no naysayer. Rather, like William Shakespeare and Emily Dickinson, he understood the dynamism and rhetorical power of the negative, in both his letters and his public speeches, and now in this note to himself.[18]

Using antithesis in his speaking and writing was second nature to Lincoln. When he offered a spontaneous farewell address on the

As I would not be a slave, so I would not be a master—

day he departed from Springfield for Washington, February 11, 1861, he declared, "Without the assistance of that Divine Being, who ever attended him [George Washington], I cannot succeed. With that assistance I cannot fail."[19] In March 1864, replying to the governor and two other leaders from Kentucky who came to complain that slaves were abandoning the state's agricultural countryside to join the Union army, Lincoln responded: "If slavery is not wrong, nothing is wrong."[20]

Lincoln's best known use of the negative occurred in the Gettysburg Address: "We cannot dedicate—we cannot consecrate—we cannot hallow—this ground."[21] Lincoln drums the negative three times—what is called an anaphora—for emphasis.

In Lincoln's thirty-three-word definition, he makes clear that the meaning of democracy in the middle of the nineteenth century must relate to the issue that was tearing the nation apart: slavery. Lincoln was fascinated with the philosophy and history undergirding the Declaration of Independence and the U.S. Constitution. Although the word "democracy" is not used in either document, the philosophical underpinnings of democracy are fully present there. He could have reached back to America's founders. But he did not.

The third and final sentence of the fragment reveals Lincoln's understanding that it is not enough to offer a positive statement of an idea: If he believes an idea to be right and true, a leader must be brave enough to name and call out contrary ideas as false. In this case, I believe he was calling out Douglas's "popular sovereignty"—his idea that each territory should be permitted to decide whether to allow slavery within its borders—as a widely circulating definition of democracy. But for Lincoln, this is "no democracy."

It is also important to note that in Lincoln's early thinking about slavery, even after 1854, he focused his attention on how and why the institution of slavery was so bad for the slave. By the summer of 1858, he began to turn his attention additionally to what slavery does to the master—the white owner. This definition, as short as it is, shows the evolution of his moral and ethical thinking.

So why did Mary Lincoln give this particular note of her husband's to the Bradwells ten years after his death? When she lived in Springfield, she valued her role as both encourager and adviser to her husband's political aspirations. In Washington, she felt pushed aside by William Seward and other members of Lincoln's cabinet; after his assassination, she believed that she alone knew what was at the heart of his political vision for the nation. Perhaps she saw that crystallized in this cherished definition she had held on to for so long.

Obviously, she could have given this definition away long before 1875. But considering her moment of crisis, when she was locked away and forbidden her own personal freedom, it is not difficult to imagine the significance of her gift to her deliverers, Myra and James Bradwell. To Mary, the two represented the ideals preserved in the definition.

Whether that interpretation is accurate or not, it is thanks to Mary Lincoln, who was criticized in her lifetime by her husband's friends and colleagues, and who has not fared well in the writings of past and present historians, that we are able to see and read this significant fragment.

In the midst of his debates with Stephen Douglas, Lincoln sat for this photograph by Calvin Jackson in Pittsfield on October 1, 1858.

CHAPTER 7

The Outraged Lincoln: Pro-Slavery Theology

[October 1, 1858?]

Suppose it is true, that the negro is inferior to the white, in the gifts of nature; is it not the exact reverse justice that the white should, for that reason, take from the negro, any part of the little which has been given him? "*Give* to him that is needy" is the Christian rule of charity; but "Take from him that is needy" is the rule of slavery.

The sum of pro-slavery theology seems to be this: "Slavery is not universally *right*, nor yet universally *wrong;* it is better for *some* people to be slaves; and, in such cases, it is the Will of God that they be such."

Certainly, there is no contending against the Will of God; but still there is some difficulty in ascertaining, and applying it, to particular cases. For instance, we will suppose the Rev. Dr. Ross has a slave named Sambo, and the question is "Is it the Will of God that Sambo shall remain a slave, or be set free?" The Almighty gives no audible answer to the question, and his revelation—the Bible—gives none—or, at most, none but such as admits of a squabble, as to its meaning. No one thinks of asking Sambo's opinion on it. So, at last, it comes to this, that *Dr. Ross* is to decide the question. And while he consider[s] it, he sits in the shade, with gloves on his hands, and subsists on the bread that Sambo is earning in the burning sun. If he decides that God Wills Sambo to continue a slave, he thereby retains his own comfortable position; but if he decides that God Will's Sambo to be free, he thereby has to walk out of the shade, throw off his gloves, and delve for his own bread. Will Dr. Ross be actuated by that perfect impartiality, which has ever been considered most favorable to correct decisions?

But slavery is good for some people!!! As a *good* thing, slavery is strikingly peculiar, in this, that it is the only good thing which no man ever seeks the good of, *for himself.*

Nonsense! Wolves devouring lambs, not because it is good for their own greedy maws, but because it is good for the lambs!!!

WE MUST NOT overlook the power of pro-slavery thought in the nineteenth century.[1] It is imperative that we acknowledge its wide reach.

Pro-slavery theology, as part of a larger pro-slavery political ideology, exerted a deep influence over sizable parts of the population, and not just in the South. Pro-slavery theology connected with a public steeped in religion by arguing that its beliefs were rooted in the Bible and the Judeo-Christian tradition.

Lincoln did not underestimate the power of this theology. At one of the most critical junctures in his life, his 1858 debates with Senator Douglas, he took the time to read a bestselling pro-slavery book and then reflect upon it in one of his most captivating notes to himself. To understand this note, we need to examine it within the larger story of the ideas and events of the pivotal year 1858.

. . .

On June 16, 1858, ecstatic Illinois Republicans nominated Lincoln to oppose Democrat Douglas in that year's campaign for the U.S. Senate. Republicans convened a convention in Springfield to enact this unanimous decision; previously, candidates had simply run for the Senate at the behest of the state legislature, as Lincoln had in his losing campaign in February 1855.

On a warm, humid Springfield evening, forty-nine-year-old Lincoln rose to speak at eight o'clock. As always, he was meticulously prepared. He began by outlining the nation's greatest problem, as he saw it: "We are now far into the *fifth* year, since a policy was initiated, with the *avowed* object, and *confident* promise, of putting an end to slavery *agitation*." The policy was unnamed, but everyone in the audience would have understood that Lincoln was referring to the Kansas-Nebraska Act. "Under the operation of that policy, agitation has not only, *not ceased,* but has *constantly augmented*."[2]

At the heart of his speech, Lincoln predicted, "'A house divided against itself cannot stand.'"[3] Using a metaphor from Jesus's admonishment of the Pharisees, Lincoln declared there could no longer be any middle position on slavery. This scriptural image would become the central theme of his senatorial campaign—affirmed by friends and attacked by opponents.

When the 35th Congress adjourned, Douglas rushed home to Illinois to begin his reelection campaign. He traveled south from Chicago, riding in a special train with flags and a banner that read "Stephen A. Douglas, the Champion of Political Sovereignty."[4]

Almost everywhere Douglas went, Lincoln followed, ready to rebut the Little Giant in town after town. Six weeks into this traveling senatorial campaign, Lincoln and his advisers came up with a plan that would change the whole nature of the contest. They proposed to Douglas the idea of an extended series of debates—up to fifty. Some of Lincoln's friends, however, knowing Douglas's greater legislative experience, feared the incumbent would run roughshod over their idealistic candidate.

Douglas countered with a plan to limit the debates to seven. They would take place in seven of the nine congressional districts, forgoing debates in the contestants' districts of Chicago and Springfield, where the two had already spoken. Lincoln agreed.

In the first two debates, Douglas attacked Lincoln's views on slavery by connecting him thirty times to what the Illinois senator called the "Black Republican Party."[5] In the third and southernmost debate, in Jonesboro, Douglas began referring to the Republican Party as the "Abolitionist Party."[6] In the fourth debate at Charleston, Douglas spoke of "Lincoln's Abolitionism and negro equality doctrines."[7]

Douglas's approach in the debates was to turn national issues into local issues. He reminded the audience that Lincoln was critical of the 1857 Dred Scott decision by the Supreme Court. In that verdict, Chief Justice Roger Taney, son of a wealthy slaveholding family in Maryland, delivered a three-part ruling for the 7–2 majority. First, he argued, slaves were not citizens and therefore, as a slave, Dred Scott was not entitled to sue in federal court. Second, admitting that the 1787 Northwest Ordinance did exclude slaves from the territories it covered, Taney nevertheless ruled that future congressional attempts to exclude slaves from new territories were unconstitutional. Third, the court ruled that Scott, even if he had been taken to the free state of Illinois, was and would continue to be a slave according to Missouri law.[8]

Pivoting from this national decision, Douglas asked the audience, "Are you in favor of conferring upon the negro the rights and privileges of citizenship?" ("No, no!") "Do you desire to strike out of our state's constitution that clause which keeps slaves and free negroes out of the State, and allow the free negroes to flow in and cover your prairies with black settlements?" ("Never!")[9] Douglas's strategy was to assault Lincoln by pandering to local prejudices and fears.

. . .

UNKNOWN TO THE large audiences clapping, speaking out, and booing at the debates, Lincoln took time between Charleston and the fifth debate at Galesburg to read a recent popular book on pro-slavery theology. This helped him to clarify his thinking in unusual and productive ways. After the first debate at Ottawa, Lincoln's advisers, Norman Judd, chairman of the Republican state central committee, and Joseph Medill and Charles Ray of the *Chicago Press and Tribune,* had encouraged him not to be defensive, but urged him instead to bolster his own arguments.[10] It was with that mindset that Lincoln set out to immerse himself in pro-slavery ideas and rhetoric.

FREDERICK A. ROSS, a Presbyterian minister in Huntsville, Alabama, published *Slavery Ordained of God* in 1857. He wrote the book in part as a response to Harriet Beecher Stowe's *Uncle Tom's*

SLAVERY

ORDAINED OF GOD.

"The powers that be are ordained of God."
ROMANS xiii. 1.

BY

REV. FRED. A. ROSS, D.D.
PASTOR OF THE PRESBYTERIAN CHURCH, HUNTSVILLE, ALABAMA.

PHILADELPHIA:
J. B. LIPPINCOTT & CO.
1857.

In the midst of his seven debates with Stephen Douglas, Lincoln took time to read Frederick A. Ross's bestselling pro-slavery book and write a note to himself about it.

Cabin. Published five years earlier, Stowe's novel had infuriated the South with its critical depiction of slave owners; many Southern towns and cities banned the novel altogether.[11]

Although many assumed that advocates of a pro-slavery position were aiming their writings solely at Southern audiences, Ross tried to speak also to Northern audiences. *Slavery Ordained of God* became a bestseller among pro-slavery advocates. A review in the London *Saturday Review* stated, "The writings of Dr. Ross are acknowledged on both sides to be the most effective retort which the South has yet offered to its antagonists."[12] Lincoln, as always, saw value in fully considering the opposition's point of view, and was drawn to it as he worked out in his mind how to respond effectively to slavery advocates.

Ross's book was based on presentations he had made at the Presbyterian general assemblies in Buffalo in 1853 and New York in 1856, as well as three letters he'd written to the Reverend Albert Barnes, influential minister of the First Presbyterian Church of Philadelphia.[13]

Ross was born in 1796 in Cumberland County, Virginia. Before the widespread founding of theological seminaries, he followed the then-common practice of studying with an experienced minister as a mentor in his preparation to be ordained. He went on to serve the Old Kingsport Presbyterian Church in northeast-

Frederick A. Ross, a Presbyterian minister from Huntsville, Alabama, gained attention as a pro-slavery writer who appealed to both Northern and Southern audiences.

ern Tennessee before accepting a call to the First Presbyterian Church in Huntsville in 1855, the oldest Presbyterian church in Alabama.[14]

In both general assembly presentations, Ross buttressed his pro-slavery arguments with passages from the Bible, referring to the so-called curse of Ham, imposed by Noah on his son in Genesis 9:20–27. The original purpose of the story may have been to defend the subjugation of the Canaanite people, but pro-slavery advocates used it to justify American slavery. Speaking in New York, Ross called "the general curse on Ham conspicuous, historic, and explanatory."[15]

Ross also advanced the timeworn arguments that slavery was an honored institution among the Jews and approved by the Apostle Paul. He further maintained that slavery was ordained by God as a beneficent institution: "The Southern slave, though degraded compared with his master, is elevated and ennobled compared with his brethren in Africa."[16] Evoking a romantic racialism, Ross contended that "Southern masters . . . hold from God, individually and collectively, the highest and the noblest responsibility ever given by Him to individual private men on all the face of the earth." And what is that responsibility? "God has intrusted to them to train millions of the most degraded in form and intellect . . . and to give them civilization, and the light and the life of the gospel of Jesus Christ."[17]

The book captured Lincoln's attention. He knew that Ross's strategy of linking pro-slavery arguments with the Bible would have a wide appeal with a highly religious public.

LINCOLN WAS A voracious self-led reader. He is best remembered for devouring newspapers. Returning home in 1849 from his single term in Congress, he began subscriptions to the *New York Tribune,* Horace Greeley's national newspaper; the *Chicago Tribune,* whose editorial policies promoted a Whig and Free Soil antislavery

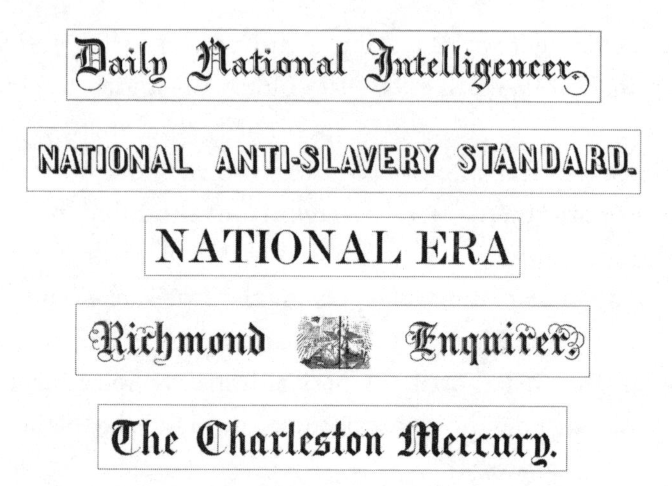

Lincoln was an avid reader of newspapers, north and south, because he was intent on knowing all points of view.

position; and the Washington *National Intelligencer,* an influential Whig newspaper that promoted Unionist principles.

Herndon encouraged him to also subscribe to antislavery newspapers. Thus, Lincoln began reading the *Anti-Slavery Standard,* the official newspaper of the American Anti-Slavery Society, and *The National Era,* an abolitionist paper published in Washington.[18]

But Lincoln believed it important to hear the other side, so he resolved to read several Southern newspapers as well, telling Herndon, "Let us have both sides at the table. Each is entitled to its day in court."[19] The *Richmond Enquirer* led the way in Southern journalism, and by 1858 had become a leading voice in the push toward secession. The *Charleston Mercury* espoused an aggressive proslavery position and attacked Northern abolitionists.[20]

These various newspapers, Northern and Southern, anti- and pro-slavery, became the intellectual grist for Lincoln's arguments about slavery in the years leading up to the Civil War. But often not recognized, he also read his share of books. In the fall of 1858, *Slavery Ordained of God* would join the newspapers in the mill of his mind.

. . .

LINCOLN STARTS THIS note: "Suppose it is true, that the negro is inferior to the white, in the gifts of nature." This is the basic assumption of Ross's book, and Lincoln understood that most white Americans started from a similar place. Rather than debating the point, Lincoln instead queries, "is it not the exact reverse justice that the white should, for that reason, take from the negro, any part of the little which has been given him?" Here he chooses not to respond with an intellectual argument but rather one based in the Christian spirit of generosity.

At this point in his life, in the late 1850s, Lincoln had become a more regular attendee of the First Presbyterian Church of Springfield.[21] His first law partner, John Todd Stuart, a member of the congregation, remembered his attendance. The mid-1850s expansion of the railroads in central Illinois allowed him to return to Springfield more frequently from the Eighth Judicial Circuit.

Lincoln's first response to Ross is a challenge from the center of Christian ethics: " 'Give to him that is needy' is the Christian rule of charity; but 'Take from him that is needy' is the rule of slavery."

Knowing that Ross and his ilk argued that slavery was the will of God, I can imagine Lincoln writing, with a twinkle in his eye, "Certainly, there is no contending against the Will of God." But he then goes on to push back against Ross, and all who avowed a divine intention behind slavery: "still there is some difficulty in ascertaining, and applying it, to particular cases." With this statement Lincoln is not denying the agency of God in human history, but rather, objecting to the hubris of Christian leaders like Ross who claimed to know the exact meaning and direction of the will of God.

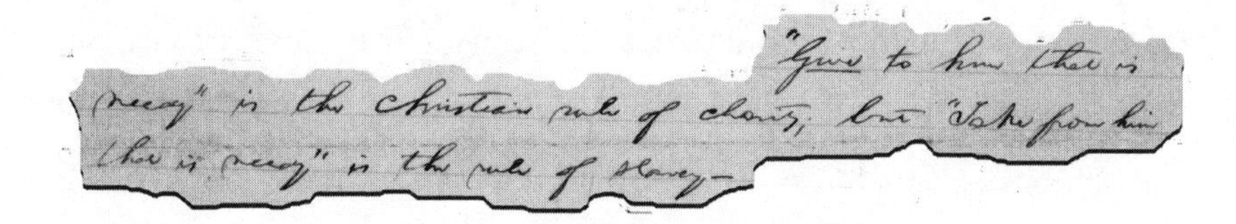

"Give to him that is needy" is the christian rule of charity; but "Take from him that is needy" is the rule of slavery—

The note next moves from the general to the particular, taking the massive national issue of slavery and making it personal by proposing a hypothetical case to test Ross's position. Lincoln imagines that Dr. Ross owns a slave named Sambo, asking, "Is it the Will of God that Sambo shall remain a slave, or be set free?"

He approaches the question from several directions. First, "The Almighty gives no audible answer to the question, and his revelation—the Bible—gives none—or, at most, none but such as admits of a squabble, as to its meaning." Right away, Lincoln challenges the validity of Ross's reading of the Bible.

Next, Lincoln introduces the autonomy and agency of the individual typically ignored in these debates: "No one thinks of asking Sambo's opinion of it." With that statement, he makes it clear that, in his mental framework, slaves are to be treated as subjects rather than objects; he advances the radical idea of African American agency in the privacy of this note.

Finally, Lincoln puts the moral accountability on Reverend Ross himself. He points out that if Ross insists that Sambo remain a slave, Ross "thereby retains his own comfortable position." Lincoln did not know Ross personally, but a Presbyterian minister in the South could be presumed to have a life of economic comfort.

Continuing his hypothetical case study, Lincoln posits that if Ross "decides that God wills Sambo to be free," it will mean that he "has to walk out of the shade, throw off his gloves, and delve for his own bread." In other words, Ross's leisurely life will change if he does not have an enslaved African American at his beck and call.

In that scenario, is it possible for Ross to be guided by "that perfect impartiality" which Lincoln suggests "has ever been considered most favorable to correct decisions"? It is clear, of course, that he believes the answer is no.

. . .

Lincoln concludes his note in a crescendo of emotion, an explosion of sarcastic fury: "But, slavery is good for some people!!!"

Later, as president, Lincoln's part-time secretary William O. Stoddard was a witness to Lincoln's writing style and observed he "is more an orator than a writer."[22] Lincoln often employed the same strategies and inflections he used in composing and delivering speeches. So, in reading this note, one can picture Lincoln's emotions escalating, his voice rising as he read it aloud. Hear him thunder: "As a *good* thing, slavery is strikingly peculiar, in this, that it is the only good thing which no man ever seeks the good of, *for himself.*" Hear him roar: "Nonsense! Wolves devouring lambs, not because it is good for their own greedy maws, but because it is good for the lambs!!!" A triplet of exclamation points appear once more, revealing the sheer absurdity Lincoln encountered as he struggled to understand how religious leaders—supposedly pious men who lived in the same country he did and read the same Bible he read—could defend the immorality of slavery.

Despite taking considerable time to explore pro-slavery theology while in the middle of seven debates with Douglas, Lincoln's mental tussles with Ross would not find a place in the final three debates with Douglas; in fact, he never mentioned Ross in any public speech.

The point of many of Lincoln's notes to himself was not to rehearse language and ideas for subsequent speeches. Instead, they served as a private pressure valve so that he could better use his persuasive combination of calm logic and humor to make the case against slavery.

Lincoln's actual attitudes toward slavery have long been the subject of debate. What were his motives in signing the Emancipation Proclamation on January 1, 1863? Was the proclamation, at its

This 1850 cartoon is critical of abolitionists by contrasting the living conditions of American slaves with those of industrial workers in England. The quotations in the mouths of Northern visitors begin, "Is it possible that we of the North have been so deceived by false Reports? Why did we not visit the South before we caused this trouble between North and South?"

base, a political and military act? In signing it, did Lincoln have any real sympathy for the slaves?

This private note provides an answer. In no uncertain terms, Lincoln reveals his thinking concerning the institution of slavery: It is fundamentally wrong, un-Christian, and rooted in economic greed. In this note, the usually rational and cool Lincoln lets his emotions explode. "Nonsense! Wolves devouring lambs, not because it is good for their own greedy maws, but because it is good for the lambs!!!"

philosophical cause— Without
tion and the Union, we could no
tained the result; but even these
primary cause of our great pros
here is something back of these,

PART THREE

PRESIDENT

rned an "apple of gold" to us—
d the Constitution, are the pict
, subsequently framed around
he picture was made, not to co
stroy the apple; but to adorn
serve it— The picture was made
le— not the apple for the picture.

Abraham Lincoln was nominated to be the candidate for president at the Republican National Convention held in Chicago in May 1860. Six months later, in a four-way race, Lincoln was elected president on November 6 with 39.8 percent of the popular vote—the lowest popular percentage vote by a victor in U.S. history.

As his March 4, 1861, inauguration approached, Lincoln leased his home at the corner of 8th and Jackson to Lucian Tilton, president of the Great Western Railroad. Shortly before leaving Springfield for Washington on February 11, Mary consigned many of the family's papers to what she called her "burn pile" in the alley behind their home.[1] In the nineteenth century it was common for people to burn their personal papers at various times during their life, lest future generations read what was for them private correspondence and notes.

It's possible that Abraham Lincoln discarded various of his private notes at this same time—such as earlier scraps from the 1830s and '40s—deeming them no longer valuable to him, yet sensitive enough in nature that he would not want them to be seen by renters or others.

When Lincoln took up residence in the White House in March 1861, he continued writing notes to himself. Nicolay and Hay continued to serve him as secretaries, but others joined his staff as assistants. While in the past his fragments were sometimes written on the run, he now worked at the Executive Mansion in a regular daily schedule, and his notes took on a more formal character.

If in this new setting Lincoln continued an old method, it was attested to by a new eyewitness. William Slade, a White House servant, would be the only person with Lincoln on many evenings as the president worked, read, and wrote. Slade, an elder in the 15th Street Presbyterian Church, a prominent African American congregation near the Executive Mansion, had earned a trusted place as a constant and confidential companion of the president.[2]

It is from Slade that we learn about another of Lincoln's habits—the president's "peculiar" manner of reading. Lincoln would frequently tear off a small piece of paper and write a note on it. Slade then observed Lincoln tucking the note in his desk, or in his pant pocket, or in his vest, before resuming his reading. "Nibbie" Slade, William's daughter, reported that her father often saved these small pieces of paper for the president.[3]

IN PART 3, I have chosen three notes from the hand of President Lincoln. The first two notes are political, while the third is theological.

The first was provoked by an exchange with a prominent Southern leader with whom Lincoln once served in the 30th Congress. Correspondence with Alexander Stephens of Georgia pushed Lincoln to express his understanding of the relationship of the Constitution to the Declaration of Independence.

The second is a long-forgotten note written in preparation for a speech Lincoln hoped to deliver in Kentucky, his native state, while on the thirteen-day pre-inaugural train trip to Washington. He never delivered the speech, but what he intended to say to the border state reveals his thinking in the weeks before his inauguration.

The third, written after a military defeat in 1862 that Lincoln knew would be dispiriting to the Northern public, prompted his reflection on the role of God in the Civil War. Examination of this note engages us in the long-debated question of Lincoln's faith—or lack thereof. This theological reflection, unknown to the public of his day, points forward to a later public speech—his remarkable second inaugural address delivered on March 4, 1865, just forty-one days before his death.

Before Lincoln's election, eleven-year-old Grace Bedell wrote, "let your whiskers grow . . . you would look a great deal better for your face is so thin." This photograph from November 25, 1860, shows the beginning of Lincoln's response.

CHAPTER 8

The Unity Lincoln: Secession and the Constitution

[circa January 1861]

All this is not the result of accident. It has a philosophical cause. Without the *Constitution* and the *Union*, we could not have attained the result; but even these, are not the primary cause of our great prosperity. There is something back of these, entwining itself more closely about the human heart. That something, is the principle of "Liberty to all"—the principle that clears the *path* for all—gives *hope* to all—and, by consequence, *enterprise*, and *industry* to all.

The *expression* of that principle, in our Declaration of Independence, was most happy, and fortunate. *Without* this, as well as *with* it, we could have declared our independence of Great Britain; but *without* it, we could not, I think, have secured our free government, and consequent prosperity. No oppressed, people will *fight*, and *endure*, as our fathers did, without the promise of something better, than a mere change of masters.

The assertion of that *principle*, at that *time*, was the word, "*fitly spoken*" which has proved an "apple of gold" to us. The *Union*, and the *Constitution*, are the *picture* of *silver*, subsequently framed around it. The picture was made,

> not to *conceal,* or *destroy* the apple; but to *adorn,* and *preserve* it. The *picture* was made for the apple—*not* the apple for the picture.
>
> So let us act, that neither *picture,* or *apple* shall ever be blurred, or bruised or broken.
>
> That we may so act, we must study, and understand the points of danger.

The America that had elected Lincoln on November 6, 1860, threatened to implode as the calendar turned to December.

Along with many Northern leaders, however, Lincoln considered Southern threats of secession bluster and bluff, believing that prudent Southern leaders would resist any moves for separation. That calculus began to change when on December 20 a South Carolina convention, meeting in Charleston, voted to secede from the Union.

Lincoln, remaining in Springfield for the transition months before his inauguration in Washington on March 4, 1861, still hoped for some positive sign from the South. As he prepared to become the nation's sixteenth president, he worked at a corner table in the Illinois governor's office on the second floor of the statehouse. Nicolay, his twenty-eight-year-old secretary, served as his one-man transition team. Friends and office seekers visited all day, every day, throughout what Henry Adams, a member of the famous Adams political family, would call the "Great Secession Winter of 1860–1861."[1]

Although Lincoln received no votes from ten Southern states, he wanted to believe strong Unionist sentiment in the South remained. He walked in the footsteps of Southerner Henry Clay,

A steady stream of visitors came and went from president-elect Lincoln's office in the Illinois State Capitol.

holding up a vision of sovereignty based in national unity, rather than the sovereignty of individual states. In his 1852 eulogy for Clay, Lincoln had praised "the Great Compromiser" as a political leader who, "whatever he did, he did for the whole country."[2] It was one of the paradoxes of Lincoln's rise to national leadership that this Illinois politician—whose only experience in federal politics had been a single term in Congress—was elected president with less than 40 percent of the national vote, yet ran his campaign with a dynamic, far-reaching national vision.

His hopes were buoyed when he learned of a recent speech delivered in Georgia by Alexander Stephens, his former Whig congressional colleague in the 30th Congress of 1847–49.

Thirteen years earlier, Lincoln had found himself drawn to Stephens, recognizing in the small Georgian, with his blazing dark eyes, a learned man who seemed an allied spirit. An intellectual with a lithe mind, Stephens impressed Lincoln as a student of the Constitution and of political institutions. He had joined Lincoln in opposition to President James Polk and the United States' War with Mexico. In a speech on the floor of Congress, Stephens cast Polk's behavior and policies as "odious and detestable."[3] Lincoln, spellbound, wrote Herndon immediately that Stephens "has just concluded the very best speech, of an hour's length, I have ever heard." He told his law partner, "My old, withered, dry eyes are full of tears yet."[4]

On November 14, 1860, following days of fury-filled speeches in Milledgeville from those advocating secession—allegations that the South had been "robbed . . . threatened . . . abused . . . vilified"—Stephens managed to change the tenor of the jam-packed chamber, striking a different tone before the Georgia House of Representatives.[5] "My object is not to stir up strife, but to allay it; not to appeal to your passions, but to your reason." He immediately focused on what he called the first question: "Shall the people of the South secede from the Union in consequence of the election of Mr. Lincoln to the Presidency of the United States?" He answered unambiguously: "My countrymen, *I tell you frankly, candidly, and earnestly, that I do not think they ought.*"[6]

Stephens reminded his listeners that the U.S. Constitution was the best in the world. He pled, "Don't give up the ship. Don't abandon her yet." When someone called out, "The ship has leaks in her," Stephens replied, "Let us stop them if we can." He concluded, "I look upon this country, with our institutions, as the Eden of the world, the paradise of the universe."[7] At no point in his dramatic speech did he reveal to his audience that he had served with Lincoln in the 30th Congress.

Anxious for any good news from Southern states, Lincoln heard of the speech and remembered his many conversations with Stephens in the nation's capital more than a decade earlier. He was intrigued. Perhaps he even thought of Stephens—a political moderate who had for decades opposed Southern radicals' calls for secession—as a potential member of his cabinet. Lincoln wanted to believe his former colleague spoke for a large number of Unionists

Lincoln knew Alexander Stephens, the Georgia congressman, from their time together in the 30th Congress.

in the South who opposed secession, or who believed it was not yet the moment for such radical action.[8]

He wrote his former Southern friend on November 30, saying, "I shall be much obliged" if Stephens would send him a copy of the speech.[9] Upon receiving the speech, Lincoln was further encouraged by both its substance and its tone. He wrote Stephens again on December 22, two days after South Carolina became the first Southern state to announce it would secede from the Union. In a letter marked, "For your own eye only," he inquired, "Do the people of the South really entertain fears that a Republican administration would, *directly,* or *indirectly,* interfere with their slaves, or with them, about their slaves? If they do, I wish to assure you, as once a friend, and still, I hope, not an enemy, that there is no cause for such fears."[10]

Lincoln could have stopped there, but concluded, "You think slavery is *right* and ought to be extended; while we think it is *wrong* and ought to be restricted."[11] If Lincoln wrote "as your friend," in his new role as president-elect he must have believed there was no point in hiding his basic belief about slavery at this moment of national crisis.

Still, Lincoln was likely surprised by Stephens's sharp reply of December 30. Not insolent, but also not shying away from vigorously stating his case, the Georgian wrote, "We both have an earnest desire to preserve and maintain the Union." Stephens told Lincoln he did not fear him, but that the South feared the Republican Party, whose "leading object" was "to put the institutions of nearly half the States under the ban of public opinion and national condemnation." He stressed he was "being not a personal enemy," and implored Lincoln to "do what you can to save our common country." He warned that a Union held together by force was "nothing short of a consolidated despotism," and encouraged Lincoln to address the nation before it was too late. He concluded his letter by appealing to the wisdom enshrined in the book of Proverbs: "A word fitly spoken by you now would be like 'apples of gold in pictures of silver.' "[12] Stephens knew Lincoln would be familiar with the verse.

Lincoln never replied to Stephens in a letter—but he did reply in a personal note to himself. Challenged by his old friend, and struck by Stephen's use of the proverb, the president-elect sat down to write his thoughts on the preservation of the Union. In the fragment, Lincoln uses the reasoning of the Southern Democrat to jump-start his own flexible mind, just as two years earlier he had used the logic of Southern pro-slavery advocate Frederick Ross to push his own antislavery ideas further.

Lincoln understood the verse from Proverbs that Stephens quoted to be an analogy. "A word fitly spoken is like apples of gold in pictures of silver." In the ancient world, gold and silver were the two most precious metals. Lincoln now builds on the analogy to declare that the gold, which is primary in the Proverbs analogy, is the Declaration of Independence. The function of the silver, secondary in value, is to adorn or enhance. Furthermore,

Lincoln asserts that the function of the Constitution, to which Stephens appeals, is not to "conceal" the primary, precious gold. Thus, "The picture was made for the apple—not the apple for the picture." In his letter, Stephens suggested that Lincoln offer his own presidential "word" that is "*fitly spoken,*" in the hope that a conciliatory word from Lincoln in the last month of 1860 might forestall the rush toward secession and the possibility of civil war.

In this fragment, Lincoln points beyond himself as president-elect to a more permanent "word": the principle of "Liberty to all," as enshrined in the Declaration of Independence.

There is no speech in which Lincoln repurposes the language of this fragment. Yet the instinctive way he points beyond himself will appear again in his two great presidential addresses. Lincoln the individual disappears in the Gettysburg Address and the Second Inaugural Address. At Gettysburg, where he calls for a new birth of freedom, he does not use a single personal pronoun. In the

In Lincoln's reemergence into politics, he grounded his speeches in the Declaration of Independence. John Trumbull's painting depicts the presentation of a draft of the Declaration to Congress.

Second Inaugural Address, where he concludes with the ethical imperative "with malice toward none, with charity for all," he uses only two personal pronouns.

Lincoln was well aware that the Constitution contained elements that made the actual attainment of "liberty to all" difficult. Abolitionists had long pointed out that clauses in the Constitution—those that permitted slavery to continue in states where it already existed, the fugitive slave clause, and the three-fifths compromise—actively impeded the achievement of this lofty goal.

In the beginning of Lincoln's political career, he shared the optimistic belief common in the early years of the nineteenth century that slavery would die a natural death as the nation matured, and that he would see that happen in his lifetime.

But slavery did not die.

FOR LINCOLN, THE concept of the Union sprang from the Declaration of Independence, which predated the Constitution; this was the foundation for all of his political ideas. He believed the Constitution did not exist by itself or for itself. That is why, in this note, he repurposes Stephens's use of the proverb: "a word fitly spoken is like apples of gold in pictures of silver." In Stephens's depiction, Lincoln's words are the apples of gold, and the current moment is the pictures of silver. Lincoln instead assigns the apples' role to the principle of "Liberty to all," and his words the role of frame, or picture, declaring, "The picture was made *for* the apple—*not* the apple for the picture." Stephens uses this particular proverb as part of his case for a states' rights view of the Constitution, a document that can be interpreted by many different constituents, whereas Lincoln uses the same proverb to advocate a view that the Constitution codified into statutes and law the underlying principle of freedom emanating from the Declaration of Independence.

preserve it— The picture was made for the apple—not the apple for the picture—

Lincoln concludes with an ethical imperative, stated twice: "So let us act" and "That we may so act." Even in his most philosophical fragments, Lincoln almost always ends his notes to himself with some kind of call to action.

However, this is a call to a more internal than external action. He recognizes a need for "study" in order to "understand the points of danger." As much as he had admired Stephens in the past, he recognized in the Georgian's letter that even so-called moderates were becoming a danger to the integrity of the Union.

If at first encouraged by Stephens's November speech, this note shows Lincoln's disappointment in his follow-up letter. While he could dismiss the passion of the Southern secessionists, Lincoln became more concerned about moderate Unionists like Stephens, as their attitudes suggested a deeper secessionist feeling than he wanted to believe. The Georgian's missive challenged Lincoln's optimism about the prospects for some kind of reconciliation with the Southern states.

Despite the frustration that triggered it, this note reveals Lincoln's remarkable ability to take an idea from someone else, friend or foe, and use it as a launchpad to expand the limits of his own thinking. Stephens's speech and subsequent letter, and Lincoln's letter and unpublished fragment, helped him understand with greater clarity his own position on states' rights and the relationship of the Constitution to the Declaration of Independence.

But why did Lincoln keep this note for his eyes only? Did he believe his ideas or language were not yet finely tuned enough for public consumption? Did he think his ideas too radical for dissemination at this moment?

The latter question may have the most value. Lincoln defines liberty in this fragment as the principle that works its way into the fabric of America in four ways: *path, hope, enterprise,* and *industry;* he emphasizes that these values are for "all."

Three times, he stresses "all." In response to the attempt by Stephens and the secessionists to limit the scope of freedom to white Americans, Lincoln muscularly implies that "all" includes African Americans as well. But this is a concept he was still struggling to fully articulate publicly, and it was a stance that was seen as radical across much of antebellum America.

Lincoln would begin to move in that direction over the next months, and the ideas from this fragment would begin to trickle out in a variety of ways. On his pre-inaugural train trip to Washington in February, he would stand in front of Philadelphia's Independence Hall on George Washington's birthday and declare, "I have never had a feeling politically that did not spring from the sentiments embodied in the Declaration of Independence."[13]

That same month, Stephens would be elected vice president of the Confederacy.[14] On March 4, 1861, Lincoln would be inaugurated the nation's sixteenth president.

This photograph by C. S. German was taken in Springfield on February 9, 1861, two days before Lincoln departed for Washington.

CHAPTER 9

The Kentuckian Lincoln: An Undelivered Speech to the South

[February 12, 1861?]

I am grateful, for the opportunity your invitation affords me to appear before an audience of my native state. During the present winter it has been greatly pressed upon me by many patriotic citizens, Kentuckians among others, that I could in my position, by a word, restore peace to the country. But what word? I have many words already before the public; and my position was given me on the faith of those words. Is the desired word to be confirmatory of these; or must it be contradictory to them? If the former, it is useless repetition; if the latter, it is dishonorable and treacherous.

Again, it is urged as if the word must be spoken before the fourth of March. Why? Is the speaking the word a "*sine qua non*" to the inauguration? Is there a Bell-man, a Breckinridge-man, or a Douglas man, who would tolerate his own candidate to make such terms, had he been elected? Who amongst you would not die by the proposition, that your candidate, being elected, should be inaugurated, solely on the conditions of the constitution, and laws, or not at all? What Kentuckian, worthy of his birthplace, would not do this? Gentlemen, I too, am a Kentuckian.

Nor is this a matter of mere personal honor. No man can be elected President without some opponents, as well as supporters; and if when elected, he cannot be installed, till he first appeases his enemies, by breaking his pledges, and betraying his friends, this government, and all popular government, is already at an end. Demands for such surrender, once recognized, and yielded to, are without limit, as to nature, extent, or repetition. They break the only bond of faith between public, and public servant; and they distinctly set the minority over the majority. Such demands acquiesced in, would not merely be the ruin of a man, or a party; but as a precedent they would ruin the government itself.

I do not deny the possibility that the people may err in an election; but if they do, the true remedy is in the next election, and not in the treachery of the person elected.

During the winter just closed, I have been greatly urged, by many patriotic men, to lend the influence of my position to some compromise, by which I was, to some extent, to shift the ground upon which I had been elected. This I steadily refused. I so refused, not from any party wantonness, nor from any indifference to the troubles of the country. I thought such refusal was demanded by the view that if, when a Chief Magistrate is constitutionally elected, he cannot be inaugurated till he betrays those who elected him, by breaking his pledges, and surrendering to those who tried and failed to defeat him at the polls, this government and all popular government is already at an end. Demands for such surrender, once recognized, are without limit, as to nature, extent and repetition. They break the only bond of faith between public and public servant; and they distinctly set the minority over the majority.

> I presume there is not a man in America, (and there ought not to be one) who opposed my election, who would, for a moment, tolerate his own candidate in such surrender, had he been successful in the election. In such case they would all see, that such surrender would not be merely the ruin of a man, or a party; but, as a precedent, would be the ruin of the government itself.
>
> I do not deny the possibility that the people may err in an election; but if they do, the true cure is in the next election; and not in the treachery of the party elected.

By the time Lincoln's inaugural train bound for Washington left Springfield on February 11, 1861, seven Southern states had seceded from the Union. Lincoln faced dual challenges: how to restore the Union without resorting to civil war, and how to preserve the Union without giving in to compromise.

The organizers of his pre-inaugural train trip arranged for him to speak in the Northern states of Indiana, Ohio, Pennsylvania, New York, and New Jersey. Lincoln hoped to make one detour from the thirteen-day route: He wanted to speak in the South. He intended to address an audience in Kentucky, the state of his birth, as a way to face both challenges at once.[1]

For some time, Lincoln had longed for Kentucky to remain within the Union. He hoped for an opportunity to speak to what he called "my native state," as part of his 1,904-mile journey to the nation's capital. He planned to cross the Ohio River at Cincinnati to speak in Kentucky.

Because Lincoln never delivered this speech, for reasons unknown, it has been nearly erased from public knowledge. This note has been sitting within the Lincoln papers for 150 years, largely unnoticed. When brought out of the shadows, it shows a compelling if complex side of Lincoln, where he is willing to see the best in the people of Kentucky, yet unwilling to mute his strong views about the Union in order to win their support.

Lincoln planned a lengthy train trip, and a zigzag route, because he was looking for every opportunity to connect with the public. From the prairies of Illinois, the train would stop in the most populous cities of the Midwest—Indianapolis, Cincinnati, Columbus, Cleveland, and Pittsburgh—before traveling on to New York and Philadelphia. Lincoln saw the journey as an opportunity to improve his tenuous relationship with an American people that had elected him with only 39.82 percent of the popular vote. William Seward, his former rival for the Republican nomination for president and now his pick for secretary of state, had originally encouraged the tour, but changed his mind as the secession crisis deepened. Worried that Southerners were plotting to seize the capital before Lincoln's inauguration on March 4, he urged Lincoln to forgo the trip and travel directly to Washington—"without announcement"—in order to get ahead of such plans.[2]

But Lincoln could not be dissuaded. He would be seen and heard by more Americans than any president before him. The whistle-stop tour was part political rally, part county fair, part carnival, and part religious revival. Between major cities, the train stopped briefly in small town after small town, all bedecked with American flags and cheering crowds—ninety-one stops in all.

Throngs of well-wishers greeted him in Indianapolis, his first overnight stop. Large portraits of George Washington and Lincoln filled windows across the bustling city of twenty thousand residents.

Lincoln had decided he would not tip his hand about the policies he intended to pursue as president, preferring to wait until his inaugural address. In response to his welcome to Indianapolis by Republican governor Oliver P. Morton, he replied, "I do not expect, upon this occasion, or any occasion, till after I get to Washington, to attempt any lengthy speech." From the balcony of the

GREAT WESTERN RAILROAD.

TIME CARD

For a Special Train, Monday, Feb. 11, 1861,

WITH

His Excellency, Abraham Lincoln, President Elect.

Leave	Springfield,	8.00 A. M.
"	Jamestown,	8.15 "
"	Dawson,	8.24 "
"	Mechanicsburg,	8.30 "
"	Lanesville,	8.37 "
"	Illiopolis	8.49 "
"	Niantic	8.58 "
"	Summit,	9.07 "
Arrive at	Decatur,	9.24 "
Leave	Decatur,	9.29 "
"	Oakley,	9.45 "
"	Cerro Gordo,	9.54 "
"	Bement,	10.13 "
"	Sadorus,	10.40 "
Arrive at	Tolono,	10.50 "
Leave	"	10.55 "
"	Philo,	11.07 "
"	Sidney,	11.17 "
"	Homer,	11.30 "
"	Salina,	11.45 "
"	Catlin,	11.59 "
"	Bryant,	12.07 P. M.
"	Danville,	12.12 "
Arrive at	State Line,	12.30 P. M.

This train will be entitled to the road, *and all other trains must be kept out of the way*.

Trains to be passed and met must be on the side track at least 10 minutes before this train is due.

Agents at all stations between Springfield and State Line must be on duty when this train passes, and examine the switches and know *that all is right before it passes*.

Operators at Telegraph Stations between Springfield and State Line must remain on duty until this train passes, and immediately report its time to Chas. H. Speed, Springfield.

All Foremen and men under their direction must be on the track and know positively that the track is in order.

It is very important that this train should pass over the road in safety, and all employees are expected to render all assistance in their power.

***Red is the signal for danger*, but any signal apparently intended to indicate alarm or danger must be regarded, the train stopped, and the meaning of it ascertained.**

Carefulness is particularly enjoined.

F. W. BOWEN,
Supt.

The Great Western Railroad printed a time card for "His Excellency, President-Elect, Abraham Lincoln," for his inaugural trip from Springfield.

Bates House, he quoted from the Old Testament book of Ecclesiastes, "There is a time to keep silence."[3]

Lincoln would follow this strategy in the more than one hundred brief remarks and responses he made during the trip. Even though he was eager to communicate his vision for national unity, he also wanted to preserve the power of announcing his plans in his inaugural address.

But there was one exception to this plan. Lincoln intended to be anything but silent in Kentucky.

HE WROTE THE proposed speech on lined notepaper. This five-page fragment remains of what were likely longer notes. On the back of the fifth page, he pasted three paragraphs from the first draft of his inaugural address. He'd had this initial version printed privately in the offices of the *Illinois State Journal* in Springfield in January. He wanted to keep this first draft from prying eyes, but he also intended to follow his practice of editing and rewriting. He would cut and paste until he was satisfied that he had arrived at the final shape of his inaugural address.

The fact that the two speeches were pasted together indicates that Lincoln prepared the Kentucky speech not from the train, but in Springfield. During the last days of December and into January, Lincoln sat each morning for Ohioan Thomas D. Jones, who was creating a bust of the president-elect—what Lincoln humorously called his "mud-head." The artist set up his modeling stand and clay in a temporary studio in his room at the St. Nicholas Hotel, Springfield's finest. While sitting with his legs crossed, Lincoln read his daily mail and worked with Faber pencils on letters and speeches—probably including one he hoped to deliver in Kentucky.[4]

WHY DID LINCOLN feel so strongly about delivering the train tour's one speech in Kentucky?

He was born at Sinking Springs farm, near Elizabethtown, Kentucky, on February 12, 1809. He resided in Kentucky until the late fall of 1816 when his father, Thomas, led the family across the Ohio River to establish a farm in southern Indiana.

Niagara-Falls! By what mysterious power is it, that
millions and millions, are drawn from all parts of the
world, to gaze upon Niagara Falls! There is no mystery about
the thing itself. Every effect is just such as any inteligent man knowing the causes, would anticipate, without
it. If the water moving onward in a great river reaches
a point where there is a perpendicular jog, of a hundred
feet in descent, in the bottom of the river, it is plain
the water will have a violent and continuous plunge
at that point. It is also plain the water, thus plunging,
will foam, and roar, and send up a mist, continuously, in which last, during sunshine, there will be
perpetual rain-bows. The mere physical of Niagara
Falls, is only this. Yet this is really a very small part
of that world's wonder. It's power to excite reflection, and
emotion, is it's great charm. The geologist will demonstrate
that the plunge or fall, was once at Lake Ontario, and
has worn it's way back to it's present position; he will
ascertain how *fast* it is wearing now, and so get a basis
for determining how *long* it has been wearing back from Lake
Ontario, and finally demonstrate by it that this world is at
least fourteen thousand years old. A philosopher of a
slightly different turn will say Niagara Falls is only the
lip of the basin out of which pours all the surplus water which rains down on two or three hundred thousand
square miles of the earth's surface. He will estimate with
approximate accuracy, that five hundred thousand tons
of water, falls with it's full weight, a distance of a
hundred feet each minute, thus exerting a force equal
to the lifting of the same weight, through the same
space, in the same time. And then the further reflection comes that this vast amount of water, constantly pouring *down*, is supplied by an equal amount constantly
lifted up, by the sun; and still he says, "If this

453

From Chapter 1, The Lyrical Lincoln: The Transcendence of Niagara Falls (1) much is lifted up, for this one space of two or three hundred thousand square miles, an equal amount must be lifted for every other equal space; and he is overwhelmed in the contemplation of the vast power the sun is constantly exerting in quiet, noiseless opperation of lifting water up to be rained down again—

But still there is more. It calls up the indefinite past— When Columbus first sought this continent— when Christ suffered on the cross— when Moses lead Israel through the Red-Sea— nay, even, when Adam first came from the hand of his Maker— then as now, Niagara was roaring here— The eyes of that species of extinct giants, whose bones fill the mounds of America, have gazed on Niagara, as ours do now— Cotemporary with the whole race of men, and older than the first man, Niagara is strong, and fresh to-day as ten thousand years ago— The Mammoth and Mastadon— now so long dead, that fragments of their monstrous bones, alone testify, that they ever lived, have gazed on Niagara— In that long— long time, never still for a single moment— Never dried, never froze, never slept, never rested,

454

From Chapter 1, The Lyrical Lincoln: The Transcendence of Niagara Falls (2)

I am not an accomplished lawyer— I find quite as much material for a lecture, in those points wherein I have failed, as in those wherein I have been moderately successful—

The leading rule for the lawyer, as for the man of every other calling, is ~~diligence~~. Leave nothing for to-morrow, which can be done to-day— Never let your correspondence fall behind— Whatever piece of business you have in hand, before stopping, do all the labor pertaining to it, which can then be done— When you bring a common-law suit, if you have the facts for doing so, write the declaration at once— If a law point be involved, examine the books, and note the authority you rely on, upon the declaration itself, where you are sure to find it when wanted— The same of defences and pleas— In business not likely to be litigated— ordinary collection cases, foreclosures, partitions, and the like,—make all examinations of titles, and note them, and even draft orders, and decrees in advance— This course has a triple advantage; it avoids omissions and neglect, saves your labor, when once done; performs the labor out of court when you have leisure, rather than in court, when you have not—

Extemporaneous speaking should be practiced and cultivated— It is the lawyer's avenue to the public— However able and faithful he may be in other respects, people are slow to bring him business, if he can not make a speech— And yet there is not a more fatal error to young lawyers, than relying too much on speech-making— If any one, upon his rare powers of speaking, shall claim an exemption from the drudgery of the law, his case is a failure in advance

~~Never encourage~~ Discourage litigation— Persuade your neighbors to compromise whenever you can— Point out to them how the nominal winner is often a real loser, in fees, expenses, and waste of time— As a peace-maker, the lawyer has a superior opertunity of being a good man— There will still be business enough—

455

From Chapter 2, The Humble Lincoln: A Lawyer's Vocation

If A. can prove, however conclusively, that he may, of right, enslave B.—why may not B. snatch the same argument, and prove equally, that he may enslave A?—

You say A. is white, and B. is black—It is *color*, then; the lighter, having the right to enslave the darker? Take care—By this rule, you are to be slave to the first man you meet, with a fairer skin than your own—~~yourself~~

You do not mean *color* exactly?—You mean the whites are *intellectually* the superiors of the blacks; and, therefore have the right to enslave them? Take care again—By this rule, you are to be slave to the first man you meet, with an intellect superior to your own—

But, say you, it is a question of *interest*; and, if you can make it your *interest*, you have the right to enslave another—Very well—And if he can make it his interest, he has the right to enslave you—

From Chapter 3, The Fiery Lincoln: Slavery and a Reentry to Politics, Fragment One dent truth—Made so plain by our good Father in Heaven, that all *feel* and *understand* it, even down to brutes and creeping insects—The ant, who has toiled and dragged a crumb to his nest, will furiously defend the fruit of his labor, against whatever robber assails him—So plain, that the most dumb and stupid slave that ever toiled for a master, does constantly *know* that he is wronged—So plain that no one, high or low, ever does mistake it, except in a plainly *selfish* way; for although volume upon volume is written to prove slavery a very good thing, we never hear of the man who wishes to take the good of it, by *being a slave himself*—

Most governments have been based, practically, on the denial of the equal rights of men, as I have, in part, stated them; *ours* began, by *affirming* those rights—*They* said, some men are too *ignorant*, and *vicious*, to share in government—Possibly so, said we; and, by your system, you would always keep them ignorant, and vicious—We proposed to give *all* a chance; and we expected the weak to grow stronger, the ignorant, wiser; and all better, and happier together—

We made the experiment; and the fruit is before us—Look at it—think of it—Look at it, in its aggregate grandeur, of extent of country, and numbers of population—of ship, and steamboat, and rails

From Chapter 3, The Fiery Lincoln: Slavery and a Reentry to Politics, Fragment Two

Twentytwo years ago Judge Douglas and
I first became acquainted— We were both
young then; he, a trifle younger than I.
Even then, we were both ambitious; I,
perhaps, quite as much so as he— With
me, the race of ambition has been a
failure— a flat failure; with *him* it has
been one of splendid success— His name
fills the nation; and is not unknown, even, in
foreign lands— I affect no contempt
for the high eminence he has reached—
So reached, that the oppressed of my
species, might have shared with me
in the elevation, I would rather stand
on that eminence, than wear the richest
crown that ever pressed a monarch's brow—

From Chapter 4, The Defeated Lincoln: Failure and Ambition

Sectionalism.

It is constantly objected to Fremont & Dayton, that they are supported by a *sectional* party, who, by their *sectionalism*, endanger the National Union— This objection, more than all others, causes men, really opposed to slavery extension, to hesitate— Practically, it is the most difficult objection we have to meet—

For this reason, I now propose to examine it, a little more carefully than I have heretofore done, or seen it done by others—

First, then, what is the ~~naked~~ question between the parties, respectively represented by Buchanan and Fremont?

Simply this: "*Shall slavery be allowed to extend into U. S. territories, now legally free?*" Buchanan says it *shall*; and Fremont says it shall *not*—

That is the *naked* issue, and the *whole* of it— Lay the respective platforms side by side; and the difference between them, will be found to amount to precisely that—

True, each party charges upon the other, *designs* much beyond what is involved in the issue, as stated; but as these charges can not be fully proved either way, it is probably better to reject them on both sides, and stick to the naked issue, as it is clearly made up on the record.

And now, to restate the question "*Shall slavery be allowed to extend into U. S. territories, now legally free?* I beg to know *how* *one* side of that question is more sectional than the other? Of course I expect to effect

From Chapter 5, The Republican Lincoln: The Birth of a Party
Fragment One: Sectionalism (1)

But, Fremont and Dayton, are both residents of
the free-states; and this fact has been vaunted,
in high places, as excessive _sectionalism_—
While interested individuals become _indignant_
and _excited_, against this manifestation of _sec-
tionalism_, I am very happy to know, that the
Constitution remains calm—keeps cool—upon
the subject— It does say that President and
Vice President shall be resident of different
states; but it does not say one must live in
a _slave_, and the other in a _free_ state—
It has been a _custom_ to take one from a slave,
and the other from a free state; but the custom
has not, at all been uniform— In 1828 Gen.
Jackson and Mr. Calhoun, both from slave-
states, were placed on the same ticket; and
Mr. Adams and Dr. Rush ~~were put~~

both from the free-states, were pitted against
them. Gen. Jackson and Mr. Calhoun were
elected; and qualified and served under
the election; yet the whole thing never suggested the idea of sectionalism—

From Chapter 5, The Republican Lincoln: The Birth of a Party
Fragment One: Sectionalism (2)

upon us—
The democratic party, in 1844, elected a Southern president— Since then, they have neither had a Southern candidate for election, or nomination— Their Conventions of 1848— 1852 and 1856, have been struggles exclusively among *Northern* men, each vieing to outbid the other for the Southern vote— the South standing calmly by to finally cry going, going, gone, to the highest bidder; and, at the same time, to make its power more distinctly seen, and thereby to secure a still higher bid at the next succeeding struggle—
"Actions speak louder than words" is the maxim; and, if true, the South now distinctly says to the North "Give us the *measures* and you take the *men*"

From Chapter 5, The Republican Lincoln: The Birth of a Party
Fragment One: Sectionalism (3)

Upon those men who are, in sentiment, opposed to the spread, and nationalization of slavery, rests the task of preventing it— The Republican organization is the embodyment of that sentiment; though, as yet, it by no means embraces all the individuals holding that sentiment. The party is newly formed; and in forming, old party ties had to be broken, and the attractions of party pride, and influential leaders were wholly wanting— In spite of old differences, prejudices, and animosities, its members were drawn together by a paramount common danger— They formed and manouvered in the face of the deciplined enemy, and in the teeth of all his persistent misrepresentations— Of course, they fell far short of gathering in all of their own— And yet, a year ago, they stood up, an army over thirteen hundred thousand strong— That army is, to-day, the best hope of the nation, and of the world— Their work is before them; and from which they may not guiltlessly turn away—

From Chapter 5, The Republican Lincoln: The Birth of a Party
Fragment Two: The Republican organization

As I would not be a *slave*, so I would not be a *master*. This expresses my idea of democracy— Whatever differs from this, to the extent of the difference, is no democracy—

From Chapter 6, The Principled Lincoln: A Definition of Democracy

Suppose it is true, that the negro is inferior to the white, in the gifts of nature; is it not the exact reverse justice that the white should, for that reason, take from the negro, any part of the little which has been given him? "Give to him that is needy" is the christian rule of charity; but "Take from him that is needy" is the rule of slavery—

Pro-slavery Theology.

The sum of pro-slavery theology seems to be this: "Slavery is not universally right, nor yet universally wrong; it is better for some people to be slaves; and, in such cases, it is the Will of God that they be such."

Certainly there is no contending against the Will of God; but still there is some difficulty in ascertaining it, and applying it, to particular cases— For instance we will suppose the Rev. Dr. Ross has a slave named Sambo, and the question is "Is it the Will of God that Sambo shall remain a slave, or be set free? The Almighty gives no audable answer to the question, and his revelation—the Bible—gives none—or at most, none but such as admits of a squabble, as to its meaning. No one thinks of asking Sambo's opinion on it— So, at last, it comes to this, that Dr. Ross is to decide the question— And while he consider it, he sits in the shade, with gloves on his hands, and subsists on the bread that Sambo is earning in the burning sun— If he decides that God Wills Sambo to continue a slave, he thereby retains his own comfortable position; but if he decides that God will's Sambo to be free, he thereby has to walk out of the shade, throw off his gloves, and delve for his own bread— Will Dr. Ross be actuated by that perfect impartiality, which has ever been considered most favorable to correct decisions?

From Chapter 7, The Outraged Lincoln: Pro-Slavery Theology

All this is not the result of accident— It has a philosophical cause— Without the Constitution and the Union, we could not have attained the result; but even these, are not the primary cause of our great prosperity— There is something back of these, entwining itself more closely about the human heart— That something, is the principle of "Liberty to all"— the principle that clears the path for all— gives hope to all— and, by consequence, enterprize, and industry to all.
The expression of that principle, in our Declaration of Independence, was most happy, and fortunate— Without this, as well as with it, we could have declared our independence of Great Brittain; but without it, we could not, I think, have secured our free government, and consequent prosperity— No oppressed, people will fight, and endure, as our fathers did, without the promise of something better, than a mere change of masters—
The assertion of that principle, at that time, was the word, "fitly spoken" which has proved an "apple of gold" to us— The Union, and the Constitution, are the picture of silver, subsequently framed around it— The picture was made, not to conceal, or destroy the apple; but to adorn, and preserve it— The picture was made for the apple— not the apple for the picture—
So let us act, that neither picture, or apple shall ever be blurred, or bruised or broken—
That we may so act, we must study, and understand the points of danger—

From Chapter 8, The Unity Lincoln: Secession and the Constitution

1

I am grateful for the opportunity your invitation affords me
to appear before an audience
of my native state. During
the present winter it has been
greatly pressed upon me by many patriotic citizens, Kentuckians
among others, that I could, by my position,
by a word, restore peace to the
country— But what word? I
have many words already before
the public; and my position was
given me on the faith of those
words— Is the desired word
to be confirmatory of these; or
must it be contradictory to them?
If the former, it is useless repetion; if the latter it is dishonorable and treacherous—
—Again, it is urged as if the word
must be spoken before the fourth

6974

From Chapter 9, The Kentuckian Lincoln: An Undelivered Speech to the South (1)

of March— Why? Is the speaking the word a "sine qua non"
to the inaugeration? Is there a
Bell-man, a Breckinridge-man,
or a Douglas man, who would
tolerate his own candidate to make
such terms, had he been elected? Who amongst you would not
die by the proposition, that your
candidate, being elected, should
be inaugerated, solely on the
conditions of the constitution,
and laws, or not at all—
What Kentuckian, worthy of
his birth place, would not do
this? Gentlemen, I too, am
a Kentuckian—

Nor is this a matter of mere
personal honor. No man can be elected President without some
~~If when a Chief~~
opponents, as well as supporters; and if when
~~Magistrate is Constitutionally~~
elected, he can not be installed, till he
~~elected he can not be installed,~~
first appeases his enemies, ~~by betraying his~~
~~till he betrays those who elected~~

6975

From Chapter 9, The Kentuckian Lincoln: An Undelivered Speech to the South (2)

~~him~~ by breaking his pledges, and betraying his friends
and, ~~surrendering to his oppo-nents~~, this government, and all popular government, is already at an end— Demands for such surrender, once recognized, and yielded to, are without limit, as to nature, extent, or repetition— They break ~~they break~~ the only bond of faith between pub-lic, and public servant; and they distinctly set the minority over the majority. Such demands acquiesced in, would not merely be the ruin of a man, or a party; but, as a precedent they would ~~be the~~ ruin ~~of~~ the government it-self—

I do not deny the possibili-ty that the people may err in an election; but if they do the true [illegible] is in the next

From Chapter 9, The Kentuckian Lincoln: An Undelivered Speech to the South (3)

The will of God prevails— In great contests each party claims to act in accordance with the will of God. Both *may* be, and one *must* be wrong. God can not be *for*, and *against* the same thing at the same time. In the present civil war it is quite possible that God's purpose is something different from the purpose of either party— and yet the human instrumentalities, working just as they do, are of the best adaptation to effect ~~his~~ His purpose. I am almost ready to say this is probably true— that God wills this contest, and wills that it shall not end yet— By his mere quiet power, on the minds of the now contestants, He could have either *saved* or *destroyed* the Union without a human contest— Yet the contest began— And having begun He could give the final victory to either side any day— Yet the contest proceeds—

8

From Chapter 10, The Theological Lincoln: A Meditation on the Divine Will

Eastman Johnson's painting portrays the young Lincoln reading by the light of a fire in his log cabin home. Painted shortly after Lincoln's death, it suggests that learning was a key to his life of meaning and purpose.

Lincoln had other connections to Kentucky, beyond its being his birthplace and boyhood home. His wife, Mary, grew up in Lexington, where her father, Robert Smith Todd, was a prominent second-generation leader of the town. Lincoln's best friend, Joshua Speed, whom he met in Springfield in 1837, also hailed from Kentucky.

After the temporary breakup of Abraham and Mary's courtship in 1841, Lincoln, battling depression, had accepted Speed's invitation to visit and recuperate at his family home, Farmington, just outside Louisville. During his stay, Lincoln met James Speed, Joshua's oldest brother. The elder Speed had long opposed slavery, and Lincoln knew he was one of the leaders who could keep Kentucky in the Union. Through both Joshua and James Speed, Lincoln had access to the shifting conversations on whether Kentucky should secede or stay.[5]

Six years later, in the fall of 1847, on Lincoln's trip to Washington to take up his seat in the 30th Congress, the family stopped in

Lexington for nearly a month to visit with Mary's family. While in Lexington, Lincoln took advantage of the singular opportunity to attend a political meeting organized by Mary's father, where Henry Clay would be delivering a speech. Lincoln had not previously met Clay, but at this event, weeks before he would begin his term in Congress, he heard Clay criticize the United States' War with Mexico. Clay stated that if the War of 1812, what he called "the British War," was defensive and "just," the war with Mexico was "no war of defense, but one unnecessary and of offensive aggression."[6] The sixty-three-year-old Clay made a speech that made an immediate and lasting impression on the thirty-eight-year-old congressman.

Lincoln clearly had numerous emotional connections to the state. But one could also argue that identifying himself as a Kentuckian when he'd lived there only until age seven was an astute politician cozying up to a crucial border state after seven Southern states had seceded from the Union. As president-elect, Lincoln was vitally concerned about Kentucky; he considered it critical to keeping all four border states—Delaware, Maryland, Missouri, and Kentucky—in the Union. Six months after his inauguration, Lincoln wrote a "Private & confidential" letter to his good friend Orville Browning, an Illinois senator. "I think to lose Kentucky is nearly the same as to lose the whole game."[7]

Lincoln knew that Kentucky's economy—largely agricultural and supported by the labor of slaves—oriented the critical border state toward its Southern neighbors. But he also believed that the long Kentucky Whig tradition represented by Clay, his political hero, would in the end be able to keep the state inside the Union.

Kentucky's strategic value consisted of its position as a middle ground between the Old Northwest states of Ohio, Indiana, and Illinois, and the Confederate state of Tennessee. Thinking militarily in his new role of commander-in-chief, Lincoln understood that whoever commanded Kentucky's natural boundaries of the Ohio and Mississippi rivers would instantly secure enormous military advantages. Whoever controlled the Cumberland and Tennessee rivers within the state would also reap large military benefits.

From his home in Illinois, Lincoln had remained attuned to the currents of opinion at play in Kentucky. He knew his native state was divided in complex ways. Northern supporters lived in southern parts of the state, while Southern partisans resided in northern areas. The westernmost area of the state, beyond the Tennessee River, was often called "Southern Kentucky," or even "the South Carolina of Kentucky." Lincoln also knew that support for the Union did not mean opposition to slavery.[8]

To further understand public opinion, Lincoln subscribed to some of the state's leading newspapers. If the state of Kentucky was largely pro-Union, the press was almost evenly divided, Union and Confederate.[9]

Three days after Lincoln's election, Lexington's fervently Democratic *Kentucky Statesman* editorialized, "No intelligent man in the South will fail to deprecate the election of Lincoln and therein the success of the Republican party as the most serious lamentable calamity which could have fallen our Republic." Nevertheless, the paper reluctantly admitted that Lincoln had been "lawfully elected."[10] *The Louisville Daily Courier* did not believe Kentucky would secede because Lincoln was elected: "We do not suppose there is one man in it who thinks she will take such a step."[11] Despite Lincoln's insistence in an earlier note that the Republican Party was not a sectional party, *The Covington Journal* did not see it that way. "For the first time," the nation had witnessed "the triumph of a purely sectional party." Despite Lincoln's personal identification with Kentucky, the paper assailed Lincoln and Vice President Hannibal Hamlin of Maine as "Northern men; they represent Northern principles; and they are elected by Northern votes exclusively."[12]

. . .

As the pre-inaugural train crossed the Indiana-Ohio border on February 12, 1861, on the way to its second overnight stop in Cincinnati, Lincoln surely looked south across the wide Ohio River toward his native state. That evening, from the balcony of Cincinnati's Burnet House, he had Kentucky on his mind as he began to speak. Realizing by now that he would not be able to cross the Ohio River and deliver his speech in Kentucky—we do not know why—he directed some of his remarks to citizens of the border state who had crossed the Ohio River to be in the audience.

"My brother Kentuckians." He reminded his audience that he had spoken in Cincinnati once before, in 1859; on that occasion he had challenged Douglas's assertion that the founding fathers would not have imagined outlawing slavery in future years. At the same time, seeking to reassure their anxieties, he said, "We mean to treat you, as near as we possibly can, as Washington, Jefferson, and Madison treated you. We mean to leave you alone, and in no way

In Cincinnati, Lincoln spoke to a crowd that included people from Kentucky who had crossed the Ohio River to hear the president-elect.

to interfere with your institution; to abide by all and every compromise of the constitution."[13]

The preserved fragment allows us to contemplate what he hoped to achieve by speaking in Kentucky. In the opening sentence, he refers to "your invitation." What a tantalizing mystery! Who offered it? A committee? An individual? Could it have been Joshua Speed? Or James Speed? Neither Lincoln, nor any other source, provides an answer.

At the outset of the fragment, Lincoln refers to the pleas coming to him from many "patriotic" citizens, "Kentuckians among others," to offer "a word" that will "restore peace" to a nation coming apart. One of the chief characteristics of Lincoln's political leadership was his constant desire to be inclusive. To do so, he imputed the best possible motives to the people of Kentucky, believing that underneath all the speeches and bluster spreading from the state, a deep Union sentiment remained.

"But what word?" he asks. His response implies that the answer should be self-evident, reminding his imagined audience that his words should already be well known. He had declined to campaign in the summer of 1860 because he believed all his ideas and positions were available to the public in his published "words." Lincoln, a man of words, took pride in the fact that he was elected to his present position "on the faith of those words." By "faith," he meant the people's trust in his integrity. In this note, he wanted his audience to know that his words were not mere campaign rhetoric; to contradict them would be "dishonorable and treacherous."

In Indianapolis, Lincoln insisted that the outpouring of patriotism was not about him as an individual or the Republican Party. He referred to himself as an "accidental instrument," a metaphor he would continue to work with in future stops, saying his role as president was "temporary" and "for a limited time."[14] He even invited supporters of the three defeated 1860 presidential candidates, Stephen Douglas, John Breckenridge, and John Bell, to ride

Gentlemen, I too, am
a Kentuckian—

with him between towns. On the eve of his inauguration as president, this was another gesture of inclusion that captured the essence of his emerging leadership.

Lincoln planned to invoke these other candidates in the Kentucky speech, to emphasize that their supporters would not "tolerate" it if these men changed the ideas on which they had campaigned. Appealing to the imagined crowd before him, he asks, "What Kentuckian, worthy of his birthplace, would not do this?" Aware that oratory was the art of persuasion, he then built a bridge with his audience: "Gentlemen, I too, am a Kentuckian."

In the longest paragraph of this fragmentary note, Lincoln makes an appeal to his integrity as a political leader. His fears about secessionist ideas in his native state are evident when he reminds Kentuckians that any politician is necessarily elected with opponents and disapproval. What should an honest politician do about these opponents? Lincoln holds out the possibility that he could "appease his enemies" by "breaking his pledges." But to do so he would "set the minority over the majority"—in other words, break the very bonds that hold a democracy together. Crucially, putting such a precedent in motion "would ruin the government itself."

Finally, Lincoln makes an unexpected concession to his opponents by admitting "that the people may err in an election." But what is the remedy for such an error? American democracy, Lincoln reminds his audience, was designed to address this very question: that is, it is the public's civic duty to vote in the next election, not attack the fairly elected political leader. Lincoln tells the Kentuckians that during the long secession winter he has been urged "by many patriotic men" to "compromise"—to "shift the ground upon which I was elected." Surely aware that what he is about to say would be unpopular among many, he then explains in some detail why he cannot break his pledges and surrender to those who opposed his election. To do so, Lincoln declares, would be to "distinctly set the minority over the majority."

In this long-forgotten note, we listen as Lincoln does a delicate dance between his natural, inclusive, magnanimous spirit, and his sense that at this moment he cannot walk back from the principles that elected him. Although the language and structure of this note differ from his inauguration speech, it echoes one of the most powerful ideas spoken in the conclusion of that address. Speaking to the audience gathered in the capital some weeks later, Lincoln proclaimed, "In *your* hands, my dissatisfied fellow countrymen, and not in *mine,* is the momentous issue of civil war."[15]

It is instructive to compare the partial text of his forgotten almost-speech to all the short addresses and responses that Lincoln gave over the course of that thirteen-day train tour. In Illinois, Indiana, Ohio, New York, New Jersey, and Pennsylvania, he knew he would be speaking to audiences that largely supported the Union. Yes, they might have favored Douglas, Bell, or Breckinridge, but three months after the election, and with the secession of seven Southern states, most Northerners were rallying to the Union.

But here, writing for an audience composed of both pro- and anti-Union supporters, Lincoln combined a cogent plea for the rule of the majority with an emotional appeal to the values of personal integrity and honor that he hoped would resonate with his "fellow Kentuckians."

This photograph by Mathew Brady in May 1861 captures the reflective Lincoln who wrote notes to himself.

CHAPTER 10

The Theological Lincoln: A Meditation on the Divine Will

[September 2, 1862?]

> The will of God prevails. In great contests each party claims to act in accordance with the will of God. Both *may* be, and one *must* be wrong. God cannot be *for*, and *against* the same thing at the same time. In the present civil war it is quite possible that God's purpose is something different from the purpose of either party—and yet the human instrumentalities, working just as they do, are of the best adaptation to effect his purpose. I am almost ready to say this is probably true—that God wills this contest, and wills that it shall not end yet. By his mere quiet power, on the minds of the now contestants, He could have either *saved* or *destroyed* the Union without a human contest. And having begun He could give the final victory to either side any day. Yet the contest proceeds.

ON SEPTEMBER 2, 1862, President Lincoln summoned an emergency cabinet meeting in the Executive Mansion. The political wolves—of both parties—were howling. Three days earlier, the Union army had been defeated in a fierce three-day battle in northern Virginia, barely thirty miles south of Washington. At the Second Battle of Bull Run—named for a winding river running several miles north of Manassas Junction—General John Pope's Union army had been outmaneuvered by Confederate troops led by General Robert E. Lee and General Thomas "Stonewall" Jackson. As Union forces retreated to Washington in confusion, the Northern press heaped criticism on Lincoln as commander in chief.

Attorney General Edward Bates, a close observer of Lincoln, took note of the president's mood at the hastily called cabinet meeting. One of Lincoln's rivals for the Republican nomination in 1860, the Missourian confided to his diary that the president spoke of his discouragement after initial forecasts of triumph had given way to reports of shocking defeat. Bates wrote that Lincoln "seemed wrung by the bitterest anguish—said he felt almost ready to hang himself."[1]

Later that same day, Lincoln sat down at his desk. The summer of 1862 had turned into a period of great discouragement for people across the North. In the East, Robert E. Lee had soundly defeated General George McClellan's Army of the Potomac in the Seven Days Battles in Virginia. In the West, Ulysses S. Grant—a new Union general just beginning to be noticed by Lincoln after a February victory at Fort Donelson in Tennessee—had emerged victorious in April at the Battle of Shiloh after initially being surprised, but suffered the highest casualties in American history up until that date. Grant would later call the summer that followed those two winter and spring victories "the most anxious period of the war."[2] Distressed by this dire outlook, that afternoon Lincoln wrote this unusual private musing, so different from anything he had yet written or spoken in public.

THE MAJORITY OF Lincoln's notes to himself remained unknown until Nicolay and Hay published their biography in 1890, but Hay held up this fragment, which he titled Meditation on the Divine Will, for audiences to see as part of a series of lectures he offered in 1871 and 1872. He had found it in a desk drawer after Lincoln's assassination, and saved it. "I have here a paper written by him, in a time of profound national gloom, with religious soul-searching, never intended to be published," he told audiences. "You shall see how this patriarch and prophet wrestled in secret with his God."[3]

Hay's was no false promise. The true nature of Lincoln's religious faith, or lack has long been fiercely debated. But this fragment reveals the intensity of his private faith journey during the Civil War.

Lincoln did not date the theological note, and throughout the years historians and editors have offered different hypotheses. In their biography, Nicolay and Hay placed it in September 1862 because they believed Lincoln wrote it "while his mind was burdened with the weightiest question of his life." They recalled, "He retired within himself and tried to bring some order into his thoughts by rising above the wrangling of men and of parties, and pondering the relations of human government to the Divine." They believed "it was not written to be seen of men."[4]

Fifteen years after publishing their biography, in the 1905 *Complete Works of Abraham Lincoln,* they added a specific date—September 30, 1862—but with a question mark.[5]

Basler, in *The Collected Works of Abraham Lincoln,* believed the September 30 date too late. He suggested, "Quite possibly the meditation was written as early as September 2, at which time, following the Second Battle of Bull Run, Lincoln seems to have plumbed his lowest depths."[6]

Lincoln scholar Douglas L. Wilson contends that the meditation "is chronologically much closer to, and perhaps even belongs to, the year 1864." Agreeing that Lincoln wrote it at a time of crisis, he argued that in 1864, three full years into the war, "the Union forces were still unable to end the rebellion." Disagreeing with Nicolay and Hay, and Basler, Wilson believes the document did not reflect the kind of "anguish" attributed to Lincoln by Attorney General Bates.[7]

Years after Hay found this fragment, it was given to Brown University, Hay's alma mater, where it remains.

Reflecting on one of the most discouraging defeats thus far in the Civil War, Lincoln seeks in this fragment to discern the purposes of God among the cacophony of voices swirling around him.

He employs theological language, beginning with "The will of God prevails." I have long pondered: Were these opening five words a statement of affirmation? Or rather, words of resignation? The language in this fragment is not centered on a merely theoretical question. In the first years of the Civil War, Lincoln received constant claims of divine preference from delegations of ministers and politicians, many assuring him: God is on our side. He knew that, just as he heard from eager leaders asserting that God was on the side of the North, Southern politicians and preachers were arriving at the Richmond White House to assure President Jefferson Davis that God was on the Confederate side. Lincoln wrote this note to reflect on the practical question of how to reconcile such divergent claims.

The logical Lincoln answers his own question. "Both *may* be, and one *must* be wrong." Just as he did in the texts of his public speeches, he underlined key words of the note for emphasis (they have been italicized here).

The conditional "*may* be" is typical of how Lincoln would think his way into a problem. He would often begin tentatively; perceiving an issue's complexity, he would want to make certain he was looking at all sides of a problem before drawing any firm conclusions.

I imagine at this point he may have stopped and thought for a while, before picking up his pen to continue on to the next intel-

In the present civil war it is quite possible that God's purpose is something different from the purpose of either party—

lectual stepping-stone: "God cannot be *for,* and *against* the same thing at the same time." The logical Lincoln here invokes a logical God. "In the present civil war it is quite possible that God's purpose is something different from the purpose of either party—and yet the human instrumentalities, working just as they do, are of the best adaptation to effect his purpose."

This sentence, at the architectural center of Lincoln's reflection, may be the best indication of Lincoln's theological thinking: God has a *purpose* in the war.

Still, never pleased with the presumptuousness of the political and religious chauvinists all around him, he qualifies this assertion with "it is quite possible." Lincoln emphasizes "the will of God" four times in this brief 147-word fragment. By repeating the word "will," he underscores the central theme of the meditation: This is a God who *acts* in history. He had become convinced that above and beyond human actors—the soldiers, the generals, the president as commander in chief—there was another, greater Actor.

HISTORICAL ATTEMPTS TO define Lincoln's religion have typically been done through the lens of fatalism. Fatalism, which Lincoln sometimes called "the doctrine of necessity," holds that all events occur by unwavering laws of causation. In Lincoln's day, fatalism was popularized as "whatever happens is bound to happen." As a young man, he resigned himself to the ordering of events outside his control.[8]

Historians and Lincoln biographers have depicted fatalism and providence as different expressions of the same determinism. But, in fact, they are very different belief systems. Providence, rather than an impersonal first cause, is belief in a God with personality, who loves human beings, and acts in history.

Indeed, this linking of fatalism and providence would have surprised Protestant theologians and Christian ministers in the nineteenth century. In 1859, Francis Wharton, an Episcopal minister soon to be professor at the new Episcopal Theological Seminary in Cambridge, Massachusetts, described fatalism as "a distinct scheme of unbelief." In his book *A Treatise on Theism, and on the Modern Skeptical Theories,* Wharton labeled fatalism as a foe of Christianity because it depersonalized God, whereas Christianity recognized a personal and providential God who acted in human events.[9]

Lincoln may have been drawn to fatalism as a young man in the 1830s, but two decades later the ideas he wrestled with in this fragment started from a quite different viewpoint, one that believes in "God's purpose."

How did Lincoln arrive at this new theological stance?

I believe this change in his thinking began when he started to hear sermons with an emphasis on providence from the Reverend James Smith at Springfield's First Presbyterian Church.[10] Later, when the Lincoln family arrived in Washington in February 1861, they were courted by a number of churches. They began attending New York Avenue Presbyterian Church on March 10, the first Sunday after Lincoln's inauguration, and would attend this congregation on a fairly regular basis during his four years as president.[11]

Lincoln quickly found himself appreciating the sermons of the congregation's minister, the Reverend Phineas Densmore Gurley. Gurley had finished first in his class at Princeton Theological Seminary, where he was a student of theologian Charles Hodge, a rising star in the Presbyterian firmament who in his lectures emphasized the providence of God. Gurley, a handsome man with a large frame, led a congregation in a denomination that prized learned preaching.[12]

Titian Ramsay Peale's 1862 photograph of the New York Avenue Presbyterian Church is what Lincoln would have seen. A log cabin and dirt road are in the picture's left foreground.

After Lincoln's death, those who commented on his religious beliefs, or lack thereof, knew nothing of Lincoln's relationship with Gurley.

On Sunday, April 14, 1861, two days after Confederate forces bombarded South Carolina's Fort Sumter, the new president was in his New York Avenue pew. It was just hours after the fort's surrender that Lincoln heard Gurley sermonize that "God, in his merciful providence," offers "another opportunity for counsel, or pause, for appeal to Him for assistance before letting loose upon the land the direct scourge which He permits to visit a people—civil war."[13]

It may be that Gurley's words that Sunday struck Lincoln deeply. Lincoln would use the same image of the "direct scourge" four years later in one of the most poignant sentences of his second inaugural address: "Fondly do we hope—fervently do we pray—that this mighty scourge of war may speedily pass away."[14]

Seven months before Lincoln wrote this fragment, in February

1862, his eleven-year-old son, Willie, died. Lincoln invited Gurley to conduct the funeral service in the East Room of the White House on February 24. Mary, so overcome with grief, did not attend.

Gurley's words of comfort included this admonition: "It is well for us, and very comforting on such an occasion as this, to get a clear and scriptural view of the providence of God."[15] Lincoln asked his pastor for a copy of the sermon.

LINCOLN CONTINUES, "I am almost ready to say this is probably true—that God wills this contest, and wills that it shall not end yet." Four years earlier, in his fragment criticizing slavery, Lincoln

In Washington, Lincoln began attending the New York Avenue Presbyterian Church, whose minister became an important influence in the president's evolving faith story.

had mused, "Certainly there is no contending against the Will of God, but still there is some difficulty in ascertaining, and applying it, to particular cases."[16]

The two qualifying adverbs, "almost" and "probably," speak once more to Lincoln's humility; he recognizes his own finitude in dealing with a transcendent God. But much more astonishing is the second part of his observation: "and wills that it shall not end yet." At the moment of writing, Lincoln, as commander in chief, is dog-tired from sleepless nights and contending with ineffective and feuding commanders; the *New-York Tribune* insinuating that Washington might be in danger of a Confederate attack; and above all, the responsibility of bringing a calamitous war to its end.[17] He confided in this private musing what he would never say in public: The end of the war seemed nowhere in sight.

"By his mere quiet power." The youthful Lincoln had met a noisy God in the Baptist churches he attended with his parents in Kentucky and Indiana. During the Civil War, he met advocates who came to the White House to speak of a strident God, a tribal God, who, jingoistic partisans self-confidently proclaimed, was "on our side."

The "power" of this God, however "quiet," is so imposing that "He could have either *saved* or *destroyed* the Union without a human contest."

Lincoln concluded his reflection with words he would never have been able to speak in public. "And having begun He could give the final victory to either side any day." From the privacy of his office in the Executive Mansion, did he think that this purposeful God might give the victory to the Confederacy? Heresy! Political and religious heresy!

In approaching this question, in humility Lincoln admitted he

The Meditation on the Divine Will was the chief antecedent of Lincoln's Second Inaugural Address, delivered on March 4, 1865.

did not know the answer. And so, he concluded, "Yet the contest proceeds."

Two and a half years later, on March 4, 1865, Lincoln delivered his second inaugural address. In 701 words, he mentioned God fourteen times, quoted the Bible four times, and invoked prayer three times. Although no one present that day was aware of Lincoln's earlier Meditation on the Divine Will, it is instructive to compare key portions of each.

Meditation on the Divine Will	Second Inaugural Address
The will of God prevails.	The Almighty has His own purposes.
Both may be, and one must be wrong. God cannot be for, and against the same thing at the same time.	The prayers of both could not be answered; that of neither has been answered fully.
I am almost ready to say that this is probably true—that God wills this contest, and wills that it shall not end.	He now wills to remove. Yet, if God wills that it continue.

Both friend and foe were surprised by Lincoln's use of theological language in a political address. African American leader, reformer, and writer Frederick Douglass was in the crowd that day. He remembered, "It sounded more like a sermon than a state paper."[18]

Neither Douglass, nor anyone in the audience, could know that behind Lincoln's second inaugural lay this earlier meditation. In this note, the private Lincoln attempted to work out the haunting question of where was God in the middle of the Civil War; he answered that question in his second inaugural.

Many were not sure what to make of Lincoln's brief address. They had expected a triumphal speech. *The New York Times* voiced that disappointment: "He makes no boasts of what he has done, or promises of what he will do."[19]

In response to a congratulatory letter from New York politician Thurlow Weed, Lincoln offered his own interpretation: "It is not immediately popular," but "I expect [it] to wear as well—perhaps better than anything I have produced." Lincoln continued, in a further echo of his meditation, "Men are not flattered by being shown that there has been a difference of purpose between the Almighty and them. To deny it, however, in this case, is to deny that there is a God governing the world." Finally, "It is a truth which I thought needed to be told."[20]

. . .

Historians and biographers have long credited Lincoln's rise to greatness to his ability to grow and change. Curiously, though, when it comes to his religious beliefs, history has not allowed him that same growth and change. Portrayals of a static Lincoln, still tethered to the fatalism he embraced as a young man, fail to do justice to the evolution in his religious thinking during the Civil War years.

Because of his early encounters with the emotional fire-and-brimstone sermons of the Baptist churches he attended in his youth, and his adult unease with sharing his most intimate feelings, Lincoln never wore his religious beliefs on his sleeve. But in the closet of his mind, in the midst of a terrible war, he wrote out his thoughts about human pretension and the presence of God. This small meditation is both the antecedent to his historic second inaugural address and the key to the long-debated riddle of Lincoln's religious faith.

Epilogue

I LOVE TALKING with high school students about Lincoln. I have spoken in public and private high schools in Massachusetts, Virginia, Florida, Tennessee, Illinois, Arizona, California, and Hawaii. Often, I speak to eleventh-grade students who are studying U.S. history. When I speak about Lincoln's notes to himself, I ask the students: How long do you think it took him to write one of the fragments?

Their answers, typically: "one minute"; "three minutes"; maybe "four minutes."

When I suggest he may have taken one or two hours to write a note, there is usually an audible gasp from the high schoolers. (On several occasions, I have seen their teachers silently applauding in the back of the classroom.) In our culture, with the distractions of our ever-present screens, I think it is difficult for them to imagine Lincoln detaching himself from all the interruptions of his day to give himself such time—or even needing such time—for this thoughtful reflection and writing. I trust that these students know the Lincoln of the Emancipation Proclamation and the Gettysburg Address, the person they have studied in their high school history books; I am eager to introduce them to the private Lincoln whose struggles with so many difficult issues laid the foundation of the public leader.

. . .

As I worked on this book, I've been asked how studying Abraham Lincoln's fragments has changed me. Years ago, as PhD students at Princeton, we were advised not to answer this kind of personal question—to practice a form of intellectual "social distancing."

I now admit that as an historian, and later as a Lincoln biographer, I knew little of the fragments for a very long time. When I finally decided to immerse myself in them, I was not even sure where nor how many there were.

At first, my most interesting findings were about his ideas—in particular, on slavery. But the more I studied the fragments, the more impressed I grew with Lincoln's mental curiosity. As we have now seen, Lincoln's purpose in his notes was intellectual, political, and moral—often all at the same time. He wrote them to probe and push his preliminary thinking about many sides of a complex problem or issue.

So how have I changed from working so closely with the fragments? I have taken up his habit of writing notes to myself. To do that, I try to give myself space and time: I am trying to be more disciplined, not allowing myself to be interrupted by texts or email. And I am trying to use these note-writing exercises to balance two of Lincoln's best qualities, which sometimes feel in opposition. He was genuinely curious and open-minded about other people's ideas and beliefs; he drove his secretaries crazy because he wanted to be accessible for conversations with ordinary citizens—what he called his "public opinion baths." But he was also forceful, passionate, and rigorous when it came to the study of ideas and issues.

At this tumultuous moment, we need Lincoln more than ever. To be sure, he cannot help us with COVID-19 or climate change, but his large-hearted spirit speaks across the years.

The example of Lincoln the public leader is referred to often. But the private Lincoln is also an example. In a world of shortened attention spans and constant interruptions, his fragments encourage us to live more thoughtful and reflective lives. In speaking to high school students, and in writing this book, I hope to point a new generation toward the rewards—personal and societal—of a habit of sustained, deep, private thought.

With the cooperation of the *Papers of Abraham Lincoln* project, I decided to include all 111 of Lincoln's fragments in this book's appendix. My hope is that readers can see the enormous depth and breadth of his thinking. Even when writing for an audience of one.

Appendix: Lincoln's Fragments and Notes

THE TRANSCRIPTIONS OF Lincoln's fragments and notes are published in cooperation with *The Papers of Abraham Lincoln* in Springfield, Illinois, a documentary editing project dedicated to identifying, imaging, transcribing, annotating, and publishing online all Lincoln documents. Editor Daniel Worthington and assistant editor Kelley B. Clausing have identified what they believe to be the complete collection of Lincoln fragments and notes: 111.

A word about symbols:

• The symbol ^ represents an insertion, meaning that Lincoln added a word or words above the line to his original note—what documentary editors call an interlineation. In a few cases where Lincoln wanted to add a larger amount of text, he added it to the margins of his notes. These insertions suggest that Lincoln not only saved his notes but went back and added to them as a new thought or circumstance came into his thinking. There will be two tags—^ ^—indicating where Lincoln's inserted text begins and ends.

• Words inside brackets [?] means it is the best guess of the editors, but the word is not entirely legible because of damage, handwriting, etc.

• Words or letters inside brackets [ ] without a question mark means the editors supplied the words or letters from a source other than the original document, usually in instances where the document is torn or damaged.

• The symbol [. . . ?] plus a strikethrough means that the word is unclear or illegible to the editor because it has been struck out.

• Strikethroughs and underlines are Lincoln's own.

• When a date includes question marks, this indicates that the following note was undated, and the date comes from former and present editors' placement in the historical time line of Lincoln's life.

Lincoln's spelling, often irregular and inconsistent, in common with most people of his time, is retained. He was fond of British spelling for particular words: "favour," "labour," etc. He also tended to use old spellings: "offence," "defence." He always used "it's" for its. As for punctuation, Lincoln often used dashes instead of periods at the end of sentences. He did the same with commas, colons, and semicolons.

I have provided a short introduction at the beginning of some notes to further explain its context and meaning.

Notes for a Speech delivered in the Illinois legislature at Vandalia, Illinois (December 1, 1834–December 8, 1839?)

Lincoln served four two-year terms, from 1834 to 1842, in the lower house of the Illinois legislature.

Show me another law like this—
Legislating in the dark—
Opening a wide door to fraud—
He who asks equity must do equity—
"Fixture"
Bring in new parties—
Redeeming creditors

Notes Regarding Plan of Campaign of 1840

(1840)

This note exemplifies Lincoln's adroit understanding of campaigning for political office.

1st Appoint one person in each county as county captain, and take his pledge to perform promptly all the duties assigned him—

Duties of the County Captain

1st To ~~appoint~~ procure from the poll-books a separate list for each Precinct of all the names of all those persons who voted the Whig ticket in August—

2nd To appoint one person in each Precinct as Precinct Captain, and, by a personal interview with him, procure his pledge, to perform promptly all the duties assigned him—

3rd To deliver to each Precinct Captain the list of names as above, belonging to his Precinct; and also a written list of his duties—

Duties of the Precinct Captain—

1st To divide the list of names delivered him by the county captain, into Sections of ten who reside most convenient to each other—

2nd To appoint one person of each Section as Section Captain, and by a personal interview with him, procure his pledge to perform promptly all the duties assigned him—

3rd To deliver to each Section Captain the list of names belonging to his Section and also a written list of his duties—

Duties of the Section Captain—

1st To see each man of his Section face to face, and procure his pledge that he will for no consideration (impossibilities excepted) stay from the polls on the first monday in November; and that he will record his vote as early in the day as possible—

2nd To add to his Section the name of every person in his vicinity who did not vote with us in August, but who will vote with us in the fall, and take the same pledge of him, as from the others—

3rd To task himself to procure at least such additional names to his Section—[3]

It shall be the duty of each [~~. . .~~ ?] ~~of~~ [~~. . .~~ ?] ~~appointed~~ ^ward & Precinct & section office^ to make a

Note regarding filing of documents

(December 9, 1844–February 11, 1861)

If Lincoln was persistent in writing notes to himself, he was not always well organized in his retention of them.

When you can't find it any where else look into this

Fragment regarding a tariff discussion

(1846–47)

Written by Lincoln between his election to Congress 1846 and taking his seat in December 1847.

Whether the protective policy shall be finally abandoned, is now the question–

Discussion and experience already had; and question now in greater dispute than ever–

Has there not been some great error in the mode of discussion?–Propose a single issue of fact, namely–

"From 1816 to the present, have protected articles [co]st us more, of labour, during the higher, than during the lower duties upon them?"

Introduce the evidence–

Analize this issue, and try to show that it embraces the true and the whole question of the protective policy–

Intended as a test of experience–

The period seclected, is fair; because it is a period of peace—a period sufficiently long to furnish a fair average under all other causes operating on prices—a period in which various modifications of higher and lower duties have occured–

Protected articles, only are embra[ce]d– Show that these only, belong to the question–

The labour price, only is embraced– Show this to be correct–

In the early days of the world, the Almighty said to the first of our race "In the sweat of thy face shalt thou eat bread, and since then, if we except the light, and the air of heaven, no good thing has been, or can be enjoyed by us without having first cost labour– And, inasmuch as ~~all~~ ^most^ good things are produced by labour, it follows that all such things of right belong to those whose labour has produced them– But it has so happened in all ages of the world, that some have laboured, and others have, ~~any~~ without labour, enjoyed a large proportion of the fruits– This is wrong, and should not continue– To [sec]ure to each labourer the whole product of his labour, or as nearly as possible, is a most worthy object of any good government– [B]ut then the question arises, how can a government best effect this? ~~object~~?– In our own country, in it's present condition, will the protective principle aid ^advance^ or ^retard^ injure this object? ~~That is the question~~– Upon this subject, ^the habits of^ our whole species fall into three great classes—useful labour~~ers~~, useless labour~~ers~~, and idleness– Of these, the first [o]nly is meritorious; and to it all the products of labour rightfully belong; but the two latter, while they exist, are heavy pensioners upon the first, robbing it of a large portion of its just rights– The only remedy for this is to, as far as possible, drive useless ~~labo~~ labour and idleness out of existence– And first, as to useless labour– Before making war upon this, we must learn to distinguish it from the useful– It appears to me, then, that all labour done directly and incendentally in carrying articles to their place of consumption, which could have been produced in sufficient abundance, with as little labour, at the place of consumption, as at the place they were carried from, is usel[ess] labour– Let us take a few examples of the application of the [principle to our] own country– Iron ^& every thing made of iron^ can be produced, in sufficient abundance[,] [and?] [wi]th as little labour, in the United States, as any where else in the [wor]ld; therefore, all labour done in bringing iron ^& it's fabrics^ from foreign countries to the United States, is useless labour– The same precisely [may be said of] Cotten, Wool, and of their fabrics respectively, as well [as many other] articles– While the uselessness of the carrying labour is [equally true?] of all the articles mentioned, and of many others not men[tioned] it is, perhaps, more glaringly obvious in relation to the [cotton] [goods we?] purchase from abroad– The raw cotten, from which they are [made, itself] grows in our own country, is carried by land and by water to [England] [is?] there spun, wove, dyed, stamped &c [*etc.*]; and then carried back [again?] and worn in the very country where it grew, and partly by the [very?] persons who grew it– Why should it not be spun, wove &c in the very neighbourhood where it both grows and is consumed, and the carrying ^labour^ thereby dispensed with? Has nature interposed any obstacles? Are not all the agents—animal power, water power, and steam power— as good [and as] abundant here as elsewhere? Will not as small an amount of human labour, answer here as elsewhere? We may easily see that the cost of this useless labour is very heavy– It includes, not only the cost of the ~~land and water~~ ^actual^ carriage, but also the insurances of every kind, and the profits the merchants through whose hands it passes– All these create a heavy burthen, necessarily falling upon the useful labour connected wi[th] such articles, either depressing the price to the producer, or enhancing it to the consumer, or, what is more probable, doing both in part A supposed case, will serve to illustrate several points now to the p[ur]pose– A. in the interior of South Carolina, has one hundred pounds of cotten, which we suppose to be the precise product of one mans labour for twenty days; B, in Manchester, England, has one hundred yards of cotten cloth, the precise product of the same amount of lab[our]– This lot of cotten, and lot of cloth are precisely equal to each other in their intrinsic value– But A. wishes to part wit[h] his cotten for the largest quantity of cloth he can get; B, al[so] wishes to part with his cloth for the greatest quantity of co[tton] he can get– An exchange is therefore necessary; but before this can be effected, the cotten must be carried to Manchester, and the cloth to South Carolina– The cotten starts to Manchester, the man that hauls ^it^ [~~. . . .~~ ?] to Chareleston in his waggon, takes a little of it out, to pay him for his trouble; the merchant, who stores it a while before the ship is ready to sail, takes a little out, for his trouble, the ship-owner, who carries it across the water, ~~will~~ takes a little out for his trouble, still before it gets to Manchester, it is tolled two or three times more for drayage, storage, commission, and so on; so that when it reaches B's hands there are but seventyfive pounds of it left– The cloth, too, in it's transit from Manchester to South Carolina ~~to~~ goes through the same process of tolling, so that when it reaches A there are but seventyfive yards of it– Now, in this case, A. and B. have each parted with twenty days labour, and each received but fifteen in return– But now let us suppose that B. has removed to the side of A's farm in South Carolina and has there made his lot of cloth– Is it not clear that he and A. can then exchange their cloth & cotten, each getting the whole of what the other parts with–

This supposed case shows the utter uselessness of the carrying labour in all similar [cases] and also, the direct burthen it imposes up[on] useful labour– And [whoever] will take up the train of reflection su[g]gested by this case, and [run] it out to the full extent of it's just application, will be [astonished,] atthe amount of useless labour will thus discover to be [done] this very way– I am mistaken, if it is not in fact many times [?] equal to all the real want in the world– ~~Those engaged in this~~ [~~. . .~~ ?] ~~would have turned~~ This useless labour I would have discontinued, and those engaged ~~it~~ in it, added to the class of useful labourers– If I [be asked whether] I would destroy all commerce, I answer "Certainly not"– I would [continue] it where it is necessary, and discontinue it, where it is not– An instance I would continue commerce, so far as it is employed [in bringing us coffee] I would discontinue it so far as it is employed in [bringing us] cotten goods–

First, then, as to useless labour– But what is useless labour? I suppose, then, that all labour done directly and incidentally in carrying articles from the place of their production to a distant place for consumption, which articles, could be produced of as good quality, and sufficient quantity, with as little labour at the place of consumption, as at the place carried from, is useless labour– Applying this principle to our own country [by] an example, let us suppose that A and B are a Penn[sy]lvania farmer, and a Pennsylvania iron-maker, whose lands [ar]e adjoining– Under the protective policy A is furnishing B. with bread and meat, and vegetables and fruits, and food for horses and oxen, and fresh supplies of horses and oxen themselves occasionly, and receiving, in exchange, all the iron, iron utensils, tools and implements he needs– In this process of exchange, each receives the whole of what the other parts [w]ith– But the change comes– The protective policy is abandoned (how, and under what expection, I will hereafter try to show) and A. determines, ~~to~~ for the future, to buy his supply of iron and iron fabrics of C an iron-maker in England– This he can only do by a direct or an indirect exchange of the products of his farm for them– The direct exchange is supposed to be adopted– In a certain instance of this sort, A desires to exchange ten barrels of flour, the precise product of one hundred days labour, for the greatest quantity of iron he can get; C, also wishes to exchange the precise product of one hundred days labour, in iron, for the greatest quantity of flour he can get– But before the exchange can take place, the flour must be carried ^from Penn[a] [Pennsylvania]^ to England and the iron ^from England^ to Pennsylvania– The flour starts– The waggoner who hauls it to Philadelphia, takes a part of it to pay him for his labour; then a merchant there, takes a little more for storage and forwarding commission; and another takes a little more for insurance; and then the ship-owner carries it across the water, and takes a little more of it for his trouble; still before it reaches C, it is tolled two or three times more for storage, drayage, commission and so on; so that when C gets it there are but seven barrels and a half of it left– The iron, too, in it's transit from England to Pensylvania, goes through the same process of tolling; so that when it reaches A, there are but three quarters of it left– Now, this carrying labour, was generally useless in this; that it diminished the quantity, while it added nothing to the quality of the articles carried; and it was useless to A, because, by continuing to buy of B, it needed not to be done

~~make the articles~~ as to useless labour.– Before proceeding however, it may be as well to give a specimen of what I co[nc]eive to be useless labour– I say, then, that all carrying ^& incidents of carrying,^ of articles from the place of their production, to a distant place for consumption, which articles could be produced of as good quality; in sufficient quantity, and with as little labour, at the place of consumption, as at the place carried from, is useless labour– Applying this principle to our own country by an example, let us suppose that A and B, are a Pensylvania farmer, and a Pennsylvania iron-maker, whose lands are adjoining–

Under the protective policy A is furnishing B with bread and meat, and vegetables, and fruits, and food for horses and oxen, and fresh supplies of horses and ox[en] themselves occasionally, and receiving, in exchange, all the iron, iron utensils, tools, and implements he needs– In this process of exchange, each receives the whole of that which the other parts with– and the reward of labour between them is perfect; each receiving the produce of just so much labour, as he has himself bestowed on what he parts with for it– But the change comes– The protective policy is abandoned, and A determines to buy his iron and iron manufactures ^of C.^ in Europe– This he can only do by a direct or an indirect exchange of the produce of his farm for them– We will suppose the direct exchange is adopted– In this A desires to exchange ten barrels of flour the precise product of one hundred days labour, for the largest quantity of iron &c that he can get; C, also wishes to exchange the precise product, in iron, of one hundred days labour, for the greatest quantity of flour he can get–^In intrinsic value, the things to be so exchanged, are precisely equal–^ But before this exchange can take place, the flour must be carried from Pennsylvania to England, and the iron form England to Pennsylvania– The flour starts; the waggoner who hauls it to Philadelphia, takes a part of it to pay him for his labours; then a merchant there takes a little more for storage and forwarding commission, and another takes a little more for insurance; and then the ship-owner carries it across the water, and takes a little more of it for his trouble; still before it reaches ~~B.~~ C. it is tolled two or three times more for storage, drayage, commission and so on, so that when C. ~~B~~ gets it, there are but ~~five~~ ^seven & a half^ barrels of it left– The iron, too, in its transit from England to Penn[a] goes through the same process [of] tolling, so that when it reaches A, there is but ~~half~~ ^three quarters^ of it left–

The result of this case is, that A and C ~~B~~ have each parted with one hundred days labour, and each received but seventy five in return– That the carrying in this case, was introduced by A ceasing to buy of B, and turning C; that it ~~is~~ ^was^ utterly useless; and that it is ruinous in its effects, upon A, are all little less than self evident– "But" asks one "if A is now only getting three quarters as much iron from C ^for ten barrels of flour^ as he used to get of B, why does he not turn back to B"?" The answer is, B has quit making iron, and so, has none to sell– "But why did B quit making?"– Because A quit buying of him, and he had no other customer to sell to– "But surely A. did not cease buying of B, with the expectation of buying of C on harder terms?–" Certainly not– Let me tell you how that was– When B was making iron as well as C, B had but one customer, this farmer A– C had four customers in Europe–

It seems to be an opinion, very generally entertained, that the condition of a nation ~~or an individual~~, is best, whe[ne]ver ~~they~~ ^it^ can buy cheapest; but this is not necessarily true; because if, at the same time, and by the same cause, it is compelled to sell correspondingly cheap, nothing is gained– Then, it is said, the best condition is, when we can buy cheapest, and sell dearest; but this again, is not necessarily true; because, with both these, we might have scarcely any thing to sell—or, which is the same thing, to buy with– To illustrate this, suppose a man in the present state of things is labouring the year round, at ten dollars per month, which amounts in the year to $120—a change in affairs enables him to buy supplies at half the former price, to get fifty dollars per month for his labour; but at the same time deprives him of employment during all the months of the year but one– In this case, though goods have fallen one half, and labour ~~raised~~ ^risen^ five to one, it is still plain, that at the end of the year, the labourer ~~would~~ ^is^ ~~be~~ twenty dollars poorer, than under the old state of things–

These reflections show, that to reason and act correctly on this subject, we must look not merely to buying cheap, nor yet to buying cheep and selling dear; but also to having constant employment, so that we may have the largest possible amount of something to sell– This matter of employment can only be secured by an ample, steady, and certain market, to sell the products of labour in–

But let us yield the point, and admit that, by abandoning the protective policy, our farmers can purchase their supplies of manufactured articles cheaper than by continuing it; and then let us see whether, even at that, they will, upon the whole, be gainers by the change– To simplify this question, let us suppose the whole agricultural interest of the country to be in the hands of one man, who has one hundred labourers in h[is e]mploy the whole manufacturing interest, to be in the hands of [an]other man, who has twenty labourers in his employ– The farmer [own]s all the plough and pasture land, and the manufacturer, all the iron-mines, and coal-banks, and sites of water power– Each is pushing on in his own way, and obtaining supplies from the [o]ther so far as he needs—that is, the manufacturer, is buying of the farmer all the cotten he can use in his cotten factory, all the wool he can use in his woollen establishment, all the bread and meat, as well as all the fruits and vegetables which are necessary for himself and all his hands in all his departments; all the corn, and oats, and hay, which are necessary for all his horses and oxen, as well as fresh supplies of horses and oxen themselves, to ^do^ all his heavy hauling about [his] iron works and generally of every sort– The farmer, in turn, is buy[ing] of the manufacturer all the iron, iron tools, wooden tools, cotten goods woolen goods &c &c. that he needs ~~fo~~ [in his] business and for his hands– But after awhile f[arm]er discovers that, were it not for the protective policy, he could buy all these supplies cheaper from a European manufacturer, owing to the fact that the price of labour is only one quarter is [as] high there as here– He and his hands are [a] majority of the whole, and therefore have the legal and moral right to have their interest~~est~~ first consulted– They throw off the protective policy, and farmer ceases buying of home manufacturer– Verry soon, however, he discovers, that to buy, even at the cheaper rate, requires something to buy with, and some how or other, he is falling short in this particular–

But let us yield the point, and admit that, by abandoning to protective policy, our farmers can purchase their supplies of manufactured articles cheaper than before; and then let us see whether, even at that, the farmers will, upon the whole, be gainers by the change– To simplify this question, let us suppose our whole population to consist of but twenty men– Under the prevalence of the protective policy, fifteen of these are farmers, one is a miller, one manufactures iron, one, implements from iron, one cotten goods, and one woolen goods– The farmers discover, that, owing to labour only costing one quarter ~~in~~ as much in Europe as here, they can buy iron, iron implements, cotten goods & woolen goods cheaper, when brought from Europe, [th]an when made by their neighbours– They are the majority, and [the]refore have both the legal and moral right to have their in[tere]st first consulted– They throw off the protective policy, [and] cease buying these articles of their neighbours– But they [soo]n discover that to buy, even at the cheaper rate, requires [som]ething to buy with– Falling short in this particular, one of [th]ese farmers, ~~st~~ takes a load of wheat to the miller, and [g]ets it made into flour, and starts, as had been his cus[to]m, to the iron furnace; he approaches the well known spot, [bu]t strange to say, all is cold and still as death—no [sm]oke rises, no furnace roars, no anvil rings– After some search, [h]e finds the owner of the desolate place, and calls out to him, "Come Vulcan, dont you want to buy a load of flour?–" "Why" says Vulcan "I am hungry enough, to be sure—have'nt tasted bread for a week—but then you see my works are stopped, and I have nothing to give for your flour– But, Vulcan, why dont you go to work and get something[?] I am ready to do so; will you hire me, farmer? Oh [no] I could only set you to raising wheat, and you see I have more of that already than I can get any thing for– But give me employment, and send your flour to Europe [for a?] market– Why, Vulcan, how silly you talk– Dont you know they raise wheat in Erope as well as here, and that labour is so cheap there as to fix the price of flour there so low, as ~~scarcl~~ scarcely to pay the long carriage of it from here, leaving nothing whatever to me– But, farmer, could'nt you pay to raise and prepare garden stuffs, and fruits, such as radishes, cabages, irish and sweet potatoes, cucumbers water melons and musk-melons, plumbs, pears, peaches, apples, and the like; all these are good things and used to sell well– So they did use to sell well, but it was to you we sold them, and now you tell us you have nothing to buy with– Of course I can not sell such things to the other farmers, because each of them raises enough for himself, and, in fact, rather wishes to sell than to buy– Neither can I send ^them^ to Europe for a market; because, to say nothing of Eropean markets being stocked with such articles at lower prices than I can afford, they are of such a nature as to rot before they could reach there– The truth is, Vulcan, I am compelled to quit raising these things altogether, except a few for my own use, and this leaves part of my own time idle on my hands, instead of my finding employment for you–

I suppose the true effect of duties upon prices to be as follows: If a ^certain^ duty be levied upon an article which, by nature can not be produced in this country, as three cents a pound upon Coffee, the effect will be, that the consumer will pay one cent more per pound than before, the producer will take one cent less, and the merchant one cent less in profits—in other words, the burthen of the duty will distributed over consumption, production, and Commerce, and not confined to either–

But if a duty ^amounting to full protection^ be levied upon an article which can be produced here with as little labour, as elsewhere, ^as iron,^ that article will ultimately, and at no distant day, in consequence of such duty, be sold to our people cheaper than before, at least by the amount of the cost of carrying it from abroad–

If at any time all labour should cease, and all existing provisions be equally divided among the people, at the end of a single year there could scarcely be one human being left alive—all would have perished by want of subsistence–

So again, if upon such division, all that sort of labour, which produces provisions, should cease, and each individual should take up so much of his share as he could, and carry it continually around his habitation, although in this carrying, the amount of labour going on might be as great as ever, so long as it could last, at the end of the year the result would be precisely the same—that is, none would be left living–

The first of these propositions shows, that universal idlene[ss] would speedily result in universal ruin; and the second shows, [th]at useless labour is, in this respect, the same as idleness–

I submit, then, whether it does not follow, that partial idleness, and partial useless labour, would, in the proportion of their extent, in like manner result, in partial ruin—whether, if all should subsist upon the labour that one half should perform, it would not result in very scanty allowance to the whole–

Believing that these propositions, and the [conclusions] I draw from them can not be successfully controverted, I, for the present, assume their correctness, and proceed to try to show, that the abandonment of the protective policy by the American Government, must result in the increase of both useless labour, and idleness; and so, in pro[por]tion, must produce want and ruin among our people–

Fragment of Note Regarding Niagara Falls (September 25–30, 1848)

. . . Niagara- Falls! By what mysterious power is it, that millions and millions, are drawn from all parts of the world, to gaze upon Niagara Falls? There is, no mystery about the thing itself– Every effect is just such as any inteligent ^man^ knowing the causes, would anticipate, without it– If the water moving onward in a great [river?], reaches a point when there is a perpendicular jog, of a hundred feet in descent, in the bottom of the river,– it is plain the water will have a violent and continuous plunge at that point– It is also plain the water, thus plunging, will foam, and roar, and send up a mist, continuously, in which last, during sunshine, there will be perpetual rain-bows– The mere physical of Niagara Falls, is only this– Yet this is really a very small part of that world's wonder– It's power to excite reflection, and emotion, is it's great charm– The geologist will demonstrate that the plunge or fall, was once at Lake Ontario, and has worn it's way back to it's present position; he will ascertain how fast it is wearing now, and so get a basis for determining how long it has been wearing back from Lake Ontario, and finally demonstrate ^by it^ that this world is at least fourteen thousand years old– A philosopher of a slightly different turn will say Niagara Falls is only the lip of the basin out of which pours all the surplus water which rains down on two or three hundred thousand square miles of the earths surface– He will estimate [with?] approximate accuracy, that five hundred thousand [tons?] of water, falls with it's full weight, a distance of a hundred feet each minute– thus exerting a force equal to the lifting of the same weight, through the same space, in the same time– And then the further reflection comes that this vast amount of water, constantly pouring down, is supplied by an equal amount constantly lifted up, by the sun; and still he says, "If this much is lifted up, for this one space of two or three hundred thousand square miles, an equal amount must be lifted for every other equal space; [and?] he is overwhelmed in the contemplation of [the?] vast power the sun is constantly exerting in [the] quiet, noisless opperation of lifting water up [to be?] rained down again–

But still there is more. It calls up the indefinite past– When Columbus first sought this continent– when Christ suffered on the cross– when Moses led Israel through the ~~red~~ Red-Sea– nay, even, when Adam ~~was made,~~ ^first came from the hand of his Maker–^ then as now, Niagara was roaring here– The eyes of that species of extinct giants, whose bones fill the Mounds of America, have gazed on Niagara, as ours do now– Cotemporary with the whole race of ~~man~~ ^men,^, and older than the first man, Niagara is ^strong and^ fresh to-day as ten thousand years ago– The Mammoth and Mastadon– now so long dead, that fragments of their monstrous bones, alone testify, that they ever lived, have gazed on Niagara– In that long– long time, never still for a single moment– Never dried, never froze, never slept, never rested, . . .

Note on What General Taylor Ought to Say

(March ??, 1848)

When Lincoln decided General Zachary Taylor would be the best Whig candidate for president in 1848, he wrote this note to himself imagining what Taylor, with no experience in politics, ought to say in a presidential campaign.

The question of a national bank is at rest; were I President I should not urge it's reagitation upon Congress; but should Congress see fit to pass an act to establish such an institution, I should not arrest it by the veto, unless I should consider it subject to some constitutional objection, from which I believe the two former banks to have been free–

It appears to me that the national debt created by the war, renders a modification of the existing tariff indispensable; and when it shall be modified, I should be pleased to see it adjusted with a due reference to the protection of our home industry– The particulars, it appears to me, must and should be left to the untramelled discretion of Congress–

As to the Mexican war, I still ^think^ the defensive line policy the best to terminate it– In a final treaty of peace, we shall probably be under a sort of necessity of taking some teritory; but it is my desire that we shall not acquire any extending so far South as to enlarge and agrivate the distracting question of slavery– Should I come into the presidency before these questions shall be settled, I should act in relation to them in accordance with the views here expressed–

Finally, were I president, I should desire the legislation of the country to rest with Congress, uninfluenced by the executive in it's origin or progress, and undisturbed by the veto unless in very special and clear cases–

Fragment of Notes Regarding Government

(July 1, 1854?)

This note was written in the first months after Lincoln reentered politics in 1854.

The legitimate object of government, is to do for a community of people, whatever they need to have done, but can not do, at all, or can not, so well do, for themselves—in their separate, and individual capacities.

In all that the people can individually do as well for themselves, government ought not to interfere.

The desirable things which the individuals of a people can not do, or can not well do, for themselves, fall into two classes; those which have relation to ~~to~~ wrongs, and those which have not. Each of these branch off into an infinite variety of subdivisions.

The first—that in relation to wrongs—embraces all crimes, misdemeanors, and non-performance of contracts. The other embraces all which, in it's nature, and without wrong, requires combined action, as public roads and highways, public schools, charities, pauperism, orphanage, estates of the deceased, and the machinery of government itself.

From this it appears that if all men were just there still would be some, though not so much need of government.

Fragment of Notes Regarding Government

(July 1, 1854?)

In this note, probably written at the same time as the previous note, Lincoln continues his discussion of the purposes of government.

Government is a combination of the people of a country to effect certain objects by joint effort. The best framed and best administered governments are necessarily expensive; while by errors in frame and maladministration most of them are more onerous than they need be, and some of them very oppressive. Why, then, should we have government? Why not each individual take to himself the whole fruit of his labor, without having any of it taxed away, in services, corn, or money? Why not take just so much land as he can cultivate with his own hands, without buying it of any one?

The legitimate object of government is "to do for the people what needs to be done, but which they can not, by individual effort, do at all, or do so well, for themselves." There are many such things—some of them exist independently of the injustice in the world. Making and maintaining roads, bridges, and the like; providing for the helpless young and afflicted; common schools; and disposing of deceased men's property, are instances.

But a far larger class of objects springs from the injustice of men. If one people will make war upon another, it is a necessity with that other to unite and coöperate for defense. Hence the military department. If some men will kill, or beat, or constrain others, or despoil them of property, by force, fraud, or noncompliance with contracts, it is a common object with peaceful and just men to prevent it. Hence the criminal and civil departments.

Fragment of Note Regarding Slavery

(July 1, 1854?)

If A. can prove, however conclusively, that he may, of right, enslave B. why may not B. snatch the same argument, and prove equally, that he may enslave A?

You say A. is white, and B. is black. It is color, then; the lighter, having the right to enslave the darker? Take care. By this rule, you are to be slave to the first man you meet, with a fairer skin than ~~yourself~~ ^your own.^.

You do not mean color exactly? You mean the whites are intellectually the superiors of the blacks; and, therefore have the right to enslave them? Take care again. By this rule, you are to be slave to the first man you meet, with an intellect superior to your own.

But, say you, it is a question of interest; and, if you can make it your interest, you have the right to enslave another. Very well. And if he can make it his interest, he has the right to enslave you.

Fragment of Note Regarding Slavery

(July 1, 1854?)

This reflection on slavery is an example of the fragmentary character of many of Lincoln's notes; it begins in the midst of a word and ends before the sentence is completed.

. . . dent truth. Made so plain by our good Father in Heaven, that all feel and understand it, even down to brutes and creeping insects. The ant, who has toiled and dragged a crumb to his nest, will furiously defend the fruit of his labor, against whatever robber assails him. So plain, that the most dumb and stupid slave that ever toiled for a master, does constantly know that he is wronged. So plain that no one, high or low, ever does mistake it, except in a plainly selfish way; for although volume upon volume is written to prove slavery a very good thing, we never hear of the man who wishes to take the good of it, by being a slave himself.

Most governments have been based, practically, on the denial of the equal rights of men, as I have, in part, stated them; ours began, by affirming those rights. They said, some men are too ignorant, and vicious, to share in government. Possibly so, said we; and, by your system, you would always keep them ignorant, and vicious. We proposed to give all a chance; and we expected the weak to grow stronger, the ignorant, wiser; and all better, and happier together.

We made the experiment; and the fruit is before us. Look at it—think of it. Look at it, in it's aggregate grandeur, of extent of country, and numbers of population—of ship, and steamboat, and rail-

Fragment in Preparation for a Speech on Sectionalism

(July 23, 1856)

It is constantly objected to Fremont & Dayton, that they are supported by a sectional party, who, by their sectionalism, endanger the National Union. This objection, more than all others, causes men, really opposed to slavery extension, to hesitate. Practically, it is the most difficult objection we have to meet.

For this reason, I now propose to examine it, a little more carefully than I have heretofore done, or seen ^it^ done by others.

First, then, what is the ~~naked~~ question between the parties, respectively represented by Buchanan and Fremomont?

Simply this: "Shall slavery be allowed to extend into U.S. teritories, now legally free?" Buchanan says it shall; and Fremont says it shall not.

That is the naked issue, and the whole of it. Lay the ^respective^ platforms side by side; and the difference between them, will be found to amount to precisely that.

True, each party charges upon the other, designs much beyond what is involved in the issue, as stated; but as these charges can not be fully proved either way, it is probably better to reject them on both sides, and stick to the naked issue, as it is clearly made up on the record.

And now, to restate the question "Shall slavery be allowed to extend into U.S. teritories, now legally free?" I beg to know how one side of that question is more sectional than the other? Of course I expect to effect nothing with the man who makes this charge of sectionalism, without caring whether it is just or not. But of the candid, fair, man ^who has been puzzled with this charge,^ I do ask "how is one side of this question, more sectional, than the other? I beg of him to consider well, and answer calmly.

If one side be as sectional as the other, nothing is gained, as to sectionalism, by changing sides; so that each must choose sides of the question on some other ground—as I should think, according, as the one side or the other, shall appear nearest right. If he shall really think slavery ought to be extended, let him go to Buchanan; if he think it ought not let go to Fremont.

But, Fremont and Dayton, are both residents of the free-states; and this fact has been vaunted, in high places, as excessive sectionalism.

While interested individuals become indignant and excited, against this manifestation of sectionalism, I am very happy to know, that the Constitution remains calm—keeps cool—upon the subject. It does say that President and Vice President shall be resident of different states; but it does not say one must live in a slave, and the other in a free state.

It has been a custom to take one from a slave, and the other from a free state; but the custom has not, at all been uniform. In 1828 Gen. Jackson and Mr Calhoun, both from slave-states, were placed on the same ticket; and Mr Adams and Dr Rush ~~were pitted both from the free-states, were pitted against them.~~ Gen. Jackson and Mr Calhoun were elected; and qualified and served under the election; yet the whole thing never suggested the idea of sectionalism.

In 1841, the president, Gen. Harrison, died, by which Mr Tyler, the Vice-President ^& a slave state man,^ became president. Mr Mangum, another slave-state man, was placed in the Vice Presidential chair, served out the term, and no fuss about it—no sectionalism thought of.

In 1853 the present president came into office. He is a free-state man. Mr King, the new Vice President elect, was a slave state man; but he died without entering on the duties of his office. At first, his vacancy was filled by Atchison, another slave-state man; but he soon resigned, and the place was supplied by Bright, a free-state man. So that right now, and for the year and a half last past, our president and vice-president are both actually free-state men.

But, it is said, the friends of Fremont, avow the purpose of electing him exclusively by free-state votes, and that this is unendurable sectionalism.

This statement of fact, is not exactly true. With the friends of Fremont, it is an expected necessity, but it is not an "avowed purpose," to elect him, if at all, principally, by free state votes; but it is, with equal intensity, true that Buchanan's friends expect to elect him, if at all, chiefly by slave-state votes.

Here, again, the sectionalism, is just as much on one side as the other.

The thing which gives most color to the charge of Sectionalism, made against those who oppose the spread of slavery into free teritory, is the fact that they can get no votes in the slave-states, while their opponents get all, or nearly so, in the slave-states, and also, a large number in the free States. To state it in another way, the Extensionists, can get votes all over the Nation, while the Restrictionists can get them only in the free states.

This being the fact, why is it so? It is not because one side of the question dividing them, is more sectional than the other; nor because of any difference in the mental or moral structure of the people North and South. It is because, in that question, the people of the South have an immediate palpable ^and immensely great^ pecuniary interest; while, ~~in~~ ^with the people of^ the North, it is merely an abstract question of moral right, with only slight, and remote pecuniary interest added.

The slaves of the South, at a moderate estimate, are worth a thousand millions of dollars. Let it be permanently settled that this property may extend to new teritory, without restraint, and it greatly enhances, perhaps quite doubles, its value at once. This immense, palpable pecuniary interest, on the question of extending slavery, unites the Southern people, ~~as~~ as one man. But it can not be demonstrated that the North will gain a dollar by restricting it.

Moral principle is all, or nearly all, that unites us of the North. Pity 'tis, it is so, but this is a looser bond, than pecuniary interest.

Right here is the plain cause of their perfect union and our want of it. ^And see how it works.^ If a Southern man aspires to be president, they choke him down instantly, in order that the glittering prize of the presidency, may be held up, on Southern terms, to the greedy eyes of Northern ambition. With this they tempt us, and break in upon us.

The democratic party, in 1844, elected a Southern president. Since then, they have neither had a ^Southern^ candidate for election, or nomination. Their conventions of 1848, 1852 and 1856, have been struggles exclusively among Northern men, each vieing to outbid the other for the Southern vote—the South standing ~~a~~ calmly by to finally ~~say~~ cry going, going, gone, to the highest bidder; and, at the same time, to make its power more distinctly seen, and thereby to secure a still higher bid at the next succeeding struggle.

"Actions speak louder than words" is the maxim; and, if true, the South now distinctly say's to the North "Give us the measures, and you take the men"

The total withdrawal of Southern aspirants, ^for the presidency,^ multiplies the number of Northern ones. These last, in competing with each other, commit themselves to the utmost verge that, through their own greediness, they have the least hope their Northern supporters will bear. Having got committed, in a race of competetion, necessity drives them into union to sustain themselves. Each, at first secures all he can, on personal attach-ments to him, and through hopes resting on him personally. Next, they unite with one another, and with the perfectly banded South, to make the offensive position they have got into, "a party measure." This done, large additional numbers are secured.

When the repeal of the Missouri compromise was first proposed, at the North there was litterally "nobody" in favor of it. In February 1854 our Legislature met in call, or extra, session. From them Douglas sought an indorsement of his then pending measure of Repeal. ~~In~~ In our Legislature were about 70 democrats to 30 whigs. The former held a caucus, in which it was resolved to give Douglas the desired indorsement. Some of the members of that caucus bolted—would not stand it—and they now divulge the secrets. They say that the caucus fairly confessed that the Repeal was wrong; and they placed their determination to indorse it, solely on the ground that it was necessary to sustain Douglas. Here we have the direct evidence of how the Nebraska-bill obtained its strength in Illinois. It was given, not in a sense of right, but in the teeth of a sense of wrong, to sustain Douglas. So Illinois was divided. So New England, for Pierce; Michigan for Cass, ~~and~~ Pensylvania for Buchan, and all for the Democratic party.

And when, by such means, they have got a large portion of the Northern people into a position contrary to their own honest impulses, and sense of right; they have the impudence to turn upon those who do stand firm, and call them sectional.

Were it not too serious a matter, this cool impudence would be laughable, to say the least.

Recurring to the question "Shall slavery be allowed to extend into U.S. teritory now legal free?

This is a sectional question—that is to say, it is a question, in its nature calculated to divide the American people geographically. Who is to blame for that? who can help it? Either side can help it; but how? Simply by yielding to the other side. There is no other way. In the whole range of possibility, there is no other way. Then, which side shall yield? To this again, there can be but one answer—the side which is in the wrong. True, we differ, as to which side is wrong; and we boldly say, let all who really think slavery ought to spread into free teritory, openly go over against us. There is where they rightfully belong.

But why should any go, who really think slavery ought not to spread? Do they really think the right ought to yield to the wrong? Are they afraid to stand by the right? Do they fear that the constitution is too weak to sustain them in the right? Do they really think that by right surrendering to wrong, the hopes of our constitution, our Union, and our liberties, can possibly be bettered?

Note Regarding George Cheney's Request

(1856–57?)

Lincoln wrote this note to remind himself of his promise to Mr. Cheney, who lived seventy miles away in McLean County. Lincoln's law partner, William H. Herndon, attested, "It is in the handwriting of Mr. Lincoln and is true and genuine." December 22, 1886. Endorsement by Herndon.

George Cheney wishes me to investigate the question whether a purchaser, with bond, but not recorded, but in actual possession of the premises, must be a party to the foreclosure of a previous mortgage, made by the person of whom be foreclosed, & duly recorded. And whether, if such person be not made a party, but afterwards yielded possession to the foreclosure title, and die, his heirs can open the foreclosure & redeem. I am to write him at Cheneys Grove, M[c]Lean Co Ills.

Note for a Speech

(1856–60?)

We were without party history, party pride, or party idols.

We were a collection of individuals, but recently in political hostility, one to another; and thus subject to all that distrust, and suspicion, and jealousy could do.

Everywhere in the ranks of the common enemy, were old party and personal friends, jibing, and jeering, and framing deceitful agreements against us.

We were scarcely met at all on the real issue.

Thousands avowed our principles, but turned from us, professing to believe we meant more than we said.

No argument, which was true in fact, made any head-way against us. This we know.

We were constantly charged with seeking an amalgamation of the white and black races; and thousands turned from us, not believing the charge (no one believed it) but fearing to face it themselves.

Note Regarding Stephen A. Douglas

(December 1, 1856?)

Twenty two years ago Judge Douglas and I first became acquainted. We were both young then; he a trifle younger than I. Even then, we were both ambitious; I perhaps, quite as much so as he. With me, the race of ambition has been a failure— a flat failure; with him it has been one of splendid success. His name fills the nation; and ~~extends~~ ^is not unknown^, even, ~~to~~ in foreign lands. I affect no contempt for the high eminence he has reached. So reached, that the oppressed of my species, might have shared with me in the elevation, I would rather stand on that eminence, than wear the richest crown that ever pressed a monarch's brow

Note Regarding Nomination of Candidates for Municipal Offices in Chicago

(February 28, 1857)

With the future of this party, the approaching city election will have something to do; not, indeed, to the extent of making or breaking it, but still to help or ^to^ hurt it ~~some~~.

Last year the city election here was lost by our friends; and more can safely say, but that fact lost us the electoral ticket at the State election.

Although Chicago recovered herself in the fall, there was no general confidence that she could do so; and the Spring election encouraged our enemies, and haunted and depressed our friends to the last.

Let it not be so again.

Let minor differences, and personal preferences, if there be such, go to the winds.

Let it be seen by the result, that the cause of free-men and free-labor is stronger in Chicago that day, than ever before.

Let the news go forth to our thirteen hundred thousand bretheren, to gladden, and to multiply them; and to insure and accelerate that consumation, upon which the happy destiny of all men, everywhere, depends.

Fragment on the Dred Scott Case

(March 6, 1857?)

The Supreme Court decided the Dred Scott case on March 6, 1857. Lincoln's words—"whatever the Supreme Court may decide"—indicate he wrote the note before that date.

What would be the effect of this, if it should ever be the creed of a dominant party in the nation? Let us analyse, and consider it.

It affirms ~~whatever decision~~ ^that whatever^ the Supreme Court may decide as to the constitutional restriction on the power of a territorial Legislature, in regard to slavery in the territory, must be obliged, and enforced by all of the departments of the federal government.

Now, if this is sound, as to this particular ^constitutional^ question, it is equally sound of all constitutional questions; so that the proposition substantially is "Whatever decision the Supreme Court makes on any constitutional question, must be obeyed, and enforced by all the departments of the federal government."

Again, it is not the full scope of this creed, that if the Supreme Court, having the particular question before them, shall decide that Dred Scott is a slave, the executive department must enforce the decision against Dred Scott. If this were it's full scope, it is presumed, no one would controvert it's correctness. But in this narrow scope, there is no room for the Legislature department to enforce the decision; while the creed affirms that all the departments must enforce it. The creed, then, has a broader scope; and what is it? It is this; that so soon as the Supreme Court decides that Dred Scott is a slave, the whole community must decide that not only Dred Scott, but that all persons in like condition, are ^rightfully^ slaves

Fragment on the Formation of the Republican Party

(February 28, 1857)

Upon those men who are, in sentiment, opposed to the spread, and nationalization of slavery, rests the task of preventing it. The Republican organization is the embodyment of that sentiment; though, as yet, it by no means embraces all the individuals holding that sentiment. The party is newly formed; and in forming, old party ties had to be broken, and the attractions of party pride, and influential leaders were wholly wanting. In spite of old differences, prejudices, and animosities, it's members were drawn together by a paramount common danger. They formed and maneuvered in the face of the deciplined enemy, and in the teeth of all his persistent misrepresentations. Of course, they fell far short of gathering in all of their own. And yet, a year ago, they stood up, an army over thirteen hundred thousand strong. That army is, to-day, the best hope of the nation, and of the world. Their work is before them; and from which they may not guiltlessly turn away.

Fragment for a Speech at Edwardsville, Illinois

(May 18, 1858?)

This is the first of three fragments Lincoln wrote in preparation for the speech at Edwardsville.

Welcome, or unwelcome, agreeable, or disagreeable, whether this shall be an entire slave nation, is the issue before us. Every incident—every little shifting of scenes or of actors—only clears away the intervening trash, compacts and consolodates the opposing hosts, and brings them more and more distinctly face to face. The conflict will be a severe one; and it will be fought through by those who do care for the result, and not by those who do not care—by those who are for, and those who are against a legalized, national slavery. The combined charge of Nebraskaism, and Dred Scottism must be repulsed, and rolled back. The deceitful cloak of "self government" wherewith "the sum of all villanies" seeks to protect and adorn itself, must be torn from it's hateful carcase. That burlesque upon judicial decisions, and slander and profanation upon the honored names, and sacred history of republican America, must be overruled, and expunged from the books of authority.

To give the victory to the right, not bloody bullets, but peaceful ballots only, are necessary. Thanks to our good old constitution, and organization under it, these alone are necessary. It only needs that every right thinking man, shall go to the polls, and without fear or prejudice, vote as he thinks.

Second Fragment for a Speech at Edwardsville, Illinois (May 18, 1858?)

We also ought to insist on knowing what the Judge now thinks on "Sectionalism." Last year, he thought it was a "clincher" against us, on the question of sectionalism, that we could get no support in the slave-states, and could not be allowed to speak, or even, breathe, South of the Ohio river. In vain did we appeal to the justice of our principles. He would have it, that the treatment we received, was conclusive evidence that we deserved it.

He, and his friends, would bring speakers from the slave-states, to their meetings, and conventions, in the free-states, and parade about, arm in arm, with them, breathing, in every gesture and tone "How we national apples do swim"

Let him cast about for this particular evidence of his own nationality now. Why, just now, he and Fremont would make the closest race imaginable, in the Southern States

In ^the^ present aspect of affairs, what ought the republicans to do?

I think they ought not to oppose any measure, merely because Judge Douglas proposes it. Whether the Lecompton constitution should be accepted, or rejected, is a question ^upon^ which, in the minds of men not committed to any of it's antecedents, and controled only by the Federal constitution, by republican principles, and by a sound morality, it seems to me, there could not be two opinions. It should be throttled, and killed, so hastily, and heartily, as a rabid dog.

What those should do, who are committed to all it's antecedents, is their business, not ours.

If, therefore, Judge Douglas' bill, secures a fair vote to the people of Kansas, without continuance to commit any one further, I think republican members of congress ought to support it. They can do so, without any inconsistency. They believe congress ought to prohibit slavery wherever it can be done, without violation of the constitution, or of good faith. And having seen the noses counted, and actually knowing that a majority of the people of Kansas are against slavery, passing an act ~~of congress~~ to secure them a fair vote, is little else than prohibiting slavery in Kansas, by act of congress.

Congress can not dictate a constitution to a new state. All it can do, at that point, is to secure the people a fair chance to form one for themselves, and then ^to^ accept, or reject it, when they ask admission into the union.

As I understand, republicans claim no more than this. But they do claim, that congress can, and ought to keep slavery out of a teritory, up to the time of it's people forming a state constitution; and they should now be careful to not stultify themselves, to any extent, on this point.

I am glad Judge Douglas has, at last, distinctly told us, that he cares not whether slavery be voted down, or voted up. Not so much that this is any news to me; nor yet, that it may be slightly new to some of that class of his friends who delight to say that they "are as much opposed to slavery as any body" I am glad, because it affords such a true and excellent a definition of the Nebraska policy itself. That policy, honestly administered, is exactly that. It seeks to bring the people of the nation to not care any thing about slavery. This is Nebraskaism, in its abstract purity—in it's very best dress.

Now, I take it, nearly every body does care something about slavery—is either for it, or against it; and that the statesmanship of a measure which conforms to the sentiments of nobody, might well be doubted in advance.

But Nebraskaism did not originate as a price of statesmanship. Gen. Cass, in 1848, invented it, as a political manoever, to secure himself the democratic nomination for the presidency. It served it's purpose ^then,^ and sunk out of sight. Six years later, Judge Douglas fished it up, and glozed it over with what he called, and still persists in calling "sacred right of self-government."

Well, I too, believe in self-government as I understand it; but I do not understand, that the previlege one man takes of making a slave of another, or holding him as such, is any part of "self government" To call it so is, to mind, simply absurd, and ridiculous.

I am for the people of the whole nation doing just as they please, in all matters which concern the whole nation; for those of each part, doing just as they choose, in all matters which concern no other part; and for each individual doing just as he chooses in all matters which concern no body else

This is the principle. Of course I am content with any exception, which the constitution, or the actually existing state of things, makes a necessity.

But neither the principle, nor the exception, will admit the indefinite spread and perpetuity of human slavery.

I think ^the^ true magnitude of the slavery element, in this nation, is scarcely appreciated by any one. Four years ago the Nebraska policy was adopted, professedly, to drive the agitation of the subject into the teritories, and out of every other place, and, especially out of congress.

When Mr Buchanan accepted the Presidential nomination, he felicitated himself with the belief, that the whole thing would be quieted, and forgotten in about six weeks. In his inaugural, and his Silliman letter, at their respective dates, he was just not quite in reach of the same happy consummation. And now, in his first annual message, he urges the acceptance of the Lecompton constitution (not quite satisfactory to him) on the sole ground of getting this little, unimportant matter out of the way.

Meanwhile, in those four years, there has really been more angry agitation of the subject, both, in and out of congress, than ever before. And just now it is perplexing the mighty ones, as no subject ever did before.

Nor is it confined to politics alone. Presbyterian Assemblys, Methodist conferences, Unitarian and single churches to an indefinite extent, are wrangling, and cracking, and going to pieces on the same question.

Third Fragment for a Speech at Edwardsville, Illinois (May 18, 1858)

From time to time, ever since the Chicago "Times" and "Illinois State Register" declared their opposition to the Lecompton constitution, and it began to be understood that Judge Douglas was also opposed to it, I have been accosted by friends of his with the question, "What do you think now?" Since the delivery of his speech in the Senate, the question has been varied a little. "Have you read Douglas's speech?" "Yes." "Well, what do you think of it?" In every instance the question is accompanied with an anxious inquiring stare, which asks, quite as plainly as words could, "Can't you go for Douglas now?" Like boys who have set a bird-trap, they are watching to see if the birds are picking at the bait and likely to go under.

I think, then, Judge Douglas knows that the Republicans wish Kansas to be a free State. He knows that they know, if the question be fairly submitted to a vote of the people of Kansas, it will be a free State; and he would not object at all if, by drawing their attention to this particular fact, and himself becoming vociferous for such fair vote, they should be induced to drop their own organization, fall into rank behind him, and form a great free-State Democratic party.

But before Republicans do this, I think they ought to require a few questions to be answered on the other side. If they so fall in with Judge Douglas, and Kansas shall be secured as a free State, there then remaining no cause of difference between him and the regular Democracy, will not the Republicans stand ready, haltered and harnessed, to be handed over by him to the regular Democracy, to filibuster indefinitely for additional slave territory,—to carry slavery into all the States, as well as Territories, under the Dred Scott decision, construed and enlarged from time to time, according to the demands of the regular slave Democracy,—and to assist in reviving the African slave-trade in order that all may buy negroes where they can be bought cheapest, as a clear incident of that "sacred right of property," now held in some quarters to be above all constitutions?

By so falling in, will we not be committed to or at least compromitted with, the Nebraska policy?

If so, we should remember that Kansas is saved, not by that policy or its authors, but in spite of both—by an effort that cannot be kept up in future cases.

Did Judge Douglas help any to get a free-State majority into Kansas? Not a bit of it—the exact contrary. Does he now express any wish that Kansas, or any other place, shall be free? Nothing like it. He tells us, in this very speech, expected to be so palatable to Republicans, that he cares not whether slavery is voted down or voted up. His whole effort is devoted to clearing the ring, and giving slavery and freedom a fair fight. With one who considers slavery just as good as freedom, this is perfectly natural and consistent.

But have Republicans any sympathy with such a view? They think slavery is wrong; and that, like every other wrong which some men will commit if left alone, it ought to be prohibited by law. They consider it not only morally wrong, but a "deadly poison" in a government like ours, professedly based on the equality of men. Upon this radical difference of opinion with Judge Douglas, the Republican party was organized. There is all the difference between him and them now that there ever was. He will not say that he has changed; have you?

Again, we ought to be informed as to Judge Douglas's present opinion as to the inclination of Republicans to marry with negroes. By his Springfield speech we know what it was last June; and by his resolution dropped at Jacksonville in September we know what it was then. Perhaps we have something even later in a Chicago speech, in which the danger of being "stunk out of church" was descanted upon. But what is his opinion on the point now? There is, or will be, a sure sign to judge by. If this charge shall be silently dropped by the judge and his friends, if no more resolutions on the subject shall be passed in Douglas Democratic meetings and conventions, it will be safe to swear that he is courting. Our "witching smile" has "caught his youthful fancy"; and henceforth Cuffy and he are rival beaux for our gushing affections.

We also ought to insist on knowing that the judge now thinks on "Sectionalism." Last year he thought it was a "clincher" against us on the question of Sectionalism, that we could get no support in the slave States, and could not be allowed to speak, or even breathe, south of the Ohio River.

In vain did we appeal to the justice of our principles. He would have it that the treatment we received was conclusive evidence that we deserved it. He and his friends would bring speakers from the slave States to their meetings and conventions in the free States, and parade about, arm in arm with them, breathing in every gesture and tone, "How we national apples do swim!" Let him cast about for this particular evidence of his own nationality now. Why, just now, he and Frémont would make the closest race imaginable in the Southern States.

In the present aspect of affairs what ought the Republicans to do? I think they ought not to oppose any measure merely because Judge Douglas proposes it. Whether the Lecompton constitution should be accepted or rejected is a question upon which, in the minds of men not committed to any of it antecedents, and controlled only by the Federal Constitution, by republican principles, and by a sound morality, it seems to me there could not be two opinions. It should be throttled and killed as hastily and as heartily as a rabid dog. What those should do who are committed to all its antecedents is their business, not ours. If, therefore, Judge Douglas's bill secures a fair vote to the people of Kansas, without contrivance to commit any one farther, I think Republican members of Congress ought to support it. They can do so without any inconsistency. They believe Congress ought to prohibit slavery wherever it can be done without violation of the Constitution or of good faith. And having seen the noses counted, and actually knowing that a majority of the people in Kansas are against slavery, passing an act to secure them a fair vote is little else than prohibiting slavery in Kansas by act of Congress.

Congress cannot dictate a constitution to a new State. All it can do at that point is to secure the people a fair chance to form one for themselves, and then to accept or reject it when they ask admission into the Union. As I understand, Republicans claim no more than this. But they do claim that Congress can and ought to keep slavery out of a Territory, up to the time of its people forming a State constitution; and they should now be careful to not stultify themselves to any extent on that point.

I am glad Judge Douglas has, at last, distinctly told us that he cares not whether slavery be voted down or voted up. Not so much that this is any news to me; nor yet that it may be slightly new to some of that class of his friends who delight to say that they "are as much opposed to slavery as anybody."

I am glad because it affords such a true and excellent definition of the Nebraska policy itself. That policy, honestly administered, is exactly that. It seeks to bring the people of the nation to not care anything about slavery. This is Nebraskaism in its abstract purity—in its very best dress.

Now, I take it, nearly everybody does care something about slavery—is either for it or against it; and that the statesmanship of a measure which conforms to the sentiments of nobody might well be doubted in advance.

But Nebraskaism did not originate as a piece of statesmanship. General Cass, in 1848, invented it, as a political manoeuver, to secure himself the Democratic nomination for the presidency. It served its purpose then, and sunk out of sight. Six years later Judge Douglas fished it up, and glozed it over with what he called, and still persists in calling, "sacred rights of self-government."

Well, I, too, believe in self-government as I understand it; but I do not understand that the privilege one man takes of making a slave of another, or holding him as such, is any part of "self-government." To call it so is, to my mind, simply absurd and ridiculous. I am for the people of the whole nation doing just as they please in all matters which concern the whole nation; for those of each part doing just as they choose in all matters which concern no other part; and for each individual doing just as he chooses in all matters which concern nobody else. This is the principle. Of course I am content with any exception which the Constitution, or the actually existing state of things, makes a necessity. But neither the principle nor the exception will admit the indefinite spread and perpetuity of human slavery.

I think the true magnitude of the slavery element in this nation is scarcely appreciated by any one. Four years ago the Nebraska policy was adopted, professedly, to drive the agitation of the subject into the Territories, and out of every other place, and especially out of Congress.

When Mr. Buchanan accepted the presidential nomination, he felicitated himself with the belief that the whole thing would be quieted and forgotten in about six weeks. In his inaugural, and in his Silliman letter, at their respective dates, he was just not quite in reach of the same happy consummation. And now, in his first annual message, he urges the acceptance of the Lecompton constitution (not quite satisfactory to him) on the sole ground of getting this little unimportant matter out of the way.

Meanwhile, in those four years, there has really been more angry agitation of this subject, both in and out of Congress, than ever before. And just now it is perplexing the mighty ones as no subject ever did before. Nor is it confined to politics alone. Presbyterian assemblies, Methodist conferences, Unitarian gatherings, and single churches to an indefinite extent, are wrangling, and cracking, and going to pieces on the same question. Why, Kansas is neither the whole nor a tithe of the real question.

A house divided against itself cannot stand.

I believe the government cannot endure permanently half slave and half free. I expressed this belief a year ago; and subsequent developments have but confirmed me. I do not expect the Union to be dissolved. I do not expect the house to fall; but I do expect it will cease to be divided. It will become all one thing or all the other. Either the opponents of slavery will arrest the further spread of it, and put it in course of ultimate extinction; or its advocates will push it forward till it shall become alike lawful in all the States, old as well as new. Do you doubt it? Study the Dred Scott decision, and then see how little even now remains to be done. That decision may be reduced to three points.

The first is that a negro cannot be a citizen. That point is made in order to deprive the negro, in every possible event, of the benefit of that provision of the United States Constitution which declares that "the citizens of each State shall be entitled to all privileges and immunities of citizens in the several States."

The second point is that the United States Constitution protects slavery, as property, in all the United States territories, and that neither Congress, nor the people of the Territories, nor any other power, can prohibit it at any time prior to the formation of State constitutions.

This point is made in order that the Territories may safely be filled up with slaves, before the formation of State constitutions, thereby to embarrass the free-State sentiment, and enhance the chances of slave constitutions being adopted.

The third point decided is that the voluntary bringing of Dred Scott into Illinois by his master, and holding him here a long time as a slave, did not operated his emancipation—did not make him free.

This point is made, not to be pressed immediately; but if acquiesced in for a while, then to sustain the logical conclusion that what Dred Scott's master might lawfully do with Dred in the free State of Illinois, every other master may lawfully do with any other one or one hundred slaves in Illinois, or in any other free State. Auxiliary to all this, and working hand in hand with it, the Nebraska doctrine is to educate and mold public opinion to "not care whether slavery is voted up or voted down." At least Northern public opinion must cease to care anything about it. Southern public opinion may, without offense, continue to care as much as it pleases.

Welcome or unwelcome, agreeable or disagreeable, whether this shall be an entire slave nation is the issue before us. Every incident—every little shifting of scenes or of actors—only clears away the intervening trash, compacts and consolidates the opposing hosts, and brings them more and more distinctly face to face. The conflict will be a sever one; and it will be fought through by those who do care for the result, and not by those who do not care—by those who are for, and those who are against, a legalized national slavery. The combined charge of Nebraskaism and Dred-Scottism must be repulsed and rolled back. The deceitful cloak of "self-government," wherewith "the sum of all villainies" seeks to protect and adorn itself, must be torn from its hateful carcass. That burlesque upon judicial decisions, and slander and profanation upon the honored named and sacred history of republican America, must be overruled and expunged from the books of authority.

To give the victory to the right, not bloody bullets, but peaceful ballots only are necessary.

Thanks to our good old Constitution, and organization under it, these alone are necessary. It only needs that every right thinking man shall go to the polls, and without fear or prejudice vote as he thinks.

Summary of a Speech at Edwardsville, Illinois

(May 18, 1858?)

The Republican County meeting at Edwardsville yesterday, was one of the most pleasant and cheering meetings ever attended in the County. Every one felt a solemn and responsible duty devolved upon them, and from a bold, outspoken expression of feeling and sentiment, there was no shrinking. Every part of the county was represented, and at no previous time were such confident expectations of success expressed.

The meeting appointed delegates to the State Convention in June, and also a Central Committee for the county.

The speeches of Hon. A. Lincoln, Hon. John M. Palmer, Col.[Colonel] Delahay and Hon. J. Gillespie were both able and eloquent, and listened to with an attention seldom witnessed. The present position and prospects of the Republican par[t]y were truthfully set forth, and although no two of the speakers perfectly agreed upon the details of political action, all were unanimons[*unanimous*] in declaring their opposition to the fraudulent attempts of the administration and the slave power to force institutions upon a free people against their consent.

We reached home at too late an hour last evening to say more this morning. Tomorrow we will publish the official proceedings, with such comments as may seem to us called for.

Fragment for A House Divided Speech at Springfield, Illinois

(June 16, 1858?)

The traditional date assigned by editors for this note, June 16, 1858, is the same as the date of the actual speech. It seems more likely that the note was written days or weeks earlier, as Lincoln thought about the content of the speech.

Why, Kansas is neither the whole, nor the tithe of the real question.

"A house divided against itself can not stand"

I believe this government can not endure permanently, half slave, and half free.

I expressed this belief a year ago; and subsequent developments have but confirmed me.

I do not expect the Union to be dissolved. I do not expect the house to fall; but I do expect it will cease to be divided. It will become all one thing, or all the other. Either the opponents of slavery will arrest the further spread of it, and put it in course of ultimate extinction; or its advocates will push it forward till it shall become alike lawful in all the states, old, as will as new. Do you doubt it? Study the Dred Scott decision, and then see, how little, even now, remains to be done.

That decision may be reduced to three points. The first is, that a negro can not be a citizen. That point is made in order to deprive the negro in every possible event, of the benefit of that provision of the U.S constitution which declares that: "The citizens of each State shall be entitled to all previliges and immunities of citizens in several States."

The second point is, that the U.S constitution protects slavery, as property, in all the U.S. territories, and that neither congress, nor the people of the territories, nor any other power, can prohibit it, at any time prior to the formation of State constitutions.

This point is made, in order that the territories may safely be filled up with slaves, before the formation of State constitutions, and thereby to embarrass the free states

Notes of Argument in a Law Case

(June 15, 1858?)

Lincoln's extensive yearly travels across the Eighth Judicial Circuit, with only a carpetbag for luggage, surely account for the fact that there are few notes from his law practice.

Legislation and *adjudication* must follow, and conform to, the progress of society.

The progress of society now begins to produce cases of the transfer, for debts, of the entire property of Railroad corporations; and to enable transferees to use, and enjoy, the transfered property, *legislation*, and adjudication, begins to be necessary.

Shall this class of legislation, just now beginning with us, be *general* or *special*?

Section Ten, of our constitution, requires that it should be general, if possible. (Read the section)

Special legislation always trenches upon the judicial department; and, in so far, violates Section Two, of the constitution (Read it).

Just reasoning—policy—is in favor of general legislation—else the legislature will be *loaded down* with the investigation of special cases—a work which the courts *ought* to perform, and can perform much more perfectly. How can the Legislature rightly decide the facts in dispute between P. & B. and S. C. & Co.

It is said that, under a general law, whenever a R. R. Co. gets tired of it's debts, it may transfer *fraudulently*, to get rid of them.

So they may—so may individuals; and which—the *legislature* or the *courts* is best suited to try the question of fraud in either case?

It is said, if a purchaser have acquired legal rights, let him not be robbed of them; but if he needs *legislation*, let him submit to just terms to obtain it.

Let him, say we, have general law in advance (guarded in every possible way against fraud) so that when he acquires a legal right, he will have no occasion to wait for additional legislation—and if he has practiced fraud, let the courts so decide.

Notes Regarding 1858 Campaign Strategy

(July 1, 1858)

This elaborate chart is evidence of how Lincoln paid close attention to historic voting patterns as he prepared to run against Stephen Douglas for the 1858 U.S. Senate seat in Illinois.

House of Representatives—Old districts.

Let all the districts go, as desparate, from one to five inclusive; seven and eight; ten and eleven; fifteen to twenty inclusive; twentythree; twentyeight, to thirty inclusive.

Struggle for the following.

			Buc.		Fre.		Fill.		Moore.		Miller.	
6th District	1	Randolph	1292		709		546		1399		996	
			1255		546				996			
			37	nett[*net*] against us.	1255				403	nett against us.		
			Buc.		Fre.		Fill.		Moore.		Miller	
9 District	1	Wabash	481		122		485		480		545	
		White	1062		27		845		1080		804	
			1543		149		1330		1560		1349	
			1479				149		1349			
			64	nett against us.			1479		111	nett against us.		
			Buc.		Fre.		Fill.		Moore.		Miller.	
12 District	2	StClair	1728		1996		973		1731		2936	
					973						1731	
					2969					nett for us.	1205	
					1728							
					1241	nett for us.						
			Buc.		Fre.		Fill.		Moore.		Miller.	
13 District	1	Clinton	840		161		362		834		514	
		Bond	607		153		659		623		785	
			1447		314		1021		1457		1299	
			1332				311		1299			
			115	nett against us.			1332		158	nett against us.		
14. District	2	Madison	1451.		1111		1658.		1489		2689	
							1111				1489	

							2769			nett for us.	1200	
							1451					
							1318	nett for us.				
21 District	1	Macoupin	1778		823		1010		1813		1771	
							823		1771			
							1833		42	nett against us.		
							1778					
							55	nett for us.				
22 District	1	Jersey	702		387		530		705.		907	
		Calhoun	391		70		163		463		239	
			1093		457		693		1168		1146	
							457		1146			
							1150		22	nett against us.		
							1093					
							57	nett for us.				
24. District	1	Edgar	1342		952		308		1337		1250	
			1260		308				1250			
			82	nett against us.	1260				87	nett against us.		
25 District	1	Coles	1178		783.		796		1303		1278	
		Moultrie	432		154		305		439		450	
			1610		937		1101		1742		1728	
							937		1728			

							2038		14	nett against us.		
							1610					
							428	nett for us.				
26 District	2	Sangamon	2475		1174		1612		2597		2450	
							1174		2450			
							2786		147	nett against us.		
							2475					
							311	nett for us.				
27 District	2	Morgan	1656		963		885		1664		1827	
		Scott	843		183		536		853		678	
			2499		1146		1421		2517		2505	
							1146		2505			
							2567		12	nett against us.		
							2499					
							68	nett for us.				
31. District	1	Hancock.	2011		1120		999		2011		2091	
					999						2011	
					2119					nett for us.	.80	
					2011							
					108	nett for us.						

32 District	1	McDonough	1370		~~1370.~~		864		1382			1406
							590				1382.	
							1454			nett for us.	24	
							1370					
							84	nett for us.				
33. District	2	Fulton	2724		2021		898		2806		2642	
					898				2642			
					2919				164	nett for us.		
					2724							
					195	nett for us.						
34.	1	Cass.	914		303		438		923		898	
		Menard	854		109		668		863		768	
			1768		412		1106		1786		1466	
			1518				412		1466			
			250	nett against us.			1518		320	nett against us.		
35.	1	Mason	737		267		553		740		794	
		Logan	823		655		484		840		1116	
			1560		922		1037		1580		1910	
							922				1580	
							1959			nett. for us.	330	
							1560					
							399	nett for us.				
36	1	Macon	821		500		393		866		804	
		DeWitt	679		623		378		691		973	
		Piatt	310		85		350		362		380	

		Champaign.	550		732		236		553		887	
			2160		1940		1357		2492		3044	
					1357						2492	
					3297					nett for us.	552	
					2160							
					1137	nett for us.						
38	1	McLean	1517		1937		560		1654		2299	
					560						1654	
					2497					nett for us.	645	
					1517							
					980	nett for us.						
39	1	Tazewell	1313		1028		757		1337		1418	
					757						1337	
					1785						41	nett for us.
					1313							
					472	nett for us.						
41	2	Peoria	2459		2082		391		2459		2380	
		Stark.	353		718		152		357		870	
			2812		2800		543		2816		3250	
			3343		543						2816	
		nett for us.	531		3343.					nett. for us.	434	

The 37th 40th 42nd and all upward we take without question.

Recapitulation

Democrats certain—	19 districts with	22 representatives.
Republicans certain	19 districts with	27 repredo.
Questionable	20 districts with	26 repredo.

Taking the Moore & Miller vote as a test, and 14 of the questionable go to the democrats, and 12 to the republicans, making the whole stand

Democrats		36
Republicans		39.

Taking the joint vote of Fremont and Fillmore against Buchanan, as a test, and the whole will stand

Democrats		27
Republicans		48.

Fight on the old districts—and first, as to Senators.

We already have Judd, Parks, Cook Henderson, and Vanderen.		5
No trouble to re-elect Gage, Talcott, Adams & Addams.		4
So many certain		9.

We must struggle for, first:

Gillespie's district,

	Buc.		Fre.		Fill.		Moore.		Miller.	
Bond	607		153		659		623		785	
Madison	1451		1111		1658		1489		2689	
Montgomery	992		162		686		1003		844	
	3050		1426		3003		3115		4318	
					1426				3115	

					4429				1203	nett for us
					3050					
					1379	nett for us.				

Palmer's district.

	Buc		Free.		Fill		Moore.		Miller.
Greene	1565		245		719		1620		825
Jersey	702		387		530		705		907
Macoupin	1778		823		1010		1813		1771
	4045		1455		2259		4138		3503
	3714				1455		3503		
	331	nett against us.			3714		635	nett against us.	

Watson's district

	Buc.		Fre.		Fill		Moore.		Miller	
Coles	1178		783		796		1303		1278	
Cumber-land	641		246		235		683		404	
Edgar	1342		952		308		1337		1250	
Vermilion	1111		1506		194		1112		1670	
	4272		3487		1533		4435		4602	
			1533						4435	
			5020						167	nett for us.

			4272							
			748	nett for us.						

Fuller's <u>district</u>.

	Buc		Fre.		Fill		Moore.		Miller	
Cass	914		303		438		923		698	
Logan	823		655		484		840		1116	
Mason	737		267		553		740		794	
Menard	854		109		668		863		768	
Tazewell	1313		1028		757		1337		1418	
	4641		2362		2900		4703		4794	
					2362				4703	
					5262				91	nett for us
					4641					
					621	nett for us.				

Arnold's <u>district</u>

	Buc		Free		Fill		Moore		Miller.	
Marshall	834		1008		115		839		1010	
Putnam	307		532		115		329		637	
Peoria	2459		2082		391		2459		2380	
~~Stark~~ ~~Woodford~~	747		596		189		794		731	
	4347		4218		810		4421		4758	

			810						4421	
			5028						337	nett for us
			4347							
			681	nett for us.						

Rose's district.

	Buc		Fre.		Fill.		Moore		Miller.
Hancock	2011		1120		999		2011		2091
Henderson	610		757		153		616		904
Schuyler	1369		388		570		1379		946
	3990		2265		1722		4006		3941
	3987		1722				3941.		
	3	nett against us.	3987				65	nett against us.	

^Desperate.^

Sutphen's district

	Buc		Fre.		Fill		Moore.		Miller
Calhoun	391		70		163		463		239
Pike	2163		1053		1010		2210		2012
Scott.	843		183		536		853		678
	3397		1306		1709		3526		2929
	3015				1306		2929		

	382	nett against us.			3015		597	nett against us.	

By this, it is seen, we give up the districts numbered 1. 2. 3. 4 5. 7. 8. 10. 11. 15. 16. 17. 18. 19. 20. 23. 28. 29. & 30, with 22 representatives.

We take to ourselves, without question 37, 40. 42. 43. 44. 45. 46. 47 48. 49. 50. 51. 52. 53. 54. 55. 56. 57, & 58. with 27 representatives.

Put as doubtful, and to be struggled for, 6. 9. 12. 13. 14. 21. 22, 24 25. 26. 27. 31. 32. 33. 34. 35. 36. 38. 39 & 41. with 26 representatives

Of these put as doubtful, taking the Moore & Miller vote as a a test, the 6. 9. 13. 21. 22. 24. 25. 26. 27. 33. & 34 with 14 representatives are against us, which added to the 22 certain against us makes 36. By the same test the 12. 14. 31. 32. 35. 36. 38. 39. & 41. with 12 representatives, are for us, which added to ~~our~~ the 27 certain for us makes 39.

Taking the joint vote of Fremont & Fillmore against Buchanan as a test; and the 21. 22. 25. 26. 27. & 33, with 9 representatives are brought over to our side— raising us to 48 & reducing our adversary to 27.

Recapitulation.

^***Desparate.***^ ***Carlin's district***

	Buc		Fre.		Fill.		Moore.		Miller.
Adams	3311		2226		662		3318		2897
Brown	903		169		433		901		586
	4214		2395		1095		4219		3483
	3490		1095				3483		
	724	nett against us.	3490				736	nett against us.	

Kuykendoll's district.

No use in trying.

Democrats hold over in all the remaining districts. 37		1		6		1		
40		1		9		1		
42		1		13		1		
43		2		21		1		1
44		1		22		1		1
45		3		24		1		
46		2		25		1		1
47		1		26		2		2
48		1		27		2		2
49		1		33		2		2
50		1		34		1		
51.		2						
52		1						
53		1						
54		2						
55		1						
56		2						
57		2						
58		1						

Fragment on the Struggle Against Slavery

(July 1, 1858?)

Lincoln wrote this note while he was running against Stephen Douglas across Illinois but had not yet challenged Douglas to a series of debates.

I have never professed an indifference to the honors of official station; and were I to do so now, I should only make myself ridiculous. Yet I have never failed—do not now fail—to remember that in the republican cause there is a higher aim than that of mere office. I have not allowed myself to forget that the abolition of the Slave-trade by Great Brittain, was agitated a hundred years before it was a final success; that the measure had it's open fire-eating opponents; it's stealthy "don't care" opponents; it's dollar and cent opponents; it's inferior race opponents; its negro equality opponents; and its religion and good order opponents; that all these opponents got offices, and their adversaries got none. But I have also remembered that ^though^ they blazed, like tallow-candles for a century, at last they flickered in the socket, died out, stank in the dark for a brief season, and were remembered no more, even by the smell. School-boys know that Wilbeforce, and Granville Sharpe, helped that cause forward; but who can now name a single man who labored to retard it? Remembering these things I can not but regard it as possible that the higher object of this contest may not be completely attained within the term of my ^natural ^ life. But I can not doubt either that it will come in due time. Even in this view, I am proud, in my passing speck of time, to contribute an humble mite to that glorious consummation, which my own poor eyes may ~~never~~ ^not^ last to see.

Definition of Democracy

(August 1, 1858?)

As I would not be a slave, so I would not be a master. This expresses my idea of democracy. Whatever differs from this, to the extent of the differences, is no democracy.

Fragment of Notes for Debates

(August 21, 1858)

The first of seven Lincoln-Douglas debates took place on August 21, thus this date, but the note was surely written days or weeks earlier.

In this age, and ^this^ country, public sentiment ^is every thing.^. With it, nothing can fail; against it, nothing can succeed. Whoever moulds public sentiment, goes deeper than he who enacts statutes, or pronounces judicial decisions. He makes possible the inforcement of them, else impossible.

Judge Douglas is a man of large influence. His bare opinion goes far to fix the opinion of others. Besides this thousands hang their hopes upon forcing their opinions to agree with his. It is a party necessity ^with them^ to say they agree with him; and there is danger they will repeat the saying till they really come to believe it. Others dread, and shrink from his denunciations, his sarcasms, and his ingenious misrepresentations. [. . . ?] The susceptable young hear lessons from him, such as their fathers never heard when they were young.

If, by all these means, he shall succeed in moulding public sentiment to a perfect accordance with his own; in bringing all men to indorse all court decisions, without caring to know whether they are right or wrong; in bringing all tongues to as perfect a silence as his own, as to their being any wrong in slavery; in bringing all to declare, with him, that they care not whether slavery be voted down or voted up; ^that if any people want slaves they have a right to have them;^ that negroes are not men, have no part in the declaration of Independence, that there is no moral question about slavery; that liberty and slavery are perfectly consistent—indeed, necessary accompaniaments; that for a strong man to declare himself the superior of a weak one, and thereupon enslave the weak one, is the very essence of liberty,—the most sacred right of self-government; when, I say, public sentiment shall be brought to all this, in the name of heaven, what barrier will be left against slavery being made lawful every where? Can you find one word of his, opposed to it? Can you not find many strongly favoring it? If for his life—for his eternal salvation—he was solely steering for that end, could he find any means so well accepted to reach the end?

If our Presidential election, by a mere plurality, and of doubtful significance, brought our Supreme court decision, that no power can exclude slavery from a Teritory; how much much ^more^ shall a public sentiment, in exact accordance with the sentiments of Judge Douglas bring another that no power can exclude it from a State?

And then, the negro being doomed, and damned, and forgotten, to everlasting bondage, is the white man quite certain that the tyrant demon will not turn upon him too?

Fragment of Note for Speeches

(September 15, 1858?)

Lincoln wrote this note sometime in the midst of the debates with Douglas.

At Freeport I propounded four distinct interrogations to Judge Douglas, all which he assumed to answer. I say he assumed to answer them; for he did not very distinctly answer any of them.

To the first, which is in these words, "If the people of Kansas shall, by means entirely unobjectionable in all other respects, adopt a State constitution, and ask admission into the Union under it, before they have the requisite number of inhabitants according to the English bill,—some ninety-three thousand,—will you vote to admit them?" the judge did not answer "Yes" or "No," "I would" or "I would not," nor did he answer in any other such distinct way. But he did so answer that I infer he would vote for the admission of Kansas in the supposed case stated in the interrogatory—that, other objections out of the way, he would vote to admit Kansas before she had the requisite population according to the English bill. I mention this now to elicit an assurance that I correctly understood the judge on this point.

To my second interrogatory, which is in these words, "Can the people of a United States Territory, in any lawful way, against the wish of any citizen of the United States, exclude slavery from their limits, prior to the formation of a State constitution?" the judge answers that they can, and he proceeds to show how they can exclude it. The how, as he gives it, is by withholding friendly legislation and adopting unfriendly legislation. As he thinks, the people still can, by doing nothing to help slavery and by a little unfriendly leaning against it, exclude it from their limits. This is his position. This position and the Dred Scott decision are absolutely inconsistent. The judge furiously indorses the Dred Scott decision; and that decision holds that the United States Constitution guarantees to the citizens of the United States the right to hold slaves in the Territories, and that neither Congress nor a territorial legislature can destroy or abridge that right. In the teeth of this, where can the judge find room for his unfriendly legislation against their right? The members of a territorial legislature are sworn to support the Constitution of the United States. How dare they legislate unfriendly to a right guaranteed by that Constitution? And if they should how quickly would the courts hold their work to be unconstitutional and void! But doubtless the judge's chief reliance to sustain his proposition that the people can exclude slavery, is based upon non-action—upon withholding friendly legislation. But can members of a territorial legislature, having sworn to support the United States Constitution, conscientiously withhold necessary legislative protection to a right guaranteed by that Constitution?

Again, will not the courts, without territorial legislation, find a remedy for the evasion of a right guaranteed by the United States Constitution? It is a maxim of the courts that "there is no right without a remedy." But, as a matter of fact, non-action, both legislative and judicial, will not exclude slavery from any place. It is of record that Dred Scott and his family were held in actual slavery in Kansas without any friendly legislation or judicial assistance. It is well known that other negroes were held in actual slavery at the military post in Kansas under precisely the same circumstances. This was not only done without any friendly legislation, but in direct disregard of the congressional prohibition,—the Missouri Compromise,—then supposed to be valid, thus showing that it requires positive law to be both made and executed to keep actual slavery out of any Territory where any owner chooses to take it. Slavery having actually gone into a territory to some extent, without local legislation in its favor, and against congressional prohibition, how much more will it go there now that by a judicial decision that congressional prohibition is swept away, and the constitutional guaranty of property declared to apply to slavery in the Territories.

But this is not all. Slavery was originally planted on this continent without the aid of friendly legislation. History proves this. After it was actually in existence to a sufficient extent to become, in some sort, a public interest, it began to receive legislative attention, but not before. How futile, then, is the proposition that the people of a Territory can exclude slavery by simply not legislating in its favor. Learned disputants use what they call the *arugmentum ad hominem*—a course of argument which does not intrinsically reach the issue, but merely turns the adversary against himself. There are at least two arguments of this sort which may easily be turned against Judge Douglas's proposition that the people of a Territory can lawfully exclude slavery from their limits prior to forming a State constitution. In his report of the 12th of March, 1856, on page 28, Judge Douglas says: "The sovereignty of a Territory remains in abeyance, suspended in the United States, in trust for the people, until they shall be admitted into the Union as a State." If so,—if they have no active living sovereignty,—how can they readily enact the judge's unfriendly legislation to slavery?

But in 1856, on the floor of the Senate, Judge Trumbull asked Judge Douglas the direct question, "Can the people of a Territory exclude slavery prior to forming a State constitution?"—and Judge Douglas answered, "That is a question for the Supreme Court." I think he made the same answer to the same question more than once. But now, when the Supreme Court has decided that the people of a Territory cannot so exclude slavery, Judge Douglas shifts his ground, saying the people can exclude it, and thus virtually saying it is not a question for the Supreme Court.

I am aware Judge Douglas avoids admitting in direct terms that the Supreme Court have decided against the power of the people of a Territory to exclude slavery. He also avoids saying directly that they have not so decided; but he labors to leave the impression that he thinks they have not so decided. For instance, in his Springfield speech of July 17, 1858, Judge Douglas, speaking of me, says: "He infers that it (the court) would decide that the territorial legislatures could not prohibit slavery. I will not stop to inquire whether the courts will carry the decision that far or not." The court has already carried the decision exactly that far, and I must say I think Judge Douglas very well knows it has. After stating that Congress cannot prohibit slavery in the Territories, the court adds: "And if Congress itself cannot do this, if it be beyond the powers conferred on the Federal Government, it will be admitted, we presume, that it could not authorize a territorial government to exercise them, it could confer no power on any local government, established by its authority, to violate the provisions of the Constitution."

Can any mortal man misunderstand this language? Does not Judge Douglas equivocate when he pretends not to know that the Supreme Court has decided that the people of a Territory cannot exclude slavery prior to forming a State constitution?

My third interrogatory to the judge is in these words: "If the Supreme Court of the United States shall decide that States cannot exclude slavery from their limits, are you in favor of acquiescing in, adopting, and following such decision as a rule of political action?" To this question the judge gives no answer whatever. He disposes of it by an attempt to ridicule the idea that the Supreme Court will ever make such a decision. When Judge Douglas is drawn up to a distinct point, there is significance in all he says, and in all he omits to say. In this case he will not, on the one hand, face the people and declare he will support such a decision when made, nor on the other will he trammel himself by saying he will not support it.

Now I propose to show, in the teeth of Judge Douglas's ridicule, that such a decision does logically and necessarily follow the Dred Scott decision. In that case the court holds that Congress can legislate for the Territories in some respects, and in others it cannot; that it cannot prohibit slavery in the Territories, because to do so would infringe the "right of property" guaranteed to the citizen by the fifth amendment to the Constitution, which provides that "no person shall be deprived of life, liberty, or property without due process of law." Unquestionably there is such a guaranty in the Constitution, whether or not the court rightfully apply it in this case. I propose to show, beyond the power of quibble, that that guaranty applies with all the force, if not more, to States than it does to Territories. The answers to two questions fix the whole thing: to whom is this guaranty given? and against whom does it protect those to whom it is given? The guaranty makes no distinction between persons in the States and those in the Territories; it is given to persons in the States certainly as much as, if not more than, to those in the Territories. "No person," under the shadow of the Constitution, "shall be deprived of life, liberty, or property without due process of law."

Against whom does this guaranty protect the rights of property? Not against Congress alone, but against the world—against State constitutions and laws, as well as against acts of Congress. The United States Constitution is the supreme law of the land; this guaranty of property is expressly given in that Constitution, in that supreme law; and no State constitution or law can override it. It is not a case where power over the subject is reserved to the States, because it is not expressly given to the General Government; it is a case where the guaranty is expressly given to the individual citizen, in and by the organic law of the General Government; and the duty of maintaining that guaranty is imposed upon that General Government, overriding all obstacles.

The following is the article of the Constitution containing the guaranty of property upon which the Dred Scott decision is based:

Article V. No person shall be held to answer for a capital or otherwise infamous crime, unless on a presentment or indictment by a grand jury, except in cases arising in the land or naval forces, or in the militia when in actual service, in time of war or public danger; nor shall any person be subject for the same offense to be twice put in jeopardy of life or limb; nor shall be compelled, in any criminal case, to be a witness against himself, nor be deprived of life, liberty, or property without due process of law; nor shall private property be taken for public use without just compensation.

Suppose, now a provision in a State constitution should negative all the above propositions, declaring directly or substantially that "any person may be deprived of life, liberty, or property without due process of law," a direct contradiction—collision—would be pronounced between the United States Constitution and such State constitution. And can there be any doubt but that which is declared to be the supreme law would prevail over the other to the extent of the collision? Such State constitution would be unconstitutional.

There is no escape from this conclusion but in one way, and that is to deny that the Supreme Court, in the Dred Scott case, properly applies this constitutional guaranty of property. The Constitution itself impliedly admits that a person may be deprived of property by "due process of law," and the Republicans hold that if there be a law of Congress or territorial legislature telling the slaveholder in advance that he shall not bring his slave into the Territory upon pain of forfeiture, and he still will bring him, he will be deprived of his property in such slave by "due process of law." And the same would be true in the case of taking a slave into a State against a State constitution or law prohibiting slavery.

Note for the Debate at Jonesboro, Illinois

(September 15, 1858?)

In this third debate with Stephen Douglas, Lincoln knew that many in this audience would have traveled to Jonesboro, the southernmost of the debate sites, from slaveholding states.

Brief Answer to his opening.
Put in the Democratic Resolutions.
Examine his Answers to my questions.
"If the people of Kansas shall, by means entirely unobjectionable in all other respects, adopt a State Constitution, and ask admission into the Union under it before they have the requisite number of inhabitants according to the English Bill—some ninetythree thousand—will you vote to admit them?"
"Can the people of a United States Territory, in any lawful way, against the wish of any citizen of the United States, exclude Slavery from its limits prior to the formation of a State Constitution?"

Fragment on Pro-Slavery Theology

(October 1, 1858?)

Suppose it is true, that the negro is inferior to the white, in the gifts of nature; is it not the exact reverse justice that the white should, for ~~this~~ ^that^ reason, take from the negro, any part of the little which has been given him? "Give to him that is needy" is the christian rule of charity; but "Take from him that is needy" is the rule of slavery.

Pro-Slavery Theology.

The sum of pro-slavery theology seems to be this: "Slavery is not universally right, nor yet universally wrong; it is better for some people to be slaves; and, in such cases, it is the Will of God that they be such."

Certainly there is no contending against the Will of God; but still there is some difficulty in ascertaining, ~~it~~, and applying it, to particular cases. For instance we will suppose the Rev. Dr Ross has a slave named Sambo, and the question is "Is it the Will of God that Sambo shall remain a slave, or be set free?["] The Almighty gives [~~. . .~~ ?] no audable answer to the question, and his revelation—the Bible—gives none. ^or, at most, none but such as admits of a squabble, as to it's meaning.^ No one thinks of asking Sambo's ~~opp~~ opinion on it. So, at last, it comes to this; that Dr ~~Rs~~ Ross is to decide the question. And while he considers it, he sits in the shade, with gloves on his hands, and subsists on the bread that Sambo is earning in the burning sun. If he decides that God Wills Sambo to continue a slave, he thereby retains his own comfortable position; but if he decides that God Will's Sambo to be free, he thereby has to walk out of the shade, throw off his gloves, and delve for his own bread. Will Dr Ross be actuated by that perfect impartiality, which has ever been considered most favorable to correct decisions?

But, slavery is good for some people!!! As a good thing, slavery is strikingly perculiar, in this, that it is the only good thing ~~that~~ ^which^ no man ever seeks the good of, for himself.

Nonsense! Wolves devouring lambs, not because it is good for their ^own^ greedy maws, but because it good for the lambs!!!

Fragment of a Speech on Slavery

(October 1, 1858)

But there is a larger issue than the mere question of whether the spread of negro slavery shall or shall not be prohibited by congress. That larger issue is stated by the Richmond Enquirer, a Buchanan paper in the South, in the language I now read.

It is also stated by the New-York Day-Book, a Buchanan paper in the North, in this language:

And, in relation to indigent white children, the same Northern paper says:

In support of the Nebraska bill, on it's first discussion in the Senate, Senator Petit of Indiana, declared the equality of men, as asserted in our Declaration of Independence, to be a "self evident lie"

In his numerous speeches, now being made in Illinois, Senator Douglas regularly argues against the doctrine of the equality of men; and while he does not draw the conclusion that the superiors ought to enslave the inferiors, he evidently wishes his hearers to draw that conclusion. He shirks the responsibility of pulling the house down, but he digs under it, that it may fall of it's own weight.

Now, it is impossible to not see that these newspapers, and Senators, are laboring at a common object; and in so doing, are truly representing the controling sentiment of their party.

It is equally impossible to not see that that common object is, to subvert, in the public mind, and in practical administration, our old and only standard of free-government, that "all men are created equal" and to substitute for it, some different standard. What that substitute is to be is not difficult to perceive. It is to deny the equality of men; and to assert ~~to~~ the natural, moral, and religious right of one class to enslave another. Whether we shall cling to the . . .

Fragment of Opinion Regarding Illinois Election Laws

(October 15, 1858)

This was written prior to the election on November 2, 1858.

It is made a question whether, under our laws, a person offering to vote, and being challenged, and having taken the oath prescribed by the act of 1849, is then absolutely entitled to vote, or whether his oath may be disproved, and his vote thereon lawfully rejected.

In Purple's Statutes Vol. 1. all our existing election laws are brought together commencing on page 514 and extending to page 532. They consist of acts and parts of acts passed at different times.

The true way of reading so much of the law as applies to the above question, is to first read (64) Sec. X., including the form of the oath, on page 528. Then turn back and read (19) Sec. XIX on page 518.

If it be said that the Section last mentioned is not now in force, turn forward to (75) Sec. XXI, on page 530, where it is expressly declared to be in force.

The result is that when a person has taken the oath, his oath may still be proved to be false and his vote thereupon rejected. It may be proved to be false by cross examining the proposed voter himself, or by any other person, or competent ~~evidence~~ ^testimony^, known to the general law of Evidence

On page 532 is an extract of a Supreme Court decision on the very Sec. 19—on page 518, in which, among other things, the Court say:

"If such person takes the oath prescribed by law, the Judges must receive his vote, <u>unless the oath be proved false</u>. Something of a definition of residence is also therein given.

Fragment of a Speech at Springfield, Illinois

(October 30, 1858)

Lincoln wrote this note after the conclusion of the seven debates with Stephen Douglas.

My friends, to-day closes the discussions of this canvass. The planting and the culture are over; and there remains but the preparation, and the harvest.

I stand here surrounded by friends—some <u>political</u>, <u>all</u> <u>personal</u> friends, I trust. May I be indulged, in this closing scene, to say a few words of myself. I have borne a laborious, and, in some respects to myself, a painful part in the contest. Through all, I have neither assailed, nor wrestled with any part of the constitution. The legal right of the Southern people to reclaim their fugitives I have constantly admitted. The legal right of congress to interfere with ~~slavery~~ ^their institution^ in the states, I have constantly denied. In resisting the spread of slavery to new territory, and with that, what appears to me to be a tendency to subvert the first principle of free government ^itself^ my whole effort has consisted. To the best of my judgment I have labored <u>for</u>, and not <u>against</u> the union. As I have not felt, so I have not expressed any harsh sentiment towards our Southern bretheren. I have constantly declared, as I really believed, the only difference between them and us, is the difference of circumstances.

I have meant to assail the motives of no party, or individual; and if I have, in any instance (of which I am not conscious) departed from my purpose, I regret it.

I have said that in some respects the contest has been painful to me. Myself, and those with whom I act have been constantly accused of a purpose to destroy the union; and bespattered with every immaginable odious epithet; and some who were friends, as it were but yesterday have made themselves most active in this. I have cultivated patience, and made no attempt at a retort. Ambition has been ascribed to me. God knows how sincerely I prayed from the first that this field of ambition might not be opened. I claim no insensibility to political honors; but ^today^ could the Missouri restriction be restored, and the whole slavery question replaced on the old ground of "toleration by necessity where it exists, with unyielding hostility to the spread of it, on principle, I would, in consideration, gladly agree, that Judge Douglas should [n]ever be out, and I never in, an office, so . . . as we be both or either, live.

Fragment of a Speech Against Slavery

(September 17, 1859)

. . . change conditions with either Canada or South Carolina? Equality, in society, alike beats inequality, whether the [~~. . .~~ ?] later be of the British aristocratic sort, or of the domestic slavery sort.

We know, Southern men declare that their slaves are better off than hired laborers amongst us. How little they know, whereof they speak! There is no permanent class of hired laborers amongst us. Twentyfive years ago, I was a hired laborer. The hired laborer of yesterday, labors on his own account to-day, and will hire others to labor for him to-morrow. Advancement—improvement in condition—is the order of things in a society of equals. As Labor is the common burthen of our race, so the effort of some to shift their share of the burthen on to the shoulders of others, is the great, durable, curse of the race. Originally a curse for transgression upon the whole race, when, as by slavery, it is concentrated on a part ^only,^ it becomes the double-refined curse of God upon his creatures.

Free labor has the inspiration of hope; pure slavery has no hope. The power of hope upon human exertion, and happiness, is wonderful. The slave-master himself has a conception of it; and hence the system of tasks among slaves. The slave whom you can not drive with the lash to break seventy-five pounds of hemp in a day, if you will task him to break a hundred, and promise him pay for all he does over, he will break you a hundred and fifty. ^You have substituted hope, for the rod.^ And yet perhaps it does not occur to you, that to the extent of your ~~again~~ gain in the case, you have given up the slave system, and adopted the free system of labor.

Notes for a Speech at Columbus, Ohio

(September 16, 1859)

Lincoln embarked on a speaking tour in Ohio in September 1859.

For Columbus

Introduction.

Purpose.

What it is.

Danger to.

What it is not.

What it is.

D. P. S.

What is genuine P. S.

What is D. P. S.

Copy right essay.

Minor points of

"Fatal heresy".

States in & States out.

Congress to say when.

Main points

Men of Revolution

History, as given

Waive inaccuracies

Admit as to real P. S.

Show they were vs. D. P. S.

Would any man but D.

Murder.

Dred Scott
At Freeport "exclude"
Since then "control" &c [etc.]"
If &c. "protect"
If &c. "goes into states"
I told him so.
"Negative, not affirmative"
How D. P. S. is dangerous
Re-opens Slave Trade
Deludes & debaches.
Conclusion.
Must treat as a "wrong."
Not to, yields all
U. S. not redeem all wrongs; but . . .
S. impairs & endangers general welfare.
Thou who do not think &c
We must think for selves.
S. where it is
Fugitive law.
But must prevent.
Have to employ means.
Must be true to purpose.
If not, what.
Our principle will triumph.

Fragment of Speech at Wisconsin State Agricultural Society

(September 30, 1859)

This is the date of the speech; the fragment was surely written earlier.

But the chief use of agricultural fairs is to aid in improving the great calling of agriculture, in all it's departments, and minute divisions—to make ~~make~~ mutual exchange of agricultural discovery, information, and knowledge; so that, at the end, all may know every thing, which may have been known to but one, or to but a few; at the beginning—to bring together especially ^all^ which is supposed to not be generally known, because of recent discovery, or invention.

The world is agreed that labor is the source from which human wants are mainly supplied. There is no dispute upon this point. From this point, however, men immediately diverge. Much disputation is maintained as to the best way of applying and controlling the labor element. By some it ^is^ assumed that labor is available only in connection with capital—that nobody labors, unless somebody else, owning capital, somehow, by the use of that capital, induces him to do it. Having assumed this, they proceed to consider whether it is best that capital shall hire laborers, and thus induce them to work by their own consent; or buy them, and drive them to it, without their consent. Having proceeded so far, they naturally conclude that all laborers are necessarily either hired laborers, or slaves. They further assume that whoever is once a hired laborer, is fatally fixed in that condition for life; and thence again, that his condition is as bad as, or worse than, that of a slave. This is the "mud-sill" theory. But another class of reasoners, hold the op . . .

Note Regarding Birthplace

(June 14, 1860)

I was born Feb. 12. 1809 in then Hardin county Kentucky, at a point within the more recently formed county of Larue, a mile, or a mile & a half from where Hodgenville now is. My parents being dead and my own memory not serving, I have no means of identifying the precise locality. It was on Nolin creek.

A. Lincoln
June 14. 1860.

Note Regarding Canal-Scrip Fraud

(October 16, 1860)

Lincoln's Whig ideas championed internal improvements, including the building of canals. The problem was always the question of how to fund these internal improvements. The Illinois and Michigan Canal, connecting Lake Michigan with the Illi-

nois River, had opened in 1848. In the weeks before the 1860 election, Republican leaders and newspapers were investigating the discovery of a fraud to print scrip to fund the canal. Lincoln may have written this note to send to a newspaper, but there is no record that he ever published an article.

It is now less than three weeks to the election. For months we have been trying to get an unequivocal declaration from democratic newspapers and democratic ~~members of~~ ^candidates for^ the Legislature, whether it is, or is not their purpose, at the next session, to release ^Gov^ Matteson from the payment of the money obtained by him through the canal script-fraud. But we have tried in vain. There is nothing left for us, but an appeal to the tax-payers. We say to them "it is your business." By your votes you can hold him to it, or you can release him." "Every year a part of the price of all you sell, from beef-cattle down to butter and eggs, is wrung from you in gold, to replenish a State Treasury" "To a certain extent, this is indispensible; but it is for you to say whether it shall be thus wrung from you to be litterally stolen, and applied to establishing banks, and building palaces for nabobs." "Will you attend to it?"

Several years ago, the auditor sold certain state lands, receiving therefor, as the law required, certain internal improvement script. This script was deposited with the then Governor, not being cancelled, or destroyed. Recently it has been discovered that a portion of this script has found it's way out of the Governor's custody, to New-York, where it has been funded and State bonds issued for it payable to Peter O Strang. Thus this script was once paid for with state lands, and then again with State bonds. But this is not the end. The bonds are brought to the Treasury here, and bought in with the gold of the tax-payers. One Lowe brings them and gets the gold for them. It turns out that the bonds are filled up in this Lowe's handwriting, and then transferred from Peter O Strang to Lowe, also in Lowe's handwriting. Who is Peter O. Strang, and how he got the script out of the Governor's custody, to treat it as his own, get State bonds for it, nobody seems to know. But this much is known. Matteson was Governor when the script may have gone from the executive custody, and Lowe was his agent at New-York, to fill up state bonds in rightful cases. Only a few days ago Lowe was in Springfield, and a suit was commenced against him for the money obtained from the State on the bonds. For a time the Sheriff could not find him; but at last he was found concealed in Matteson's house. And this too, after the Sheriff had been once turned away from the house, by Matteson himself.

Notes Regarding Votes for Curtin and Foster

(October 1860)

Lincoln, deeply concerned about winning Pennsylvania in the 1860 election, here closely follows the contest for governor between Republican Andrew Curtin and Democrat Henry Donnel Foster.

Curtin		Foster		600.		200
1.000		100		100.		1000
700		200		700.		1000
800.		4.000		300.		
600.		300		50.		
3500		1.000		29.200		21000
800		200		30.900		23.2.00
500		800				
1.000		400.				
1.800		100				
1.000		1.000				
1.000		300				
2.000		200				
300		400				
500.		200				
1.500.		1.000				
150.		100				
3.500		200				

500		1000				
1.000		400				
.300		1.500				
800		2.500				
600		300				
500.		2.000				
1000		1.000				
400		600				
1000		200				
2.500						

Notes Regarding Election Returns for 1860 Presidential Election in Illinois

(November 1860)

In this note, Lincoln is following Illinois results of the 1860 presidential election.

Stark Co—large gains
Stephenson Co 15 towns gain 159 over 1856—860 Maj.
Marshall Co.—Lincoln gain 47.
[Bethado?] Boone Co. complete L. 1758 D 310
10 towns in Knox Co. give L 1397 maj—gain of 560
Champaign—all but 2 towns L maj 650 may reach 700
DuPage Co 940 Rep maj—1 town not heard strong Rep.
Marshall Co 188 Rep maj—entire Rep ticket elected
McDonough gone 100 Rep

Note Regarding Commercial and Financial Uneasiness

(November 9, 1860)

After winning the presidential election, Lincoln is aware that many are voicing concerns about the financial stability of the country. As during the presidential campaign, he wants people "to examine his views already before the public."

I find Mr Lincoln is not insensible to any uneasiness in the minds of candid men, ~~or~~ ^nor^ to any commercial, or financial, depression, or disturbance, in the country ^if there be such;^ still he does not, so far as at present advised, deem it necessary, or proper for him to make, or authorize, any public declaration. He thinks candid men need only to examine his views already before the public.

Fragment of the House Divided Speech

(December 7, 1860)

People in Lincoln's day sought the autographs of famous people.
In this note, he wrote out the first lines of his famous House
Divided speech and signed his name to it.

We are now far into the fifth year since a policy was instituted, with the avowed object, and confident promise, of putting an end to slavery agitation. Under the operation of that policy, that agitation has not only not ceased, but has constantly augmented. I believe it will not cease till a crisis shall have been reached, and passed. "A house divided against itself can not stand. I believe this government can not endure permanently half slave and half free. I do not expect the Union to be dissolved, I do not expect the house to fall; but I do expect it will cease to be divided. It will become all one thing or all the other. Either the opponents of slavery will avert the further spread of it, and place it where the public mind shall rest in the belief that it is in course of ultimate extinction; or it's advocates will push it forward till it will become alike lawful in all the States old as well as new North as well as South.

The foregoing, in pencil, in my own hand, is a copy of an extract of a speech of mine delivered June 16. 1858, which I now state at the state at the request of M[r] E. B. Pease.

A. Lincoln
Dec. 7. 1860.
Speech A Lincoln
Autograph of Abraham Lincoln made for [Asher?] Taylor, 1860

Note of Recommendations for Applicants for Register and Receiver in Springfield, Illinois

(December 28, 1860)

In this note, Lincoln weighs applicants for local positions.

Brief.

Register and Receiver, Springfield, Illinois

For Register.

A.—	1.—		Arny Robinson,	Illinois.		
		By	Harry W. Gourley,		Feb. 22/	61.
	2.—	"	J. A. M[c]Neill		"	"
	3.—	"	Sundry Citizens			
	4.—	"	Applicant letter			
	5.—	"	O. J. Ketchum			
	6.—	"	Presco Wright			
B.—	1.—		William F. Elkin,	Illinois.		
		By	Stephen F. Logan & others		Dec. 28/	60
			For Receiver.			

C.—	1.—		James Garland,	Illinois		
			Applicants letter			
D.—	1.—		John H. Littlefield,	Illinois		
			Applicants letter			
E.—	1.—		Protest of J. Robt	against re-appointment of Archer G. Herndon		

Brief.
Register & Receiver, Springfield, Illinois.

Memorandum on the Appointment of Simon Cameron

(December 31, 1860)

Because Pennsylvania proved important in Lincoln's election victory, he knew he needed to appoint someone from the state to his cabinet. Simon Cameron, U.S. senator from Pennsylvania, ran as a candidate for the Republican nomination for president, but withdrew and supported Lincoln. In this note Lincoln weighs whether he should appoint Cameron and to which position in his cabinet.

J. K. Moorhead - M.C.

"I have no hesitation in saying that if Penna. receives the honor, it should be in the person of Gen[l] Cameron"

Wm Nichols.	lst Sen. Dist	}		
G. Rush Smith.	2nd " "			
Jno. H. Parker	3rd " "			Joint letter from Philad[a]
Geo. Conwell	4th " "			

"He (Cameron) is the universally acknowledged head and representative man of the "Peoples Party" of the State, and it is not only the claim of the people of the State, in view of the position he thus occupies, as well as his practical business qualifications and life devotion to the material interests of the State, that he should be at the head of the Treasury Department under your administration, but also of the great love of your friends in this city"

F. W. Thomas	}		
Theodore Kell			Joint letter from, Germans, Propritor, Editor & President of
F.T. Loes			Rep. Assocation at Philad[a]
Peter Ford			

"Feeling assured as we do that the appointment of the Hon Simon Cameron would be hailed with joy by the citizens of this State, and that it would secure to our city and our state future triumphs for the Republican party, we respectfully present his name for your kind and favorable consideration.

2.

Jos. Casey-	Harrisburg -	Ex. M.C. & Del. to Chicago.	Many letters from him
J. S. Haldeman -	Fairview.	Form. Pa. Pres. of State Ag Soc. & Del. to Chicago -	Long letter
J. P. Sanderson -	Philad[a]		
Wm F. Small-	Philada -		Long letter.
John Z. Goodrich -	Stockbridge, Mass.		Long letter
Charles T. Jones -	Philad[a]		Letter.
Russell Essett -	Pittsburgh		Letter.
Francis Blackburne,	Philad[a]	^Del. to Chicago.^	Long letter

Levi Kline -	Lebanon, Pa.	Del. to C. & Com ^man^	Long letter -
Hazlehurst.	Philad[a]		Letter.
Isaac G. Gordon -	Brookville, Pa. -	^Rep. in Leg.^	Letter
David Wilmot.	Towanda, Pa.		Letter.
A. H. Reeder	Easton, Pa.		Letters & visit.
Leonard Ulmer.	Williams~~burgh~~^port^. Pa.		Letter
J. W. Killinger,	Lebanon, Pa.	MC -	Letter

3

John M. Butler,		M.C. almost,	Phila[ia]	Letter.	
Henry D. Moore.		State Treasurer, that is to be.	Phil -	Letter.	
J. S. Rightmyer	}				
Jesse Hillman			William-sport, [Pa.]		Joint letter -
L. Ulmer					
S. H. Walters					
Jno A Hiestand.	Editor	Lancaster, Pa.	Letter.		
Geo. A. Coffey -		Phil -	Letter		
A. R. McIlvaine.	Ex. M.C.	Brandywine Manor Pa.	Letter		
Geo. R. Hendrickson -		Mountjoy - Lancaster Co. Pa.	Letter -		

John M. Butler	}				
Wm Elliott					
Joseph S. Morey		Joint letter from Phil.			
E. Ward					
John W. Wallace.		New Castle, Pal	Letter		
G. S. Vliet	}				
Robert M. Palmer					
Jacob. G. Frick		Dels. to Chicago.			
S. A. Bergstresser		Letter from Pottsville Pa			
Wm C. Lawson					

4

G. Rush Smith -		Phil -	Letter.
John C. Myers,	Editor -	Reading Pa.	Letter
John Strohm,	Ex. M.C.	Lancaster Co Pa.	Letter
B. Rush Petrikin.		Pa.	Letter
Wm B. Thomas -	Pres. of Rep. Cent Club	Phil -	Letter
Wm H. Kerr.	Sheriff of Phil. City & Co.		Letter -
Daniel G. Thomas.	Rep. in Leg	Phil	Letter -
R. P. King -	Elector -	Phil -	Letter.
James M. Moore -		Phil -	Letter -

David Taggart,	Elector -	Northumberland, Pa.	Letters
Joseph Buffington,		Kittaning Pa	Letter
John F. Long		Lancaster Pa.	Letter.
Hon. F. P. Stanton,			Letter.
James Pollock.	Ex. MC. & Ex. Gov.	Milton, Pa.	Letter.
David Mumma, Jr	Head elector,	Harrisburg. Pa	Letter.

Notes on the Constitution and the Union

(January 1861)

All this is not the result of accident. It has a philosphical cause. Without the Constitution and the Union, we could not have attained the result; but even these, are not the primary cause of our great prosperity.

There is something back of these, entwining itself more closely about the human heart. That something, is the principle of "Liberty to all"—the principle that clears the path for all—gives hope to all—and, by consequence, enterprize, and industry to all.

The expression of that principle, in our Declaration of Independence, was most happy, and fortunate. Without this, as well as with it, we could have declared our independence of Great Brittain; but without it, we could not, I think, have secured our free government, and consequent prosperity. No ^oppressed,^ people will fight, and endure, as our fathers did, without the promise of something better, than a mere change of masters.

The assertion of that principle, at that time, was the word, "fitly spoken" which has proved an "apple of gold" to us. The Union, and the Constitution, are the picture of silver, subsequently framed around it.

The picture was made, not to conceal, or destroy the apple; but to adorn, and preserve it. The picture was made for the apple—not the apple for the picture.

So let us act, that neither picture, or apple shall ever be blurred, ^or bruised^ or broken.

That we may so act, we must study, and understand the points of danger.

. . . ^ . . . ^ . . . ^the^ . . . ^of "Liberty to all"^ . . .

Fragment of Speech Intended for Kentuckians

(February 12, 1861?)

1

I am grateful for the oppertunity your invitation affords me to appear before an audience of my native state. During the present winter it has been greatly pressed upon me by many patriotic citizens, Kentuckians among others, that I could ^in my position^ by a word, restore peace to the country— But what word? I have many words already before the public; and my position was given me on the faith of those words— Is the desired word to be confirmatory of these; or must it be contradictory to them?

If the former, it is useless repetion; if the latter, it is dishonorable and treacherous—

Again, it is urged as if the word must be spoken before the fourth of March— Why? Is the speaking the word a "sine qua non" to the inaugeration? Is there a Bell-man, a Breckinridge-man, or a douglas man, who would tolerate his own candidate to make such terms, had he been elected? Who amongst you would not die by the proposition, that your candidate, being elected, should be inaugerated, solely on the conditions of the constitution, and laws, or not at all—

What Kentuckian, worthy of his birth place, would not ^do^ ~~say~~ this? Gentlemen, I too, am a Kentuckian—

Not is this a matter of mere personal honor. ^No man can be elected President without some opponents, as well as supporters; and if when elected, he can not be installed, till he first appeases his enemies, ~~by betraying his~~^~~If, when a Chief Magistrate is Constitutionally elected he can no be installed, till he betrays those who elected him,~~ by breaking his pledges, and ^and betraying his friends^ ~~surrendering to his opponents~~, this government, and all popular government, is already at an end— Demands for such surrender, once recognized, and yielded to, are without limit, as to nature, extent, or repetition— They break ~~they break~~ the only bond of faith between public, and public servant; and they distinctly set the minority over the majority. Such demands acquiesed in, would not merely be the ruin of a man, or a party; but ^as a precedent^ they would ~~be the~~ ruin ~~of~~ the government itself—

election, and not in the treachery of the person elected -

During the winter just closed, I have been greatly urged, by many patriotic men, to lend the influence of my position to some compromise, by which I was, to some extent, to shift the ground upon which I had been elected. This I steadily refused. I so refused, not from any party wantonness, nor from any indifference to the troubles of the country. I thought such refusal was demanded by the view that if, when a Chief Magistrate is constitutionally elected, he cannot be inaugurated till he betrays those who elected him, by breaking his pledges, and surrendering to those who tried and failed to defeat him at the polls, this government and all popular government is already at an end. Demands for such surrender, once recognized, are without limit, as to nature, extent and repetition. They break the only bond of faith between public and public servant; and they distinctly set the minority over the majority.

I presume there is not a man in America, (and there ought not to be one) who opposed my election, who would, for a moment, tolerate his own candidate in such surrender, had he been successful in the election. In such case they would all see, that such surrender would not be merely the ruin of a man, or a party, but, as a precedent, would be the ruin of the government itself.

I do not deny the possibility that the people may err in an election; but if they do,

Notes Regarding Appointment of Freeman H. Morse, (March 1861?)

Starting in March 1861, many of the notes Lincoln wrote as president concern appointments to governmental and military positions.

Mr. Senator Fessenden is exceedingly anxious that that Hon: Freeman H. Morse shall be consul to London- & he says when he first mentioned Mr Morris' name for that place, I said it was the first application-

U. S. Consulate
London.
F. H. Morse
of Maine
Memorandum.

Notes Regarding the Nomination of Isaac N. Weston as Deputy Postmaster at Westfield, Massachusetts

(March 6, 1861–April 15, 1865?)

No 180
Nomination of Isaac N. Weston. D.PM. Wesfield. Mass
(withdrawn by the President)

Notes Regarding Recommendations for Appointments in Connecticut (August 1862?)

1st District

Collector Alphonso C Crosby recommended by both the senator & the Representatives
Assessor Edward Goodman recommended by the same

2d District

Collector John Woodruff recommended by the same
Assessor John B. Wright recommended by Dixon & Representative Loomis the Republican State Com. & nearly the entire State Senate

3. District

Collector x Henry Hammond x recommended by Senators Dixon & Foster, J. F. Babcock N D Sperry & Rep. State Com.
Assessor Jesse S. Ely no opposition

4th Dist

Collector. David H. ^F.^ Hollister x recommended by ^Foster^ Dixon Loomis Rep State Com. Babcock Sperry & many others
Assessor Henry S. Griswold by Dixon & Loomis ^Babcock, Sperry^

Executive Mansion,

Washington, , 186.

1st Dt

Assessor Edward Goodman
Collector A. C. Crosby

2nd Dt

Assessor John B. Wright
Collector John Woodruff

3d D

Assessor Jesse C. Ely
Collector Henry Hammond

4th D

Assessor Henry S. Griswold
Collector David S. Hollister
The above named are recommended by Senators Dixon and Foster & Representative Loomis-
Senator Dixon's recommendations

Note Regarding California Appointments

(April 1, 1861)

About appointments in California.
Consult Leland Stanford & Eugene L. Sullivan.
California.

Notes Regarding Baltimore, Maryland Appointments

(April 1, 1861?)

Baltimore—Maryland.

Collector— Dep.	Henry W. Hoffman.
Surveyor of P—	William L. Marshall
Naval Officer— Dep.	Francis S. Cockran.
Appraiser Genl. .	Frederick Schley.
1. Appraiser—	Charles P. Montague
2. Do.—	Joseph F. Meredith
Navy Agent—	Wm Pinckney Ewing
Post-Master—	William H. Purnell.
Attorney—	
Marshal—	Washington Bonifant.

Note Regarding New York Appointments

(April 1, 1861)

Hon Conkling's card for N. Y. City

Thinks Mr. Denison preferable to eithe Mr Dorsheimer, Draper, or Welch, partly because they all at present hold offices.

Collector

Hiram Barney
Surveyor
Henry B. Stanton
Naval Officer
Abraham Wakeman
District Attorney

Wm Curtis Noyes
Marshall
Jedediah W. Harbt
Navy Agent
D. D. T. Marshall
Superintendent of the Assay Office
Alfred Wells
Assitant Treasurer
George Opdyke
New York City
M^{r}. Conkling's Card.

Note Regarding California Appointments

(April 1, 1861)

California.

Sacramento—				
	Collector—	L. H. Foote	$	3430—00
Monterey.			.	~~3055—50~~
	Collector—	John F. Porter	"	3055—50
^Santa Barbara, Collector Samuel B. Brinkerhoff^Sonoma.				
	Collector	Seth M. Swain.	"	3165.71
San Joaquin				
	Collector	S. W. Sperry.	"	3174.55
San Diego				
	Collector	Joshua Sloan.	"	2250—00

San Pedro				
	Surveyor—	Oscar Macy.	"	3000—00
San Francisco				
	Collector—	Ira P. Rankin	"	7900—00
	Dep. & Aud—		"	3125.00
	Dep—		"	3125.00
	Dep—		"	3125.00
	Appraiser Genl	Samuel J. Bridge.	"	3125.00
	Appraiser.	Benj. W. Mudge.	"	3125.00
	do—	John P. Zane.	"	3125.00
	Naval officer		"	6250—00
	Surveyor		"	5625.00
Mint				
	Superinten-dent—	Robert J. Stevens	"	4500—00
	Treasurer—	David W. Cheese-man.	"	4500—00
	Melter	Walter S. Denio—	"	3000—00
	Assayer.	Conrad Wiegand	"	3000—00
	Corner	William Schmolz	"	3000.00
Navy				
	Navy Agent—			

2

		Judicial Department—			
	Northern District.				
		Attorney.	William H. Sharp		
		Marshal.	William Rabe.		
	Southern District				
		Attorney.	Dimmick		
		Marshal.	Henry D. Barrows		
83	Surveyor General—			$	4500—00
85-86	San Francisco L. O				
		Register.	George B. Tingley	"	3000—00
		Receiver.	Royal H. Waller.	"	3000—00
	Los Angelos L—O				
		Register	Antonio Maria Pico.	"	3000—00
		Receiver.	Lewis Sperry.	"	3000—00
	Marysville L. O.				
		Regester.	A. J. Snyder,	"	3000—00
		Receiver.	J. Compton.	"	3000—00
	Humboldt L. O				
		Register.	John M. Eddy.	"	3000—00
		Receiver.	William H. Pratt.	"	3000—00
	Stockton L. O				

		Register.	George D. Webster	"	3000—00
		Receiver.	G. C. Havens.	"	3000—00
	Visalia L. O				
		Register.	Henry W. Briggs.	"	3000—00
		Receiver.	George M. Gerrish.	"	3000—00
95	California Indian Dept.				
	^North.^	Superintendency (S. F).	Geo. M. Hanson.	"	4000.00
	^South—^	Do	Miner Frink, Jr		
	Klamath Sub-Agency—			"	1500—00
	Cal— Agency ([?])			"	3000—00
	Sub— do— (Mendocino)			"	1500—00
	Sub. do —			"	1500—00

3

California	Indian Dep[t] Con[t]		
	Tejon Agency	$	3000—00
	Klamath Agency	"	3000—00

Note Regarding New Mexico Appointments

(April 1, 1861)

New-Mexico

	Governor			
	Secretary			
	C. J			
	Ass— J.			
	Ass J—			
	Attorney			
	Marshal—			
	Land Dep[t]			
84.		Surveyor-Genl—	$	3000—00
85.6	Santa Fe L. O.			
		Register	"	3000—00
		Receiver	"	3000—00
94	Indian Dept			
		Superintendent— Santa. Fe	"	2000—00
		Utah Agency	"	1550—00
		Apache Agency	"	1550—00
		Abiqun Agency	"	1550—00
		Santa Fe Agency	"	1550—00
		Navajoe Agency	"	1550—00
		Do	"	1550.00

249035:

Utah

	Governor			
	Secretary			
	C.J.			
	Ass—J			
	Ass—J.			
	Attorney			
	Marshal			
84	Land Dept			
		Surveyor General	$	3000—00
		~~Olympia~~ ^Salt Lake^ L. O		
		Register	"	3000.00
		Receiver	"	3000.00
94	Indian Dep[t]			
		Superintendent (S. L. C)	"	2500—00
		Agent	"	1550—00
		Agent	"	1000—00
		Agent	"	1000—00

Note Regarding Washington and Oregon Appointments (April 1, 1861)

Washington & Oregon

		Governor—	William H. Wallace	
		Secretary	Leander J. S. Turney	

		C J.	C. C. Hewitt	
		Ass— J.	James E. Wyche	
		Ass— J.		
		Attorney	John J. M[c]Gilvra	
		Marshal		
84	Land Dep[t]			
		Surveyor Gener[al]		$3000—00
		Olympia L— O		
		Register.	Arthur A. Denny,	2500—00
		Receiver.	Joseph Cushman,	2500.00
94	Indian Dep[t]			
		Superintendent		2500—00
		Puget Sound Agency		1500—00
		Squakson Agency		1000—00
		Siltez Agency		1500—00
		Umpqua Agency		1000—00
		Grand Ronde Agency		1500—00
		E. Oregon Agency		1500—00
		Cayuse Agency		1000—00
		Col. River Agency		1500—00
		Local do.		1000—00
		Flathead Agency		1500—00
		Astoria Agency		1000—00

		Collector at Fort-Townsend,	Victor Smith	
		Collector at Nesqualley,	Henry C. Wilson—	

Notes Regarding Nebraska Appointments

(April 1, 1861)

Nebraska—

		Governor	Nebraska		
		Secretary			
		C. J.			
		Ass. J			
		Ass. J			
		Attorney			
		Marshal			
84	Land Dep^{t} (Kansas & Nebraska				
		Surveyor General			$2000—00
		Lecompton L. O			
			Register		
			Receiver		
		Kickapoo L. O			
			Register		
			Receiver		
		Fort Scott L. O			
			Register		
			Receiver		
		Ogden L— O			
			Register		

			Receiver		
		Omaha L. O			
			Register		
			Receiver		
		Brownville L. O			
			Register		
			Receiver		
		Nebraska City L. O			
			Register		
			Receiver		

Nebraska & Kansas

	Land Dept cont			
		Dakota City L. O		
			Register	
			Receiver	
91	Indian Dept			
		Superintendent (St L)		2000—00
		Blackfeet Agency		1500—00
		Upper Mo. Agency		1500—00
		Yancton Sioux Agency		1500—00
		Upper Platte Agency		1500—00
		Omaha Agency		1500—00
		Ottoe & Mo. A		1500—00
		Pawnee A		1500—00
		Kickapoo A		1500—00
		Delaware A		1500—00

		Shaw— & Wy— A		1500—00
		Pottawatamie A		1500—00
		Great Nemaha A.		1500—00
		Sac & Fox A		1500—00
		Kansas A		1500—00
		Osage R. A.		1500—00

Notes Regarding Appointment of James S. C. Boal

(April 1, 1861?)

Dr. Robert Boal of Lacon, Ills, wishes his son, James St. C. Boal, to be Assistant Sec. of Leg. to Paris - & I want him to be obliged.

Note Regarding Appointment of Simeon Smith

(April 2, 1861)

This 2nd day of April 1861 Mr Senator Preston King appears in person, and presses that Simeon Smith, of Minnesota be appointed Commissioner of Pensions. Mr King makes a personal appeal in the case.

Note Regarding Theodore C. Dorsey as Potential Cadet at West Point

(July 9, 1861)

To-day, July 9, 1861— Miss. Isabella Dorsey, of Baltimore, presents the name of her brother— Theodore C. Dorsey— to be a Cadet at West-Point— He will be sixteen years of age the 19th of November this year— When he shall be old enough, I should like to oblige his sister—

A. Lincoln

Note Regarding Commissions of James Shields and Michael Corcoran

(July 1861)

Private

Thomas Francis Meagher, ~~and~~ as well as Senator Latham & Gen. Denver, desire the appointment of Shields.

Bishop Hughes thinks Corcoran should be appointed; and my own judgment concurs in both cases.

887. P. AGO. 1861.

Note Regarding James Churchman

(July 1861)

James Churchman, wishes to be Consul to Vapairaso, Chili; and I have a strong desire to oblige him.

James Churchman, for Consul to Valparaiso—

1861

Notes Regarding Furnishing Officers to Volunteers

(August 28, 1861)

17

Dated St Louis Aug 25 1861.

Rec'd, Washington, 1861, o'clock, min. M.
To Hon M Blair

Jefferson C Davis a Lieut in the US army was sent here by the Governor of Indiana in command of Reg[t] He is informed by adjutant Thomas that he cannot retain his command I will ask if he and a few army officers I have found may be allowed to retain command of their Regts

J C Fremont
[?] Commdg

55.415 ad
343. P. C 1861
President U. S
A. Lincoln

Approves the proposition of the Postmaster Genl and Secretary of War,- that officers of the grade of Captain and below be furnished to Volunteers, and those now acting with Vols, be permitted to remain with them to the extent of one hundred; and that their places be partially supplied by appointment of Cadets to [?]
(2 Communications within)
Rec[d] (AGO) Aug. 28. 1861,

(October 1, 1861)

This note, about Lincoln's desire to move on the Cumberland Gap, near the junction of Kentucky, Tennessee, and Virginia, indicates his increasing interest in Union military strategy.

On, or about the 5th of October, (the exact day to be determined hereafter) I wish a movement made to seize and hold a point on the Railroad connecting Virginia and Tennessee, near the Mountain pass called Cumberland Gap.

That point is now guarded against us by Zolicoffer, with 6000 or 8000, rebels at Barboursville, Kentucky, say twentyfive miles from the Gap towards Lexington.

We have a force of 5000 or 6000, under General Thomas, at Camp Dick Robinson, about twentyfive miles from Lexington, and seventy five from Zollicoffer's camp on the road between the two, which is not a Railroad, anywhere between Lexington and the point to be seized—and along the whole length of which the Union sentiment ^among the people^ largely predominates.

We have military possession of the Railroads from Cincinnati to Lexington, and from Louisville to Lexington. ^and some Home Guards under General Crittenden are on the latter line.^

We have possession of the Railroad from Louisville to Nashville, Tenn, so far as Muldrough's Hill, about forty miles, and the rebels have possession of that road all South of there.

At the Hill we have a force of 8000 under Gen. Sherman; and about an equal force of rebels is a very short distance South, under under Gen. Buckner.

We have a large force at Paducah, and a smaller at Fort-Holt, both on the Kentucky side, with some at Bird's Point, Cairo, Mound City, Evansville, & New-Albany, all on the other side; and all which, with the Gun-Boats on the River, are, perhaps, sufficient to guard the Ohio from Louisville to it's mouth.

About supplies of troops, my general idea is that all from Wisconsin, Minnesota, Iowa, Illinois, Missouri, and Kansas, not now elsewhere, be left to Fremont.

All from Indiana and Michigan, not now elsewhere, be sent to Anderson at Louisville.

All from Ohio, needed in Western Virginia be sent there; and any remainder, be sent to Mitchell at Cincinnati, for Anderson.

All East of the Mountains be appropriated to McClellan, and to the coast.

As to movements, my idea is that the one for the coast, and that on Cumberland Gap be simultaneous; and that, in the mean time, preparation, vigilant watching, and the defensive only be acted upon—(this however, not to apply to Fremonts operations in Northern and middle Missouri)—that before these movements, Thomas and Sherman shall respectively watch, but not attack Zollicoffer, and Buckner.

That when the coast and Gap movements shall be ready, Sherman is merely to stand fast; while all at Cincincinnati, and all at Louisville with all on the lines, concentrate rapidly at Lexington, and thence to Thomas' camp joining him, and the whole thence upon the Gap.

It is for the Military men to decide whether they can find a pass through the Mountains at or near the Gap, which can not be defended by the enemy, with a greatly inferior force, and what is to be done in regard to this.

The Coast and Gap movements made, Generals McClellan and Fremont, in their respective Departments, will avail themselves of any advantages the diversions may present.

Washington DC
1861
President Lincoln's views of a plan of campaign.

Note Regarding a Letter about Mr. Penfield

(December 31, 1861)

The foregoing is ^the copy of^ a letter I wrote on the day of it's date; and I now wish the officers of the government to settle with and pay Mr Penfield, according to the terms of the letter, and his performance of the conditions stated.

A Lincoln
Dec. 31. 1861

Note Regarding William McKay

(1861–1865)

William McKay, wishes to be a Judge in Colorado— He was recommended for Judge of Kansas, & his papers are in the Atty Gen^{ls} Dep^{t}

Notes Regarding Senators' Preferences for Minister to Rome

(1861-1862?)

	Senators- J. R. Doolittle		
	T. O. Howe		
Reps	S. Hanchett		Wisconsin
A S. Sloan	A S. Sloan		
"	J. F. Potter		
"			
Sen	Rufus King & Staff		
Sena	& other citizens		
Senators	McDougal	}	California
	& Latham		

Senators	Wade		
	Trumbull		
	Wilson of Mass		
	& others		

Letters from Alex[r] Mitchell & others-all uniting in the same request.
Judge Abram D. Smith, of Wisconsin, Backers' for Minister of Rome-

A L.

Notes Regarding Appointment of William B. Richmond

(1861)

William B. Richmond
Tennessee
Consul to Paris. address him to the care of
B G Wainwright & Co
13 rue du [Fonbonsy?]
Montmartre
Paris.
Mr. Richmond resides in Tenn. and is recommended by Messrs Bell, Johnson, Maynard & Nelson. also by Senator Simmons & other Rhode Islanders.
1861
MParis Consul
W[m]B Richmond
Tennessee
Richmond

Notes Regarding the Appointment of William W. Richmond

(1861)

William B Richmond
Memphis
Tennessee
App. Consul at Paris or Havre. Recommended by Senator Simmons & also Messrs Bell & Johnson.

Note Regarding Vacancy as Appraiser

(1861)

Arad B. Newton, if there shall be a vacancy, in Appraisership, wishes the place.

Note Regarding Appointment of William B. Richmond

(1861)

Wm M. Richmond, of New-Orleans, wishes to be Consul to Paris— He has lived abroad many years, & understands the languages— M^{r} [Bonliquy?] is his acquaintance—

Note on Appointment of Mark H. Dunnell

(1861)

The Vice President, and the United congressional delegation of Maine urge the appointment of Mark H. Dunnell as Consul General for Canada, always bearing in mind that M^{r}Fessenden, first of all, wishes M^{r}Morse to be consul to London

Note Regarding Recruitment of Free Negroes

(July 22, 1862)

To recruiting free negroes, no objection.
To recruiting slaves of disloyal owners, no objection.
To recruiting slaves of loyal owners, with their consent, no objection.
To recruiting slaves of loyal owners without conent, objection, unless the necessity is urgent.
To conducting offensively, while recruiting, and to carrying away slaves not suitable for recruits, objection.

Note Regarding Appointment of Jediah F. Alexander

(July 31, 1862)

Executive Mansion,
Washington, July, 31, 1862

To-day, Jediah F. Alexander of Bond Co. Ills. tells me he has papers on file for Collector in his District. I [aim?] to give him fair consideration.

A.L.
July 31. 1862.

Note Regarding Appointment of John Parkinson

(August 8, 1862)

To-day. Aug. 8. 1862. J. R. Bell, Calls to say a good word for John Parkinson, to be assessor for Hon. Mr Brown's District, in Western Virginia. I slightly know Mr Parkinson—

Note Regarding Appointment of Gabriel R. Paul

(August 23, 1862)

Executive Mansion,
Washington, Aug. 23, 1862.

To-day, Mrs Major Paul of the Regular Army calls and urges the appointment of her husband to a Brig. Genl. She is a saucy woman and I am afraid she will keep tormenting till I may have to do it.

Note Regarding Appointment of J. D. Webster

(August 29, 1862)

I personally know Col Webster, to be a competent & most worthy gentleman; and should be glad for him to make the examination & report indicated within, if he can be spared from the field, and if the Sec. of War approves.

A Lincoln
Aug. 29, 1862.

Fragment on Divine Will

(September 2, 1862?)

The will of God prevails. In great contests each party claims to act in accordence with the will of God. Both may be, and one must be wrong. God can not be for, and against the same thing at the same time. In the present civil war it is quite possible that God's purpose is something different from the purpose of either party, and yet the human instrumentalities, working just as they do, are of the best adaptation to effect ~~His~~I ^His^ purpose. I am almost ready to say this is probably true—that God wills this contest, and wills that it shall not end yet. By his mere quiet power, on the minds of the now contestants, He could have either saved or destroyed the Union without a human contest. Yet the contest began. And having begun He could give the final victory to either side any day. Yet the contest proceeds.

Note Regarding Father Joseph O'Hagan

(September 22, 1862)

Executive Mansion,
Washington, Sep. 22, 1862.
To-day, Sister Mary Carroll calls and asks that Father Joseph O'Hagan, now chaplain to 4th Regt of Excelsior Brigade, be made a hospital chaplain. She says that nearly all the Catholics of his regt are now in hospital, and that the Catholic chaplains already appointed cannot possibly attend all the Catholic soldiers in hospital.

Note Regarding William H. Channing as Unitarian Chaplain

(October 16, 1862)

Executive Mansion,
Washington, Oct 16, 1862.

To-day, Mr Goodloe calls with Rev. Mr Channing of the Unitarian church here, (now used as a hospital) to be chaplain there, or elsewhere here. I believe him entirely worthy, but I have not now an appointment to make.

A. Lincoln

Note Regarding the Army of the Potomac

(October 20, 1862)

This note is an example of Lincoln's close attention to military leadership and the strength of the Union army.

War Department
Washington City, D.C.
1862

A report of the A. P. Oct. 20. 1862. shows.

Grand total	231.997—	of these
Fit for duty	144.662	
Ab. with leave.	66.808.	Remainder of Grand total, pres. sick.
		pres in arrest
		& Ab without leave
Defence of W.	90.613.	
	60.426	
	17.673	

Gen—Burnside

Sumner.
Couch
Wilcox
Franklin.
Smith
Reynolds—
Hooker.
Butterfield
Stoneman

Note Regarding Strength of Confederate Army

(October 20, 1862)

Lincoln also kept track of the strength of the Confederate army.

Va	21.580
Ala.	8.205
La	6.263
NC.	14.189
Ga.	16—725

Tenn.	2.400
S. C.	12.850
Ark	500
Florida	1650
Texas	1250
Miss	3957
	89.563

Note Regarding Capture of Confederate Naval Vessel

(November 6, 1862)

Executive Mansion,
Washington, 1862.

First idea

Purchase one of those now being constructed for our enemies— or some other of not let less speed or power, deliverable at a given point fully equipped. Then take possession.

Second idea

Charter for twelve months with the previlege of purchasing and taking possession at any point for a certain sum within that period. Then advertise for some Port in the vicinity of the intended cruising ground.

Charter also another on the same conditions, dispatch her with fuel, stores and the armament to an unfrequented harbor, under the direction of a reliable man, there to await orders. After getting information as we can with the first ~~vessel~~ ^named^ steamer join the tender and arm the cruiser, Pursue the enemy, exhibit your authority only when absolute necessity requires it

I was asked to inquire what the Gov^{t} would pay, on delivery, for the Capture of a "Secesh vessel" I could not answer & so refer the question to the Sec. of the Navy.

A. Lincoln
Nov. 6. 1862.

Notes Regarding Recent Appointments and Vacancies

(December 1, 1862)

Minister Resident.

Richard Milford Blatchford, of New York, Minister Resident, Rome.
Thomas H. Clay, of Kentucky, Minister Resident to the Republic of Nicaragua.

Consuls.

B.O. Duncan, of So: Carolina, Consul at Ravenna.
Noah L. Wilson, of Indiana, Consul at La Union.
Rollin C. M. Hoyt, of Massachusetts, Consul at Minatillan.
George W. Holley, of New York, Consul at Naples.
Jay T. Howard, of Pen[a], Consul at San Juan del Sur.
John J. Hyde, of Connecticut, Consul at San Juan, P.R.
William Walton Murphy, ^of Michg,^ Consul for the Duchy of Brunswick.
Deodat Brastow, of Maine, Consul at Rio Grande, Brazil
Frederic Wippermann, of Dist: of Col. Consul at Galatza
F. Cosby, of Kentucky, Consul at Geneva.
James Monroe, of Ohio, Consul at Rio de Janeiro.
Richard A. Edes, of Dist: of Col. Consul at Maracaibo.
Arthur Folsom, of Illinois, Consul at Cape Haytien
Ingersoll Lockwood, of New York, Consul at Hanover
Edwin J. Eastman, a Citizen of the U.S. Consul of Cork.
William E. Phelps, of Illinois, Consul at St: Petersburg.
William W. Thomas, Jr., of Maine, Consul at Gottenburg.
J. H. Mansfield, of Wisconsin, Consul at Tabasco.
James De Long, of Ohio, Consul at Aux Cayes.

Consuls- con-

Marquis D. L. Lane, of Maine, Consul at Vera Cruz.
William F. Brown, of N. Jersey, Consul at Cape Town.

Alexander Schwartz, Consul at Riga.
John Xantus, of the Dist. of Col., Consul at Manzanillo.
Señor Don Cirilo Molina, Consul at Carthagena, Spain.
L. W. Hall, of Penna Consul at Dundee.
Lockwood L. Doty, of New York, Consul at Nassau, N.P.
Vincent St. Vrain, of Texas, Consul at Paso el Norte.
Charles Gilbert Wheeler, of Missouri, Consul at Nuremburg.
Hugh J. Hastings, of N. York, Consul at Ravenna.
Judge & Arbitrators
Under the Treaty with Her Britannic Majesty, of the 7th April, last, for the suppression of the African Slave Trade.
Alonzo S. Upham, of New York, Judge at Cape Town.
Cephas Brainerd, ^of N. York,^ Arbitrator at New York City.
William L. Avery of N. Hampshire, Arbitrator at Cape Town
Timothy R. Hibbard, of New York, Arbitrator at Sierra Leone.
Secretaries of Territories.
W. F. M. Arny, of Kansas, Secretary of the Territory of N. Mexico
Elwood Evans, of Washington Territory, Secretary of said Territory.
Zenas C. Robbins, of Dist. of Columbia, Register of Wills, in & for the County of Washington, D.C.

List of offices now vacant.

Judgeship under the Treaty with Her Britannic Majesty, of the 7th April, last, for the suppression of the African Slave Trade at Sierra Leone.
Secretary of Legation at Lima.

Consulate at	Martinique.
" "	Guadaloupe.
" "	Algiers.
" "	Mozambique.
" "	Liege.

" "	Vienna.
" "	Brunai.
" "	Trebizond.
" "	Copenhagen.
" "	Port au Prince.
" "	Monterey.
" "	Campeachy.
" "	San Blas.
" "	Laguna.
" "	Chihuahua.
" "	Guatmala
" "	Omoa & Truxillo.
" "	Santa Martha
" "	Bogata.

Vacant Consulates-continued-

Consulate at	Puerto Cabello.
" "	Guayaquil.
" "	Asuncion.

Secy. State.

Transmitting list of Ministers, Consuls &c to be sent to the Senate for confirmation.

Dec 1. 1862

Note on Extract of John Bright Speech in Birmingham, England

(December 1862)

Lincoln deeply admired John Bright, British liberal statesman. When some in England advocated recognizing the Confederacy, Bright remained a strong supporter of Lincoln and the Union. In this note, Lincoln appreciates a quotation from one of Bright's speeches, delivered at Birmingham, England, December 18, 1862.

"I can not believe that civilization, in its journey with the sun, will sink into endless night, to gratify the ambition of the leaders of this revolt, who seek to wade through slavery to a throne, and shut the gate of mercy on mankind."

Note Regarding Promotions

(December 24, 1862)

Executive Mansion,
Washington, December 24, 1862.
To-day Hon. M[r] Cox calls, and asks that Col. Samuel A. Gilbert, of Ohio be a Brigadier Gen[l]. He is now near Lexington, Ky. Has been in service from the beginning Papers on file in his favor from Gen. Wright & others.

He also says a word for Co[l]. Wood, as also does Senator Sherman. Papers on file in this case also.

Note Regarding Wesley Greene

(December 1862)

After inquiry, I believe it is true that a man calling himself J. Wesley Greene, and professing to reside at Pittsburg, Pa. called on the President some time in November, and stated to him that he, Greene, had had two interviews with Jeff. Davis, at Richmond, Va. on the last day of October; and also related certain statements which he said Davis had made to him upon the occasion. The President became satisfied that Green had not seen Davis at all, and that the whole thing was a very shallow attempt at humbuggery. Jeff. Davis can redeem Green's character if he will, by verifying his statement.

Note Regarding Appointment of William Holman as Chaplain

(1862)

Mr Crittenden is for Mr Holman for Chaplain at Louisville.

Note Regarding Francis J. Heron

(1862)

Col. Francis J. Herron, of Iowa, to be a Brigadier General—
See Iowa delegation.

Note Regarding Meredith Clymer

(January 6, 1863)

Executive Mansion,
Washington, Jan. 6,, 1863.
To-day, Col Ulmann calls & urges that Dr ^Meredith^ Clymer be appointed one of the new Medical Inspectors. Thinks he is of superior fitness for the place

Note Regarding Transfer of Richard Johnson

(February 13, 1863)

Executive Mansion,
Washington, Feb. 13, 1863.
To-day, Hon. Mr Yeaman, of Ky. calls and asks that Gen. R. W. Johnson, may be transferred from Gen. Rosecrans command to that of Gen. Wright. Mr Yeaman says he does this at the request of Gen. Johnson

A. Lincoln

Note Regarding Henry Baxter

(March 6, 1863)

Executive Mansion,
Washington, March 6., 1863.
Senator Chandler says Co^{l} Baxter crossed the Rappahannock with boats when Pontoniers shrunk back.

Note Regarding Joseph Snider

(March 9, 1863)

Executive Mansion,
Washington, March 9., 1863.
To-day, Senator Bowden, with Mr Boyd, & Mr. Hawxhurst, one an editor & one a Member of the Legislature, call and ask that Co^{l} Joseph Snider, of the 7th Va. now in the A. P. be a Brigadier General. He has been three times hit,—twice at Antietam and with slight injury, and once very severly at Fredericksburg— Also has had two horses shot under him—They say Gov. Pierpoint & ~~the whole~~ ^many of the^ Legislature ~~is~~ for him. He resides in Monongalia Co, West Virginia.

Note Regarding William W. Wallace

(March 9, 1863)

Executive Mansion
March 9. 1863.
Col. Rose, of Ia, recommends Wm Wirt Wallace, of 9th Dist. for P. Marshal— Says he is a tip-top man.

Note Regarding Appointment of Odon Guitar

(March 11, 1863)

Executive Mansion,
Washington, March 11., 1863.
Major Rollins calls and again urges that, if possible, Co[l] Odon Guitar, be a Brigadier General. I believe the case is a meritorious.

Note Regarding Promotion of George Sangster

(March 14, 1863)

Executive Mansion,
Washington, March 14, 1863.
To-day, Gov. Hicks, with Col. Walton, Member of Md. Leg. & Mr. Ireland, Post. Master at Anapolis, and ask that Co[l] George Sangster, of N.Y. be promoted— These Md— people make his acquaintance his commanding paroled Camp at Anapolis— Senator Harris. is also for him.

Note Regarding Isaac H. Duval

(March 16, 1863)

March 16, 1863
H. W. Crothers, aid to Gov. Pierpoint, on behalf of the Governor & himself, asks that Co[l] Isaac. H. Duval, of W. Virginia, & now at Winchester with Milroy, be a Brigadier General— They want him in West-Virginia, Lightburn being in Tennessee with Rosecrans. Senator Bowden joins in the request.

Both say they wish Milroy to command in West- Virginia

Note Regarding Military Promotions

(March 27–30, 1863)

Executive Mansion,
Washington, March 27., 1863.
To-day m^{r} Blake, of ~~Illinois,~~ Indianapolis, asks

1. Capt Aiken be promoted
2. Col. William H. Blake of the 9th be promoted.
3. Co^{l} John W. Blake of the 40th be promoted.
4. That himself, James Blake, have something.

Submitted to the Secretary of War.

A. Lincoln
March, 30. 1863,

Note Regarding Harbor Defenses

(April 4, 1863)

On this general subject, I respectfully refer Mr Browne to the Secretaries of War and Navy for conferrence and consultation.

I have a single idea of my own about harbor defence. It is a Steam-ram, built so as to sacrifice nearly all capacity for carrying, to ~~that~~ those of speed and strength, so as to be able to split any vessel having hollow enough in her to cary supplies for a voyage of any distance. Such ram, or course could not ^her self^ cary supplies for a ~~voage~~ voyage of considerable distance; and her business would be to guard a particular harbor, as a Bull-dog guards his master's door

A. Lincoln
April 4, 1863.

Note Regarding Alonzo Wood and John H. Knapp

(April 14, 1863)

Executive Mansion
Washington, April 14, 1863.
To-day, Hon. Thos T. Davis, Rep-elect 23rd Dist of N.Y. personally recommends that Alonzo Wood, Esq be Provot-Marshal, Dr John H. Knapp, for the medical [member?]

A L.

Note Regarding John G. Foster

(April 22, 1863)

Executive Mansion,
Washington, April 22., 1863.
To-day, Gov. Stanley, calls and asks that Gen. Foster, may have his commission dated back. Gen. F.'s conduct at Washington N.C. I think, entitles him to additional consideration.

A. Lincoln

Note Regarding Samuel A. Pancoast

(April 23, 1863)

Executive Mansion,
Washington, April 23, 1863.
To-day Samuel A. Pancoast, an elderly "friend" residing in Hampshire Co, West-Virginia, calls and asks to be Provost-Marshal, for District in which his county is situated— He is a vigourous old man, who has been imprisoned by the "Secesh" for seventeen months in succession having now been at liberty only about three weeks.

Note Regarding John C. Holland

(May 9, 1863)

Executive Mansion,
Washington, May 9, 1863.
To-day M[r] Bonifant, Marshal of Maryland, and Mr J. F. Wagner, an Appraiser at Baltimore call and ask that Co[l] John C. Holland may be Provost-Marshal, for 5th Dis[t] of Maryland.

Note Regarding Appointment of Lawrence Kipp

(May 28, 1863)

Executive Mansion,
Washington, May 28, 1863.
To-day Senator M[c]Dougal asks that 1st Lieut Lawrence Kip, now on Gen. Wool's Staff, may be a Brigadier General. The Senator makes this a personal request—almost—and I wish to oblige him.

Note Regarding Jacob B. Julian

(January 11, 1864)

Jan, 11, 1864
Today Hon. Geo. W. Julian mentions that heretofore his brother Jacob B. Julian, was recommended for District Judge of Ia

Note Regarding Eric C. Crippen

(January 16, 1864)

Executive Mansion,
Washington, Jan. 16, 1864.
Upon condition that Earl C. Crippen of Co F. 73rd Ohio Volunteers, returns to his regiment, within a reasonable time, and faithfully serves

out his term, including time lost by his desertion, or until he shall be honorably discharged, he is fully pardoned for any desertion of which he is heretofore and now guilty.

A. Lincoln

Fragment of Note on Slavery

(March 22, 1864)

I never knew a man who wished to be himself a slave. Consider if you know any good thing, that no man desires for himself.

A. Lincoln
March 22, 1864

Note Regarding the Probability of Reelection

(August 23, 1864)

On August 22, 1864, Lincoln received a pessimistic report from his advisers about his prospects for reelection. Henry B. Raymond, editor of The New York Times, *convening the Republican National Committee, wrote Lincoln that he would lose New York, Pennsylvania, and Illinois. The want of military success was a huge part of the problem.*

Lincoln was resigned to the possibility that he might not be reelected. Six days before the Democratic convention would select his opponent, he wrote this private memorandum. He brought it to that day's cabinet meeting. Lincoln presented it, folded so that none of the text was visible, and asked each person to sign the back of the document. Lincoln never explained why he did not read or show the members of his cabinet the memo's content. He believed that if a Democrat was elected president, that person would end the war on terms that guaranteed Confederate independence.

Executive Mansion,
Washington, Aug. 23^{d}, 1864.
This morning, as for some days past, it seems exceedingly probable that this Administration will not be re-elected. Then it will be my duty to

co-operate with the President-elect, as to save the Union between the election and the inauguration; as he will have secured his election on such ground that he cannot possibly save it afterwards.

(Signed) A. Lincoln
William H Seward
W. P. Fessenden
Edwin M. Stanton
Gideon Welles
Edw'd Bates
M. Blair
J. P. Usher
August 23. 1864

Note Regarding Estimated Electoral Vote

(October 13, 1864)

Time

Office U.S. Military Telegraph,
WAR DEPARTMENT,
Washington, D.C., October 13th 1864.

Supposed Copperhead Vote.			Union Vote, for President	
New-York	33		New England States	39
Penn	26		Michigan	8
New Jersey	7		Wisconsin	8
Delaware	3		Minnesota	4
Maryland	7		Iowa	8
Missouri	11		Oregon	3
Kentucky	11		California	5
Illinois	16		Kansas	3

	114		Indiana	15
			Ohio	21
			W. Virginia	5
				117
			Nevada	3
				120

Note Projections of November Election

(October 1864)

War Department
Washington City,
1864

Genl. M^c^Clellan			Abraham Lincoln	
New-York	33		New-England	39
Pennsylvania	26		Michigan	8
New Jersey	7		Wisconsin	8
Delaware	3		Minesota	4
Maryland	7		Iowa.	8
Missouri	11		Oregon	3
Kentucky	11		California	5
Illinois	16		Kansas.	3
	114		Indiana	13
			Ohio	21
			W. Virginia	5
				117

Note Regarding John C. Lewis

(November 12, 1864)

Executive Mansion,
Washington, Nov 12, , 1864.
Whenever proper evidence shall be brought to me along with this paper that a substitute has been procured, received and duly ~~mus~~ mustered in, in place of John C. Lewis, private in Company B. 188th Regt N.Y. Vols. I will will discharge the latter.

A. Lincoln
Nov. 12. 1864

Note Regarding New Jersey and New York

(November 1864)

Lincoln, known from his earliest days of keeping tabs on vote totals, records the total votes cast in New York and New Jersey in the 1864 presidential election. His source is the New-York Daily Tribune.

Taken from Tribune	{	New-Jersey	128.680
		New-York	730.664

New-Jersey & New-York.

Note Regarding Conditions for Peace

(April 5, 1865)

As to peace I have said before, and now repeat, that three things are indispensable.

1. The restoration of the national authority throughout all the States.
2. No receding by the Executive of the United States on the slavery question from the position assumed thereon in the late Annual Message to Congress, and in preceding documents.

3. No cessation of hostilities short of an end of the war, and the disbanding of all force hostile to the government.

That all propositions coming from those now in hostility to the government, and not inconsistent with the foregoing, will be respectfully considered, and passed upon in a spirit of sincere liberality.

I now add that it seems useless for me to be more specific with those who will not say they are ready for the indispensable terms, even on conditions to be named by themselves. If there be any who are ready for those indispensable terms, on any conditions whatever, let them say so, and state their conditions, so that ~~they~~ ^such conditions^ can be distinctly known, and considered.

It is further added that, the remission of confiscations being within the executive power, if the war be now further persisted in, by those opposing the government, the making of confiscated property at the least to bear the additional cost, will be insisted on; but that confiscations (except in cases of third party intervening interests) will be remitted to the people of any state which shall now promptly, and in good faith, withdraw it's troops and other support from further resistance to the government.

What is now said as to remission of confiscation has no reference to supposed property in slaves.

Copy of paper read to and left with Judge Campbell at Richmond

April 5. 1865

Acknowledgments

My long and winding road leading to writing about Lincoln's private fragments and notes has benefited from many friends and institutions along the way.

The journey began with the decision to teach an initial seminar on Abraham Lincoln in the history department at UCLA. To enhance the students' experience, I took them across freeway traffic to the Huntington Library in San Marino to view their new exhibit, *The Last Best Hope on Earth: Abraham Lincoln and the Promise of America*.

In our class readings, I found myself drawn to Lincoln's second inaugural address. When I wanted to learn if there were any antecedents to his remarkable address, my quest took me to Brown University in Providence, Rhode Island.

I will not forget my first encounter with a Lincoln fragment. As I sat in the John Hay Library, librarian Mary-Jo Kline let me hold in my hands a single, blue-lined sheet of paper. Though it was not titled by Lincoln, Hay had later inscribed, "Meditation on the Divine Will." At the time, my interest was in this one fragment; I did not know that Lincoln had written so many other notes to himself.

In recent years, in a desire to offer a new presentation on Lincoln, I began to explore other Lincoln fragments. Audiences at Lincoln Memorial University in Harrogate, Tennessee; the Abraham Lincoln Presidential Library in Springfield, Illinois; then the Huntington Library and the Jonathan Club in Southern California offered enormously helpful comments as they listened to various versions of this book.

Deeply immersed in my next biography—the compelling and complex story of Joshua Lawrence Chamberlain, hero of Little Round Top at Gettysburg who went on to become the four-time governor of Maine and president of Bowdoin College—I decided that Chamberlain would need to pause at Gettysburg as Lincoln intervened once again.

I want to thank many who have helped me see the private Lincoln more clearly. I begin by expressing gratitude to the editors of *The Papers of Abraham Lincoln*. Director Daniel E. Worthington and assistant editor Kelley Clausing generously offered their advice and help at every step of the way. I was the beneficiary of their expert advice on the origin and scope of Lincoln's fragments and notes.

I am indebted once again also to friends at the Abraham Lincoln Presidential Library in Springfield, Illinois, who welcomed this book project and were encouraging in their support of it. I thank Alan Lowe, who, when executive director, invited me to speak on Lincoln fragments in September 2017 when I was in the initial steps of conceiving this book. Samuel Wheeler, then the Illinois state historian and director of research and collections at the library, offered his encouragement, as did Christopher Schnell, manuscripts manager.

Once again, I offer my appreciation to the talented staff of the Huntington Library. I have been assisted in countless ways in researching and writing now my seventh book while serving as a reader in this distinctive library.

I am grateful to Allan Aubrey, who teaches history and civics at Sullivan East High School in Bluff City, Tennessee. He drove one hundred miles to attend my Lincoln presentation at Lincoln Memorial University in Harrogate, Tennessee, in September 2015.

After our conversation that day, he let me read his excellent master's thesis, *The Lincoln Fragments: The Thought Behind the Timeless Words*.

I thank James Marcus, former editor of *Harper's Magazine,* who published "Notes to Self: Lincoln's Private Thoughts on Fate, Slavery, and Belief," in the February 2018 issue.

I am delighted to acknowledge exceptional persons who helped in various ways with four chapters of the book.

For chapter 2, I thank Guy C. Fraker, Bloomington (Illinois) lawyer, author, and longtime friend, who offered invaluable assistance in thinking through Lincoln's notes for lawyers. Some years ago, on a memorable day, I joined Guy when he guided a group of us on the meandering route of Lincoln's travels on the Eighth Judicial Circuit.

For chapter 3, my thanks to Harlan Crow, who invited me to his remarkable private library in Dallas, Texas. Librarian Sam Fore made available Lincoln's 1854 fragment on slavery.

For chapter 7, I thank Dr. Beth S. Hessel (my former student), at the time executive director of the Presbyterian Historical Society in Philadelphia, and Lisa Jacobsen, senior research archivist, for providing biographical material on Presbyterian minister and pro-slavery author Frederick Ross.

Jonathan White, a friend and marvelous historian, suggested I should include a chapter on Lincoln's correspondence with Alexander Stephens, which resulted in the notable "apple of gold" fragment that became the foundation of chapter 8.

I am grateful for friends who read the entire manuscript. Jim McPherson, my teacher at Princeton, and dean of Civil War historians; Harold Holzer—I can't keep up with the many splendid Lincoln books Harold has written; Richard Norton Smith, who knows more about the American presidency than anyone; John Marszalek, Civil War historian and executive director and managing editor of the Ulysses S. Grant Association, who brought his editorial pen to the manuscript; and Ernie Cortes, Jr., national co-chair of the Industrial Areas Foundation, who offered insightful reading of draft after draft, informed by his wide-ranging reading as he leads community organizers in this tumultuous time in our nation. This book is better because of each of their counsel.

Once again, the remarkable Dr. Nancy Macky, professor of English and drama, has brought her love of writing to thinking with me about Lincoln's remarkable gift of language in his notes to himself. As a dear friend, and fellow reader at the Huntington Library, I express my gratitude to her for being part of every aspect of this book. Thank you, Nancy!

Karen Needles, director of the Lincoln Archives Digital Project, is a Lincoln co-conspirator. Karen both suggests and can find photographs and artwork anywhere. She and I worked together fulfilling my intent to put images at the exact sentence where the reader encounters a particular aspect of the Lincoln story.

This is my fourth book with Random House. I am grateful for their team of talented people led by Gina Centrello, president and publisher, and Tom Perry, senior vice president.

At Random House, it all begins and ends with my editor, the incredible Caitlin McKenna. She believed in this book from the start. Caitlin suggested printing the twelve key fragments in full color. She advocated printing—for the first time—the complete trove of Lincoln's notes in a special appendix. In a world that relies too exclusively on electronic communication, she and I regularly speak by telephone, to the betterment of our communication about each facet of the book. Caitlin's intelligence, insights, and suggestions have again and again sharpened my understanding and made the private Lincoln come into clearer focus, always with the reader in mind.

Editor Marie Pantojan stepped in at a crucial time in the manuscript's trajectory to offer her always helpful advice. Associate editor Emma Caruso kept all the moving parts of the book transitioning together. For a second book, I thank Victoria Wong, the interior designer, and—also for a second book—Joseph Perez, who designed the cover. My gratitude also to Richard Elman, production designer, and Katie Tull, marketer. What a pleasure to work once more with Dennis Ambrose, who managed the entire editorial production of the book.

I thank Michelle Daniel for her excellent job in the important and detailed work of copy editing.

My literary agent, Mary Evans, believed wholeheartedly in this book project. When flying east from California I always look forward to insightful conversations with Mary, at her office in New York, or at her farm in the Hudson Valley. We have been literary partners for twenty-two years. I trust her instincts and rely on her counsel. Mary, this is book five together. Thank you!

Finally, my profound thanks to my wife, Cynthia. She has long experienced living with Lincoln like he was a member of our family. She tells friends that if I am unable to give a presentation on Lincoln, she is ready to do so. She is my in-house editor: an insightful reader and editor of multiple drafts of each new book. In this unprecedented pandemic, we have spent more time than ever with each other—and with Lincoln—to my delight.

Notes

Abbreviations and Short Titles Employed in Notes

AL—Abraham Lincoln.

ALPLC—Abraham Lincoln Presidential Library and Museum, Springfield, Illinois.

AL MSS DLC—Abraham Lincoln Papers, Library of Congress.

Burlingame, *Abraham Lincoln*—Michael Burlingame, *Abraham Lincoln: A Life,* two volumes (Baltimore, MD: Johns Hopkins University Press, 2009).

Carwardine, *Lincoln*—Richard Carwardine, *Lincoln: A Life of Purpose and Power* (New York: Alfred A. Knopf, 2006).

CW—The Collected Works of Abraham Lincoln, 9 volumes, ed. Roy P. Basler (New Brunswick, NJ: Rutgers University Press, 1953–55) and *Supplement, 1832–1865,* 2 volumes (Westport, CT: Greenwood Press, 1974).

CWAL—Complete Works of Abraham Lincoln, ten volumes, ed. John G. Nicolay and John Hay (New York: F. D. Tandy, 1905).

Donald, *Lincoln*—David Herbert Donald, *Lincoln* (New York: Simon & Schuster, 1995).

Nicolay and Hay, *Abraham Lincoln*—John G. Nicolay and John Hay, *Abraham Lincoln: A History,* ten volumes (New York: Century, 1890).

White, *A. Lincoln*—Ronald C. White, Jr., *A. Lincoln: A Biography* (New York: Random House, 2009).

Prologue

1. For the story of the Copperheads, see Jennifer L. Weber, *Copperheads: The Rise and Fall of Lincoln's Opponents in the North* (New York: Oxford University Press, 2006).
2. Frank L. Klement, *The Limits of Dissent: Clement L. Vallandigham and the Civil War* (Lexington: University of Kentucky Press, 1970), 178–81.
3. James F. Wilson, "Some Memories of Lincoln," *North American Review* 163 (December 1896), 670–71. Although Wilson is writing three decades later, his recol-

lection of Lincoln's conversation about his notes rings true with similar reports from a number of witnesses that we will encounter in this book. See also Douglas L. Wilson, *Lincoln's Sword: The Presidency and the Power of Words* (New York: Alfred A. Knopf, 2007), 165–66.

4. I am grateful to Kelley Clausing, assistant editor of the Papers of Abraham Lincoln in Springfield, Illinois, for her insights on Lincoln's evolving handwriting.
5. AL, "Fragment of a Tariff Discussion," [Dec. 1, 1847?] *CW* 1:408–16.
6. Richard N. Current, *The Lincoln Nobody Knows* (New York: McGraw Hill, 1958), 12.
7. Ibid., 12.
8. David C. Mearns, *The Lincoln Papers* (Garden City, NY: Doubleday, 194), vol. 1, 15; Jason Emerson, *Giant in the Shadows: The Life of Robert T. Lincoln* (Carbondale: Southern Illinois University Press, 2012), 106; Joshua Zeitz, *Lincoln's Boys: John Hay, John Nicolay, and the War for Lincoln's Image* (New York: Viking, 2014), 231–32.
9. Mearns, *The Lincoln Papers,* vol. 1, 18; Zeitz, *Lincoln's Boys,* 231–32.
10. Zeitz, *Lincoln's Boys,* 294.
11. Ibid., 232; Emerson, *Giant in the Shadows,* 109.
12. Nicolay and Hay serialized their biography in forty excerpts in the *Century Magazine* between 1890 and 1896.
13. See Michael Burlingame, *Abraham Lincoln: The Observations of John G. Nicolay and John Hay* (Carbondale: Southern Illinois University Press, 2007), especially 1–16. Burlingame, mindful of those who have criticized it for its biases, repositions it as ten volumes of primary documents and reminiscences, to which he adds insightful analysis of the diaries, journals, and letters on which the biography was based.
14. Nicolay and Hay, *Abraham Lincoln,* vol. 6, 342.

Part One: Lawyer

1. White, *A. Lincoln,* 43–48.
2. Ibid., 77–80.
3. AL to Samuel D. Marshall, November 11, 1842, *CW* 1:305.
4. Michael Burlingame, *Abraham Lincoln: A Life,* vol. 1, 259.

Chapter 1: The Lyrical Lincoln: The Transcendence of Niagara Falls

1. Oliver G. Steele, *Steele's Book of Niagara Falls,* 10th ed. (Buffalo, NY: Oliver G. Steele, 1847).
2. G. Morton Weed, *School Days of Yesterday: Buffalo Public School History* (Buffalo, NY: Buffalo Board of Education, 2002), 2.
3. Steele, *Steele's Book of Niagara Falls,* 10.
4. David Donald describes Lincoln's note about Niagara Falls as "momentary rhapsody," Donald, *Lincoln,* 132.
5. As with all his notes, Lincoln did not date it. Nicolay and Hay dated it July 1,

1850—with a question mark. Basler believed a more accurate dating would be the last week of September 1848, when Lincoln left a political speaking tour in Massachusetts to travel home to Springfield via Albany and Buffalo, New York. This route would give him the opportunity to visit Niagara Falls sometime between September 25 and 30. I agree with Basler's dating. Additionally, Lincoln wrote this note on the same kind of paper he used for several political speeches he made in Congress in 1848. AL, Fragment: "Niagara Falls" [September 25–30, 1848], *CW* 2:11, n. 1.

6. AL to Thomas S. Flournoy, February 17, 1848, *CW* 1:452.
7. AL to Jesse Lynch, April 10, 1848, *CW* 1:463.
8. *Old Colony Republican* (Taunton, MA), September 23, 1848; White, *A. Lincoln,* 159; Donald, *Lincoln,* 131–32; Burlingame, *Abraham Lincoln,* vol. 1, 280–83.
9. White, *A. Lincoln,* 159; Donald, *Lincoln,* 131.
10. White, *A. Lincoln,* 159–60; Donald, *Lincoln,* 131–32.
11. Burlingame, *Abraham Lincoln,* vol. 1, 283; White, *A. Lincoln,* 160.
12. *Boston Daily Atlas,* September 23, 1848; *New York Tribune,* September 25, 1848; Walter Stahr, *Seward: Lincoln's Indispensable Man* (New York: Simon & Schuster, 2012), 110; Glynden G. Van Deusen, *William Henry Seward* (New York: Oxford University Press, 1967), 109–10.
13. White, *A. Lincoln,* 160; Burlingame, *Abraham Lincoln,* vol. 1, 283.
14. Linda L. Revie, *The Niagara Companion: Explorers, Artists, and Writers at the Falls, from Discovery Through the Twentieth Century* (Waterloo, Ontario: Wilfrid Laurier University Press, 2003), 21; Paul Gromosiak and Christopher Stoianoff, *Images of America: Niagara Falls 1850–2000* (Charleston, SC: Arcadia Publishing, 2012), 9; Peter Porter, "Historic Niagara," in William Dean Howells, *The Niagara Book* (New York: Doubleday, Page, 1892), 96.
15. William Irwin, *The New Niagara: Tourism, Technology, and the Landscape of Niagara Falls, 1776–1917* (University Park: Pennsylvania State University Press, 1996), xiv–xv; John F. Sears, *Sacred Places: American Tourist Attractions in the Nineteenth Century* (New York: Oxford University Press, 1989).
16. Nathaniel Hawthorne, "My Visit to Niagara," in *The Centenary Edition of the Works of Nathaniel Hawthorne* (Columbus: Ohio State University Press, 1974), 2:281–83.
17. Charles Dickens, *American Notes for General Circulation* (New York: Harper and Brothers, 1842), 74.
18. Sears, *Sacred Places,* 5–7.
19. John Quincy Adams, 1843 Speech on Niagara Falls, in *Souvenir of Niagara* (Buffalo, NY: Sage Publishers, 1864), 128. Adams describes his visit to Niagara Falls in *Memoirs of John Quincy Adams, His Diary from 1795 to 1848,* vol. 11, ed. Charles Francis Adams (Philadelphia: J. B. Lippincott, 1876), 392–97.
20. Jeremy Elwell Adamson, *Niagara* (Washington, D.C.: Corcoran Gallery of Art, 1985), 37.
21. Orin Dunlap, "Dramatic Incidents," in *The Niagara Book,* 58–63.
22. *Buffalo Commercial Advertiser,* March 30, 1848; *Buffalo Express,* March 31, 1848;

David Phillips, *The Day Niagara Falls Ran Dry* (Toronto, Ontario: Key Porter Books, 1993), 62–64.

23. David C. Mearns, *The Lincoln Papers* (Garden City, NY: Doubleday, 194), vol. 1, 150; Allen C. Guelzo, *Abraham Lincoln: Redeemer President* (Grand Rapids, MI: William B. Eerdmans Publishing, 1999), 108.
24. Robert Chambers, *Vestiges of the Natural History of Creation* (New York: Wiley and Putnam, 1845).
25. Charles Lyell, *Principles of Geology Being an Attempt to Explain the Former Changes of the Earth's Surface, by Reference to Causes Now in Operation,* 3 vols. (London: J. Murray, 1830–33).
26. Guelzo, *Abraham Lincoln: Redeemer President,* 108.
27. Chambers, *Vestiges of the Natural History of Creation,* 278–79.
28. Ibid., 256.
29. William H. Herndon and Jesse W. Weik, *Herndon's Lincoln,* ed. Douglas L. Wilson and Rodney O. Davis (Urbana: Knox College Lincoln Studies Center and the University of Illinois Press, 2006), 187–88. See also James Tackach, *Lincoln and the Natural Environment* (Carbondale: Southern Illinois University Press, 2019), 52.
30. Herndon and Weik, *Herndon's Lincoln,* 187–88.
31. Ibid., 187–88.
32. Ibid.

Chapter 2: The Humble Lincoln: A Lawyer's Vocation

1. These searches resulted in the publication of *The Law Practice of Abraham Lincoln: Complete Documentary Edition* on three DVD-ROM discs in 2000, and the publication of the four-volume *The Papers of Abraham Lincoln: Legal Documents and Cases,* ed. Daniel W. Stowell (Charlottesville: University of Virginia Press, 2008). See especially "Historical Introduction," vol. 1, xxix–xlii.
2. John J. Duff, *A. Lincoln: Prairie Lawyer* (New York: Rinehart, 1960), 9–10, lists Lincoln's law colleagues with some higher education: Henry E. Dummer, Bowdoin College, and later at Harvard Law School; John T. Stuart, Centre College; Dan Stone, Middlebury College; Ninian Edwards and John J. Hardin, Transylvania College Law School; Edward Jones, Virginia Law School, and his partner, William H. Herndon, who attended Illinois College briefly.
3. In 1850, of the twenty-four thousand lawyers in the United States, only four hundred were graduates of law schools. Mark E. Steiner, *An Honest Calling: The Law Practice of Abraham Lincoln* (De Kalb: Northern Illinois University Press, 2006), 30.
4. Mark W. Granfors and Terrence C. Halliday, "Professional Passages: Caste, Class and Education in the 19th Century Legal Profession," table 1, "Educational Pattern by Date of Bar Admission" (American Bar Foundation Working Paper, 1987), cited by Steiner, *An Honest Calling,* 186, note 28.
5. AL, "Autobiography Written for John L. Scripps," [c. June 1860], *CW* 4:65. John Locke Scripps, editor of the *Chicago Press and Tribune,* interviewed Lincoln in

Springfield in June 1860. Republicans called Scripps's campaign biography, published in mid-July 1860, "Campaign Document No. 1." The cheap thirty-two-page pamphlet sold more than one million copies.

6. "Historical Introduction," *Papers of Abraham Lincoln, Legal Documents and Cases,* vol. 1, xxix.
7. Ibid. For the process of Lincoln's admission to the bar, see Steiner, *An Honest Calling,* 37–40.
8. AL, "'Spot' Resolutions in the United States House of Representatives," December 22, 1847, *CW* 1:420–22; Burlingame, *Abraham Lincoln,* vol. 1, 264–65; Carwardine, *Lincoln,* 22–23; Donald, *Lincoln,* 123–24.
9. *Illinois State Register* (Springfield), March 10, 1848; White, *A. Lincoln,* 152; Burlingame, *Abraham Lincoln,* vol. 1, 269.
10. "Historical Introduction," *Papers of Abraham Lincoln, Legal Documents and Cases,* vol. 1, xxxix.
11. For the boundaries of the Eighth Judicial Circuit, see Guy C. Fraker's two books, *Lincoln's Ladder to the Presidency: The Eighth Judicial Circuit* (Carbondale: Southern Illinois University Press, 2012), 10; *Looking for Lincoln in Illinois: A Guidebook to Lincoln's Eighth Judicial Circuit* (Carbondale: Southern Illinois University Press, 2017), 1.
12. Albert J. Beveridge, *Abraham Lincoln, 1809–1858,* vol. 1 (Boston: Houghton Mifflin, 1928), 493.
13. Albert A. Woldman, *Lawyer Lincoln* (New York: Carroll and Graf, 1936), 89.
14. "Historical Introduction," *Papers of Abraham Lincoln, Legal Documents and Cases,* vol. 1: xxxv–xxxvi.
15. Willard J. King, *Lincoln's Manager: David Davis* (Cambridge, MA: Harvard University Press, 1962).
16. David Davis interview, September 30, 1866, in *Herndon's Informants: Letters, Interviews, and Statements About Abraham Lincoln,* ed. Douglass L. Wilson and Rodney O. Davis (Urbana: University of Illinois Press, 1998), 349.
17. *CW* 2:140–43; AL, "Fragment: Notes for a Law Lecture," [July 1, 1850], *CW* 2, 82, note. Basler adds in footnote 1, "It seems probable that Lincoln wrote these observations on the legal profession several years later."
18. *Papers of Abraham Lincoln, Legal Documents and Cases,* vol. 1, 12–13, suggests the date of 1859.
19. AL to Jesse W. Fell, Enclosing Autobiography, December 20, 1859, *CW* 3:512.
20. I am grateful to Guy Fraker for this insight.
21. AL, "Communication to the People of Sangamo County," March 9, 1832, *CW* 1:5–9; White, *A. Lincoln,* 49; Donald, *Lincoln,* 42–43; Burlingame, *Abraham Lincoln,* vol. 1, 72–73; Sidney Blumenthal, *A Self-Made Man: The Political Life of Abraham Lincoln,* vol. 1, *1809–1849* (New York: Simon & Schuster, 2016), 56–57.
22. Benjamin Franklin, *Poor Richard's Almanack,* 1785, in *Autobiography, Poor Richard, and Later Writings* (New York: Library of America, 1987), 556.
23. David Davis interview, September 20, 1866, *Herndon's Informants,* 349.
24. Paul Simon, *Freedom's Champion: Elijah Lovejoy* (Carbondale: Southern Illinois University Press, 1994).

25. AL, "Address Before the Young Men's Lyceum of Springfield, Illinois," January 27, 1838, *CW* 1:108.
26. Ibid., 109.
27. Steiner, *An Honest Calling*, 76–81.
28. Edwards is quoted in Steiner, *An Honest Calling*, 85; Fraker, *Lincoln's Ladder to the Presidency*, 20, 26.
29. Noah Webster, *American Spelling Book* (Boston: John West, 1807), 164.

Part Two: Politician

1. AL, "Speech at Peoria, Illinois," October 16, 1854, *CW* 2:282; Lewis E. Lehrman, *Lincoln at Peoria: The Turning Point* (Mechanicsburg, PA: Stackpole Books, 2008).
2. The Kansas-Nebraska Act stated, "All questions pertaining to slavery in the territories were to be left to the decision of the people residing therein." David M. Potter, *The Impending Crisis: 1848–1861*, ed. Don Fehrenbacher (New York: Harper and Row, 1976), 250–53; Eric Foner, *Free Soil, Free Labor, Free Men: The Ideology of the Republican Party Before the Civil War* (New York: Oxford University Press, 1995), 155–59.
3. For the Missouri Compromise, see Robert Pierce Forbes, *The Missouri Compromise and Its Aftermath: Slavery and the Meaning of America* (Chapel Hill: University of North Carolina Press, 2007); Robert V. Remini, *Henry Clay: Statesman for the Union* (New York: W. W. Norton, 1991), 177 ff.
4. For the story of the Compromise of 1850, see Remini, *Henry Clay*, 730 ff; Robert V. Remini, *At the Edge of the Precipice: Henry Clay and the Compromise That Saved the Union* (New York: Basic Books, 2010); and John C. Waugh, *On the Brink of the Civil War: The Compromise of 1850 and How It Changed the Course of American History* (New York: Rowman and Littlefield, 2003).
5. AL, "Autobiography Written for John L. Scripps," [c. June 1860], *CW* 4:67.

Chapter 3: The Fiery Lincoln: Slavery and a Reentry to Politics

1. AL, "Fragment on Slavery," [July 1, 1854], *CW* 2:222-23. I thank Harlan Crow, who owns Lincoln's 1854 fragment on slavery, and librarian Sam Fore, who made it available to me.
2. *Illinois State Register* (Springfield), September 27, 1854.
3. Robert W. Johannsen, *Stephen A. Douglas* (Urbana: University of Illinois Press, 1973), 447.
4. Lincoln made the same speech at Bloomington, at Springfield on October 4, and at Peoria on October 16. The only full text is one Lincoln provided after his Peoria speech. Thus, AL, "Speech at Peoria, Illinois," October 16, 1854, *CW* 2:248.
5. AL, "Speech at Peoria, Illinois," October 16, 1854, *CW* 2:265–66.
6. AL, "Speech at Peoria, Illinois," October 16, 1854, *CW* 2:276.
7. Eric Foner, *The Fiery Trial: Abraham Lincoln and American Slavery* (New York:

W. W. Norton, 2010), 63–65, observes, "Lincoln had finally found a subject worthy of his intellectual talent and political ambition."

8. James M. McPherson, *Tried by War: Abraham Lincoln as Commander in Chief* (New York: Penguin Press, 2008), 157–59; White, *A. Lincoln,* 541–44.
9. George Fitzhugh, *Sociology for the South; or The Failure of a Free Society* (Richmond, VA: Morris, 1854), 83. See also Harvey Wish, *George Fitzhugh: Conservative of the Old South, Southern Sketches* 11 (Charlottesville, VA: Green Bookman, 1938). (For Lincoln and Fitzhugh, see Arthur Charles Cole, *Lincoln's "House Divided" Speech: Did It Reflect a Doctrine of Class Struggle?: An Address Delivered Before the Chicago Historical Society on March 15, 1923* (Chicago: University of Chicago Press, 1923).
10. AL to Henry L. Pierce and Others, April 6, 1859, *CW* 3:374–76.
11. Fitzhugh, *Sociology for the South,* 177–79.
12. Ibid., 180–82.
13. AL, "Second Inaugural Address," March 4, 1865, *CW* 8:332.
14. Emmanuel Hertz, *The Hidden Lincoln: From the Letters and Papers of William H. Herndon* (New York: Viking Press, 1938), 96–97.

Chapter 4: The Defeated Lincoln: Failure and Ambition

1. For a comparison of Lincoln and Douglas, see Roy Morris, Jr., *The Long Pursuit: Abraham Lincoln's Thirty-Year Struggle with Stephen Douglas for the Heart and Soul of America* (New York: HarperCollins, 2008).
2. Robert W. Johannsen, *Stephen A. Douglas* (Urbana: University of Illinois Press, 1973), 3–15; Morris, *The Long Pursuit,* 8–12.
3. Johannsen, *Stephen A. Douglas,* 28–29; White, *A. Lincoln,* 70–72.
4. AL, "Communication to the People of Sangamo County," *Sangamo Journal* (Springfield), March 9, 1832, *CW* 1:8.
5. Daniel Walker Howe, *Making the American Self: Jonathan Edwards to Abraham Lincoln* (Cambridge, MA: Harvard University Press, 1997), especially chapter 4, "The Emerging Ideal of Self-Improvement," 107–35.
6. Donald, *Lincoln,* 41–42; Burlingame, *Abraham Lincoln,* vol. 1, 72–75; White, *A. Lincoln,* 48–49.
7. Donald, *Lincoln,* 46; Burlingame, *Abraham Lincoln,* vol. 1, 74–75; White, *A. Lincoln,* 52.
8. Burlingame, *Abraham Lincoln,* vol. 1, 81–85; Donald, *Lincoln,* 52–53; White, *A. Lincoln,* 59–60.
9. *Illinois State Register* (Springfield), November 23, 1839; Douglas L. Wilson, *Honor's Voice: The Transformation of Abraham Lincoln* (New York: Alfred A. Knopf, 1998), 199.
10. Joseph Gillespie to William H. Herndon, January 31, 1866, *Herndon's Informants,* 181.
11. William H. Herndon to Isaac N. Arnold, October 24, 1883, cited in Michael Burlingame, *The Inner World of Abraham Lincoln* (Urbana: University of Illinois Press, 1994), 5.

12. Donald, *Lincoln,* 90–92; White, *A. Lincoln,* 113–14.
13. Burlingame, *Abraham Lincoln,* vol. 1, 190–93; White, *A. Lincoln,* 113–16.
14. The Seventeenth Amendment modified article 1, section 3, of the Constitution, allowing voters to cast direct votes for U.S. senators. The amendment was passed by Congress on May 13, 1912, and ratified on April 8, 1913.
15. AL to Hugh Lemaster, November 29, 1854, *CW* 2:289.
16. Hugh Lemaster to AL, December 11, 1854, AL MSS DLC.
17. "List of Members of the Illinois Legislature in 1855," [January 1, 1855?], *CW* 1:296–98.
18. AL to Elihu B. Washburne, January 6, 1855, *CW* 2:303–04.
19. Shields, realizing his political ambitions in Illinois were doomed, would move to Minnesota, where he was elected to the Senate, and later to Missouri, where he was elected once again to the Senate.
20. Don E. Fehrenbacher, *Prelude to Greatness: Lincoln in the 1850s* (Stanford, CA: Stanford University Press, 1962), 38–39; White, *A. Lincoln,* 207; Donald, *Lincoln,* 183–84; Carwardine, *Lincoln,* 64.
21. Fehrenbacher, *Prelude to Greatness,* 39.
22. White, *A. Lincoln,* 208; Donald, *Lincoln,* 183–84; Burlingame, *Abraham Lincoln,* vol. 1, 401–02.
23. Fehrenbacher, *Prelude to Greatness,* 175, note 30.
24. AL to Elihu Washburne, February 9, 1854, *CW* 2:306.
25. Catherine Clinton, *Mrs. Lincoln: A Life* (New York: HarperCollins, 2009), 99–100; Jean H. Baker, *Mary Todd Lincoln: A Biography* (New York: W. W. Norton, 1987), 150.
26. Willard L. King, *Lincoln's Manager: David Davis* (Cambridge, MA: Harvard University Press, 1962), 108.
27. Joseph Gillespie, memorandum, April 22, 1880, Joseph Gillespie Papers, Chicago History Museum.
28. AL to Jesse Sandford, Mortimer Porter, and Ambrose K. Striker, March 10, 1855, *CW* 2:308.
29. AL to Elihu Washburne, February 9, 1854, *CW* 2:306.
30. Robert Henry Parkman, "The Patent Case That Lifted Lincoln into a Presidential Candidate," *Abraham Lincoln Quarterly* 4, no. 3 (September 1946), 105–22.
31. For Stanton, see Benjamin P. Thomas and Harold M. Hyman, *Stanton: The Life and Times of Lincoln's Secretary of War* (New York: Alfred A. Knopf, 1962); William Marvel, *Lincoln's Autocrat: The Life of Edwin Stanton* (Chapel Hill: University of North Carolina Press, 2015); Walter Stahr, *Stanton: Lincoln's War Secretary* (New York: Simon & Schuster, 2017).
32. Thomas and Hyman, *Stanton,* 64; Stahr, *Stanton,* 76–77; White, *A. Lincoln,* 212–13.
33. Thomas and Hyman, *Stanton,* 64–66; Marvel, *Lincoln's Autocrat,* 74–75; Stahr, *Stanton,* 77–78. Stahr points out that many of the quotes about Lincoln attributed to Stanton, such as "Why did you bring that damned long-armed ape here . . . he does not know any thing and can do you no good," are all from reminiscences at a much later time.

34. William H. Herndon and Jesse W. Weik, *Herndon's Lincoln,* ed. Douglas L. Wilson and Rodney O. Davis (Urbana: Knox College Lincoln Studies Center and the University of Illinois Press, 2006), 220; White, *A. Lincoln,* 213–14.
35. Johannsen, *Stephen A. Douglas,* 843.

Chapter 5: The Republican Lincoln: The Birth of a Party

1. For the story of the multiplicity of parties, see Corey M. Brooks, *Liberty Power: Antislavery Third Parties and the Transformation of American Politics* (Chicago: University of Chicago Press, 2016). For the intersection of religion and politics in the Liberty Party, see Douglas M. Strong, *Perfectionist Politics: Abolitionism and the Religious Tensions in American Democracy* (Syracuse, NY: Syracuse University Press, 1999).
2. Lincoln complained to Williamson Durley, an abolitionist and "Liberty man," "If the Whig abolitionists of New York had voted with us last fall, Mr. Clay would now be president." AL to Williamson Durley, October 3,1845, *CW* 1:347.
3. For the Free Soil Party, see Eric Foner, *Free Soil, Free Labor, Free Men: The Ideology of the Republican Party Before the Civil War* (New York: Oxford University Press, 1995); David M. Potter, *The Impending Crisis: 1848–1861,* ed. Don Fehrenbacher (New York: Harper and Row, 1976), 250–53; Michael F. Holt, *The Political Crisis of the 1850s* (New York: W. W. Norton, 1983); Brooks, *Liberty Power,* 129–30, 171–76, 192–95.
4. For the birth of the Republican Party, see William E. Gienapp, *The Origins of the Republican Party 1852–1856* (New York: Oxford University Press, 1987); Lewis L. Gould, *The Republicans: A History of the Grand Old Party* (New York: Oxford University Press, 2003).
5. For nativism, see Tyler G. Anbinder, *Nativism and Slavery: The Northern Know-Nothings and the Politics of the 1850s* (New York: Oxford University Press, 1994).
6. AL to Joshua Speed, August 24, 1855, *CW* 2:323.
7. Ibid.
8. AL, "Speech at Galena, Illinois," *Galena Weekly North-Western Gazette,* July 23, 1856, *CW* 2:353.
9. Ibid., 354.
10. Alexis de Tocqueville, *Democracy in America* (New York: George Dearborn, 1838), 329.
11. Foner, *The Fiery Trial: Abraham Lincoln and American Slavery,* 47–49; Carwardine, *Lincoln,* 20–21; White, *A. Lincoln,* 276.

Chapter 6: The Principled Lincoln: A Definition of Democracy.

1. For the trial, see Jason Emerson, *The Madness of Mary Lincoln* (Carbondale: Southern Illinois University Press, 2007), 44–61. Up until Emerson's book, our under-

standing of the trial of Mary Lincoln was through the correspondence of her son Robert Lincoln. See Mark E. Neely and R. Gerald McMurtry, *The Insanity File: The Case of Mary Lincoln* (Carbondale: Southern Illinois University Press, 1986). For the trial, see also Emerson, *Giant in the Shadows;* Clinton, *Mrs. Lincoln,* 299–303; and Baker, *Mary Todd Lincoln,* 316–25.

2. Robert Lincoln to Mary Harlan, October 16, 1867, quoted in Katherine Helm, *The True Story of Mary, Wife of Lincoln* (New York: Harper, 1928), 267–77; Emerson, *Madness of Mary Lincoln,* 5, 23, 27–28.
3. Emerson discovered these letters at Hildene, the summer home Robert built in Manchester, Vermont, in 1905, *Madness of Mary Lincoln,* 2–3. Emerson balances Robert's motives by probing two theories of the insanity case:

   > (1) she was mentally ill, and her loving son Robert committed her to a sanitarium in 1875 because he felt it was his duty, difficult as it was, to keep her safe from herself as well as from others; or (2) she was the sane victim of a male chauvinist society that sought to shut away her embarrassment to the Lincoln legacy, while the cold-blooded and rapacious Robert was politically and monetarily motivated to incarcerate her against her will. [Ibid., 1. See also Emerson, *Giant of the Shadows,* 162–68.]

4. Emerson, *Madness of Mary Lincoln,* 59.
5. Ibid., 60; Baker, *Mary Todd Lincoln,* 325.
6. Baker, *Mary Todd Lincoln,* 335.
7. Emerson, *Madness of Mary Lincoln,* 71.
8. Ibid., 38–39. Jane M. Friedman, *America's First Woman Lawyer: The Biography of Myra Bradwell* (Buffalo, NY: Prometheus Books, 1993), 18–19.
9. Friedman, *America's First Woman Lawyer,* 29–30.
10. Emerson, *Madness of Mary Lincoln,* 38–39; Clinton, *Mrs. Lincoln: A Life,* 295.
11. For Myra and James Bradwell's strategy in securing Mary Lincoln's release, see Friedman, *America's First Woman Lawyer,* 47–67; Emerson, *Madness of Mary Lincoln,* 100; and Neely and McMurtry, *Insanity File,* 58–68.
12. Friedman, *America's First Woman Lawyer,* 71.
13. AL, "Definition of Democracy," August 1, 1858?, *CW,* 2:532.
14. Historian Philip Paludan researched the use of "democracy" in Lincoln's speeches and writings. See *Lincoln's Legacy: Ethics and Politics,* ed. Philip Paludan (Urbana: University of Illinois Press, 2008), 4. Burlingame, *Abraham Lincoln* v. 1, 255–56.
15. Stephen Douglas, First Joint Debate at Ottawa, August 21, 1858, *The Lincoln-Douglas Debates,* edited and with an introduction by Harold Holzer (New York: HarperCollins, 1993), 56.
16. Ibid., 84.
17. Abraham Lincoln, Reply, Fifth Joint Debate at Galesburg, October 7, 1858; Ibid., 257.
18. I am indebted to Douglas L. Wilson for the insight of Lincoln's use of the negative. His perceptive essay "Lincoln's Rhetoric," *Journal of the Abraham Lincoln Association* 34, no. 1, (Winter 2013): 1–17, reminds us that Lincoln stated many of his

most poignant ideas in the negative; 14. Shakespeare, in *Richard III,* used a triple negative: "I never was nor never will be false," Stanley to Richard III: Act IV, iv, 493.

19. AL, Farewell Address at Springfield, Ill., February 11, 1861, *CW,* 4:190–91.
20. AL to Albert G. Hodges, April 4, 1864, *CWAL,* 7:281.
21. AL, Gettysburg Address, November 19, 1863, *CW,* 7:17–23.

Chapter 7: The Outraged Lincoln: Pro-Slavery Theology

1. For the larger story of pro-slavery thought, see Faust, *Ideology of Slavery.*
2. AL, "A House Divided": Speech at Springfield, Illinois, June 16, 1858, *CW,* 2:461.
3. Ibid.
4. Johannsen, *Stephen A. Douglas,* 456–57; Morris, *Long Pursuit,* 73–74.
5. First Joint Debate, Ottawa, August 21, 1858, and Second Joint Debate, Freeport, August 27, 1858, *The Lincoln-Douglas Debates of 1858,* edited by Robert W. Johannsen (New York: Oxford University Press, 1965), 37–115.
6. Ibid., Third Debate at Jonesboro, September 15, 1858, 118–19.
7. Ibid., Fourth Debate at Charleston, September 18, 1858, 179.
8. James F. Simon, *Lincoln and Chief Justice Taney: Slavery, Secession and the President's War Powers* (New York: Simon & Schuster, 2006), 115–16.
9. First Debate at Ottawa, August 21, 1858, *The Lincoln-Douglas Debates,* ed. Rodney O. Davis and Douglas L. Wilson (Urbana, University of Illinois Press, 2008), 14.
10. White, *A. Lincoln,* 269.
11. Mark A. Noll, *The Civil War as a Theological Crisis* (Chapel Hill: University of North Carolina Press, 2006), 88.
12. Frederick Augustus Ross, "Slavery Ordained of God," *Saturday Review* (London), July 4, 1857.
13. Biographical material on Ross is found in Frederick Augustus Ross, Vertical File, RG 414, Series II, Presbyterian Historical Society, Philadelphia, PA.
14. "Frederik Augustus Ross," *Appleton Cyclopedia of American Biography* (New York: D. Appleton, 1888), Vol. 5, 328.
15. Ross, *Slavery Ordained of God,* 31–32. For the prevalence of this argument from the Bible, see Larry E. Tise, *Proslavery: A History of the Defense of Slavery in America, 1701–1840* (Athens: The University of Georgia Press, 1987), 118, 189.
16. Ross, *Slavery Ordained of God,* 17.
17. Ibid., 43.
18. Herndon and Weik, *Herndon's Lincoln,* 224.
19. White, *Abraham Lincoln,* 169, and Woldman, *Lawyer Lincoln* (New York: Carroll and Graf, 1936), 55.
20. White, *A. Lincoln,* 169.
21. John T. Stuart to J. A. Reed, December 17, 1872, *Scribner's Monthly* 6 (July 1973), 336.
22. William O. Stoddard, *Inside the White House in War Times: Memoirs and Reports of*

Lincoln's Secretary, edited by Michael Burlingame (Lincoln: University of Nebraska Press, 2000), 130.

Part Three: President

1. Catherine Clinton, *Mrs. Lincoln: A Life* (New York: HarperCollins, 2009), 120.
2. Joseph Washington, *They Knew Lincoln,* 157–60.
3. Washington, *They Knew Lincoln,* 110–11.

Chapter 8: The Unity Lincoln: Secession and the Constitution

1. Harold Holzer cites Adams's phrase in *Lincoln President-Elect: Abraham Lincoln and the Great Secession Winter, 1860–1861* (New York: Simon & Schuster, 2008), 1.
2. AL, "Eulogy on Henry Clay," July 16, 1852, *CW* 2:126.
3. Thomas Edwin Schott, *Alexander Stephens of Georgia: A Biography* (Baton Rouge: Louisiana State University Press, 1988), 57–58.
4. AL to William Herndon, February 2, 1848, *CW* 1:448.
5. Schott, *Alexander H. Stephens of Georgia,* 305–06.
6. *The Assertions of a Secessionist: From the Speech of A. H. Stephens,* November 14, 1860 (New York: Loyal Publications Society, 1861), 2; Holzer, *Lincoln President-Elect,* 138.
7. Schott, *Alexander H. Stephens of Georgia,* 305–06; Michael P. Johnson, *Toward a Patriarchal Republic: The Secession of Georgia* (Baton Rouge: Louisiana State University Press, 1977), 18.
8. William C. Davis, *Look Away: A History of the Confederate States of America* (New York: Free Press, 2002), 37.
9. AL to Alexander H. Stephens, November 30, 1860, *CW* 4:146.
10. AL to Alexander H. Stephens, December 22, 1860, *CW* 4:160.
11. Ibid.
12. Alexander H. Stephens to AL, December 30, 1860, *CW* 4:160–61, note 1. For the correspondence between Stephens and Lincoln, see Alexander Stephens, *A Constitutional View of the Late War Between the States: Its Causes, Character, Conduct, and Results, Presented in a Series of Colloquies at Liberty Hall,* 2 vols. (Philadelphia: National Publishing, 1868–70), vol. 2, 266–70. Lincoln would have known the wording of the verse from Proverbs 25:11 from the King James Version of the Bible, used by Protestants in the nineteenth century.
13. AL, "Speech in Independence Hall," February 22, 1861, *CW* 4:240.
14. On March 21, 1861, Stephens presented the justification for the Confederacy seceding from the United States in a speech at the Athanaeum in Savannah, Georgia. He declared that disagreements over the enslavement of African Americans were the "immediate cause" of secession. In what became known as his Cornerstone Speech, he stated, "Our new government's foundations are laid, its cornerstone rests, upon the great truth that the negro is not equal to the white man." Schott, *Alexander H. Stephens of Georgia,* 334.

Chapter 9: The Kentuckian Lincoln: An Undelivered Speech to the South

1. Inaugurations took place on March 4 until the second inauguration of Franklin D. Roosevelt, when the date was moved to January 20. For Lincoln and the thirteen-day trip, see Ted Widmer, *Lincoln on the Verge: Thirteen Days to Washington* (New York: Simon & Schuster, 2020); Victor Searcher, *Lincoln's Journey to Greatness: A Factual Account of the Twelve-Day Inaugural Trip* (Philadelphia: John C. Winston, 1960); and Ronald C. White, *The Eloquent President: A Portrait of Lincoln Through His Words* (New York: Random House, 2005), 23–61. Widmer cites the undelivered Kentucky speech in one paragraph, 149. Holzer is the only Lincoln author who gives attention to the speech, *Lincoln President-Elect,* 313–16.
2. William H. Seward to AL, December 29, 1860, *CW* 4:170, note 1.
3. AL, "Speech from the Balcony of the Bates House in Indianapolis, Indiana," February 11, 1860, *CW* 4:195; Ecclesiastes 3:7 [King James Version]; Widmer, *Lincoln on the Verge,* 133–35; Searcher, *Lincoln's Journey to Greatness,* 50–51.
4. Holzer, *Lincoln President-Elect,* 184–86; White, *The Eloquent President,* 8–9.
5. William H. Townsend, *Lincoln and the Blue Grass: Slavery and the Civil War in Kentucky* (Lexington: University of Kentucky Press, 1955), 273–74.
6. Henry Clay, "Speech at Lexington , KY, November 13, 1847," *The Papers of Henry Clay,* ed. Melba Porter Hay (Lexington: University Press of Kentucky, 1991), 10:361–64; Robert V. Remini, *Henry Clay: Statesman for the Union* (New York: W. W. Norton, 1991), 692–93.
7. AL to Orville Browning, September 22, 1861, *CW* 4:532.
8. Berry Craig, *Kentucky Confederates: Secession, Civil War, and the Jackson Purchase* (Lexington: University Press of Kentucky, 2014), 1–10.
9. The study of the press in the South has focused more on Virginia and South Carolina. For a study of Kentucky, see Berry Craig, *Kentucky's Rebel Press: Pro-Confederate Media and the Secession Crisis* (Lexington: University Press of Kentucky, 2018).
10. *Kentucky Statesman* (Lexington), November 9, 1860; Berry, *Kentucky's Rebel Press,* 51–52.
11. *Louisville Daily Courier,* November 10, 1860.
12. *Covington (Kentucky) Journal,* November 10, 1860.
13. AL, "Speech at Cincinnati, Ohio," February 12, 1861, *CW* 4:199; Widmer, *Lincoln on the Verge,* 150–51, 161–65.
14. AL, "Reply to Oliver P. Morton at Indianapolis, Indiana," February 11, 1861, *CW* 4:194.
15. AL, "First Inaugural Address," March 4, 1861, *CW* 4:271.

Chapter 10: The Theological Lincoln: A Meditation on the Divine Will

1. AL, "Meditation on the Divine Will," [Sept 2, 1862?], *CW* 5:404, note 1.
2. Ulysses S. Grant, *Personal Memoirs* (New York: Charles L. Webster, 1885), 1:394–95.

3. *At Lincoln's Side: John Hay's Civil War Correspondence and Selected Writings,* ed. Michael Burlingame (Carbondale: Southern Illinois University Press, 2000), 127.
4. Nicolay and Hay, *Abraham Lincoln,* 6:341–42.
5. AL, "Meditation on the Divine Will," *CWAL* 8:52–53.
6. AL, "Meditation on the Divine Will," *CW* 5:403–4, note 1.
7. Douglas L. Wilson, *Lincoln's Sword: The Presidency and the Power of Words* (New York: Alfred A. Knopf, 2007), 255–56, 329–30.
8. On fatalism and the doctrine of necessity, see Donald, *Lincoln,* 15, 114, 514–15. For a contrary view, see Ronald C. White, Jr., *Lincoln's Greatest Speech: The Second Inaugural* (New York: Simon & Schuster, 2002), 133–38, 148–49.
9. Francis Wharton, *A Treatise on Theism, and on the Modern Skeptical Theories* (Philadelphia: J. B. Lippincott, 1859), 147, 152; White, *Lincoln's Greatest Speech,* 146.
10. Carwardine, *Lincoln,* 36–38; Burlingame, *Abraham Lincoln,* vol. 1, 359; White, *A. Lincoln,* 180–82.
11. White, *Lincoln's Greatest Speech,* 128.
12. On Gurley, see Ronald C. White, Jr., "Abraham Lincoln's Minister: Phineas Densmore Gurley," in *Capital Witness: A History of the New York Avenue Presbyterian Church in Washington, D.C.,* ed. Dewey D. Wallace, Jr., Wilson Golden, and Edith Holmes Snyder (Franklin, TN: Plumbline Media, 2011), 112–32; John A. O'Brien, "Seeking God's Will: President Lincoln and Rev. Dr. Gurley," *Journal of the Abraham Lincoln Association* 39, no. 2 (Summer 2018): 29–54; and White, *Lincoln's Greatest Speech,* 131–33, 138–40.
13. White, *Lincoln's Greatest Speech,* 154–55; Phineas D. Gurley, "Congress Versus the Constitution," *Southern Review,* July 1868, 72; David Ranking Barbee, "President Lincoln and Doctor Gurley," *Abraham Lincoln Quarterly* 5, no. 1 (March 1948): 5.
14. AL, "Second Inaugural Address," March 4, 1865, *CW* 8:333.
15. Phineas D. Gurley, "Funeral Address on the Occasion of the Death of William Wallace Lincoln" (Washington, D.C., 1862), 3–4; White, *A. Lincoln,* 476–77.
16. AL, "Fragment on Pro-Slavery Theology," October 1, 1858?, *CW* 3:204.
17. For Lincoln's struggles as commander in chief, see James M. McPherson, *Tried by War: Abraham Lincoln as Commander in Chief* (New York: Penguin, 2008), 117–20.
18. Frederick Douglass, *Autobiographies* (1893; reprint, New York: Library of America, 1994), 801; David W. Blight, *Frederick Douglass: Prophet of Freedom* (New York: Simon & Schuster, 2018), 458–60; White, *Lincoln's Greatest Speech,* 184.
19. *New York Times,* March 6, 1865.
20. AL to Thurlow Weed, March 15, 1865, *CW* 8:356.

Select Bibliography

Books, Dissertations, Diaries, Letters

Adams, John Quincy. *Memoirs of John Quincy Adams, Comprising Portions of His Diary from 1795 to 1848*. Vol. 11., edited by Charles Francis Adams. Philadelphia: J. B. Lippincott, 1876.

Adamson, Jeremy Elwell. *NIAGARA*. Washington, D.C.: Corcoran Gallery of Art, 1985.

Anbinder, Tyler G. *Nativism and Slavery: The Northern Know Nothings and the Politics of the 1850s*. New York: Oxford University Press, 1992.

Arnold, Isaac N. *The Life of Abraham Lincoln*. Chicago: Jansen, McClurg, 1885.

Aubrey, Allan. *The Lincoln Fragments: The Thought Behind the Timeless Words*. MA thesis, Ashland University, 2016.

Baker, Jean. *Mary Todd Lincoln: A Biography*. New York: W. W. Norton, 1987.

Barnes, Albert. *Church and Slavery*. Philadelphia: Parry & McMillan, 1857.

Beveridge, Albert J. *Abraham Lincoln, 1809–1858*. Vol. 1. Boston: Houghton Mifflin, 1928.

Blight, David W. *Frederick Douglass: Prophet of Freedom*. New York: Simon & Schuster, 2018.

Blumenthal, Sidney. *The Political Life of Abraham Lincoln*. 3 vols. New York: Simon & Schuster, 2016–19.

Brooks, Corey M. *Liberty Power: Antislavery Third Parties and the Transformation of American Politics*. Chicago: University of Chicago Press, 2016.

Burlingame, Michael. *Abraham Lincoln: A Life*. 2 vols. Baltimore, MD: Johns Hopkins University Press, 2008.

———. *Abraham Lincoln: The Observations of John G. Nicolay and John Hay*. Carbondale: Southern Illinois University Press, 2007.

———. *The Inner World of Abraham Lincoln*. Urbana: University of Illinois Press, 1994.

Carwardine, Richard. *Lincoln: A Life of Purpose and Power*. New York: Alfred A. Knopf, 2006.

———. *Lincoln's Sense of Humor.* Carbondale: Southern Illinois University Press, 2017.

Chambers, Robert. *Vestiges of the Natural History of Creation.* 2nd ed. New York: Wiley and Putnam, 1845.

Clinton, Catherine. *Mrs. Lincoln: A Life.* New York: Harper, 2009.

Cole, Arthur Charles. "Lincoln's 'House Divided' Speech: Did It Reflect a Doctrine of Class Struggle?" An Address Delivered Before the Chicago Historical Society on March 15, 1923. Chicago: University of Chicago Press, 1923.

Complete Works of Abraham Lincoln, edited by John G. Nicolay and John Hay. 12 vols. New York: Francis D. Tandy, 1905.

Craig, Berry. *Kentucky Confederates: Secession, Civil War, and the Jackson Purchase.* Lexington: University Press of Kentucky, 2014.

———. *Kentucky's Rebel Press: Pro-Confederate Media and the Secession Crisis.* Lexington: University Press of Kentucky, 2018.

Current, Richard N. *The Lincoln Nobody Knows.* New York: McGraw Hill, 1958.

Davis, William C. *Look Away: A History of the Confederate States of America.* New York: Free Press, 2002.

Dickens, Charles. *American Notes for General Circulation.* New York: Harper & Brothers, 1842.

Dirck, Brian R. *Lincoln the Lawyer.* Urbana: University of Illinois Press, 2007.

Donald, David Herbert. *Lincoln.* New York: Simon & Schuster, 1995.

———. *Lincoln's Herndon: A Biography.* New York: Alfred A. Knopf, 1948. Reprint, Da Capo Press, 1989.

———. *"We Are Lincoln Men": Abraham Lincoln and His Friends.* New York: Simon & Schuster, 2003.

Duff, John J. *A. Lincoln: Prairie Lawyer.* New York: Rinehart, 1960.

Emerson, Jason. *Giant in the Shadows: The Life of Robert T. Lincoln.* Carbondale: Southern Illinois University Press, 2012.

———. *The Madness of Mary Lincoln.* Carbondale: Southern Illinois University Press, 2007.

Etcheson, Nicole. *Bleeding Kansas: Contested Liberty in the Civil War Era.* Lawrence: University Press of Kansas, 2004.

Faust, Drew Gilpin, ed. *The Ideology of Slavery: Proslavery Thought in the Antebellum South, 1830–1860.* Baton Rouge: Louisiana State University Press, 1981.

Fehrenbacher, Don E. *The Dred Scott Case: Its Significance in American Law and Politics.* New York: Oxford University Press, 1978.

———. *Prelude to Greatness: Lincoln in the 1850s.* Stanford, CA: Stanford University Press, 1962.

Ferguson, Robert A. *Law and Letters in American Culture.* Cambridge, MA: Harvard University Press, 1984.

Fitzhugh, George. *Sociology for the South, or The Failure of Free Society.* Richmond, VA: A. Morris, 1854.

Foner, Eric. *The Fiery Trial: Abraham Lincoln and American Slavery.* New York: W. W. Norton, 2010.

———. *Free Soil, Free Labor, Free Men: The Ideology of the Republican Party Before the Civil War.* New York: Oxford University Press, 1970.

Forbes, Robert Pierce. *The Missouri Compromise and Its Aftermath: Slavery and the Meaning of America*. Chapel Hill: University of North Carolina Press, 2007.

Fraker, Guy C., *Looking for Lincoln in Illinois: A Guide to Lincoln's Eighth Judicial Circuit*. Carbondale, Southern Illinois University Press, 2017.

———, *Lincoln's Ladder to the Presidency: The Eighth Judicilal Circuit*. Carbondale, Southern Illinois University Press, 2012.

Frank, John P. *Lincoln as a Lawyer.* Urbana: University of Illinois Press, 1961.

Friedman, Jane M. *America's First Woman Lawyer: The Biography of Myra Bradwell*. Buffalo, NY: Prometheus Books, 1993.

Frothingham, Paul Revere. *Edward Everett: Orator and Statesman*. Port Washington, NY: Kennikat Press, 1925.

Gienapp, William E. *The Origins of the Republican Party 1852–1856*. New York: Oxford University Press, 1987.

Gould, Lewis L. *The Republicans: A History of the Grand Old Party.* New York: Random House, 2003.

Grant, Ulysses S. *Personal Memoirs*. 2 vols. New York: Charles L. Webster, 1885.

Gromosiak, Paul, and Christopher Stoianoff. *Images of America: Niagara Falls 1850–2000*. Charleston, SC: Arcadia Publishing, 2012.

Guelzo, Allen C. *Abraham Lincoln: Redeemer President*. Grand Rapids, MI: William B. Eerdmans, 1999.

———. *Lincoln and Douglas: The Debates That Defined America*. New York: Simon & Schuster, 2008.

Gurley, Phineas D. "Funeral Address on the Occasion of the Death of William Wallace Lincoln." Washington, D.C.: n.p., 1862.

Hay, John. *At Lincoln's Side: John Hay's Civil War Correspondence and Selected Writings*. Edited by Michael Burlingame. Carbondale: Southern Illinois University Press, 2000.

Helm, Katherine. *The True Story of Mary, Wife of Lincoln*. New York: Harper, 1928.

Herndon, William H. *Herndon's Informants: Letters, Interviews, and Statements About Abraham Lincoln*. Edited by Douglas L. Wilson and Rodney O. Davis. Urbana: University of Illinois Press, 1998.

Herndon, William H., and Jesse W. Weik. *Herndon's Lincoln*. Edited by Douglas L. Wilson and Rodney O. Davis. Urbana: University of Illinois Press, 2006.

———. *Herndon's Lincoln: The True Story of a Great Life*. 3 vols. New York: Belford, Clarke, 1889.

Hertz, Emanuel. *The Hidden Lincoln: From the Letters and Papers of William H. Herndon*. New York: Viking, 1938.

Holt, Michael F. *The Political Crisis of the 1850s*. New York: W. W. Norton, 1983.

———. *The Rise and Fall of the American Whig Party: Jacksonian Politics and the Onset of the Civil War.* New York: Oxford University Press, 1999.

Holzer, Harold. *Lincoln President-Elect: Abraham Lincoln and the Great Secession Winter 1860–1861*. New York: Simon & Schuster, 2008.

Howe, Daniel Walker. *Making the American Self: Jonathan Edwards to Abraham Lincoln*. Cambridge, MA: Harvard University Press, 1997.

———. *The Political Culture of the American Whigs*. Chicago: University of Chicago Press, 1979.

———. *What Hath God Wrought: The Transformation of America 1815–1848*. New York: Oxford University Press, 2007.

Howells, William Dean, Mark Twain, Nathaniel Shaler, et al. *The Niagara Book*. New York: Doubleday, 1893.

Hurst, James Willard. *The Growth of American Law: The Law Makers*. Boston: Little, Brown, 1950.

Irwin, William R. *The New Niagara: Tourism, Technology, and the Landscape of Niagara Falls, 1776–1917*. University Park: Pennsylvania State University Press, 1996.

Jaffa, Harry F. *Crisis of the House Divided: An Interpretation of the Lincoln-Douglas Debates*. Chicago: University of Chicago Press, 1959, 1982.

Johannsen, Robert W. *Stephen A. Douglas*. Urbana: University of Illinois Press, 1973.

Johnson, Michael P. *Toward a Patriarchal Republic: The Secession of Georgia*. Baton Rouge: Louisiana State University Press, 1977.

Kaplan, Fred. *Lincoln: The Biography of a Writer*. New York: HarperCollins, 2008.

King, Willard L. *Lincoln's Manager: David Davis*. Cambridge, MA: Harvard University Press, 1960.

Klement, Frank L. *The Limits of Dissent: Clement L. Vallandigham and the Civil War*. Lexington: University of Kentucky Press, 1970.

Lehrman, Lewis E. *Lincoln at Peoria: The Turning Point*. Mechanicsburg, PA: Stackpole Books, 2008.

Lincoln, Abraham. *Complete Works of Abraham Lincoln*. Edited by John G. Nicolay and John Hay. 12 vols. New York: Francis D. Tandy, 1905.

———. *Lincoln's Legacy: Ethics and Politics*. Edited by Philip Paludan. Urbana: University of Illinois Press, 2008.

Lincoln, Abraham, and Stephen A. Douglas. *The Lincoln-Douglas Debates*. Edited and with an introduction by Harold Holzer. New York: HarperCollins Publishers, 1993.

———. *The Lincoln-Douglas Debates*. Edited by Rodney O. Davis and Douglas L. Wilson. Urbana: University of Illinois Press, 2008.

The Lincoln-Douglas Debates of 1858. Edited by Robert W. Johannsen. New York: Oxford University Press, 1965.

Marvel, William. *Lincoln's Autocrat: The Life of Edwin Stanton*. Chapel Hill: University of North Carolina Press, 2015.

McPherson, James M. *Tried by War: Abraham Lincoln as Commander in Chief*. New York: Penguin, 2008.

Mearns, David C. *The Lincoln Papers: The Story of the Collection, with Selections to July 4, 1861*. Vol. 1. Garden City, NY: Doubleday, 1948.

Morris, Roy, Jr. *The Long Pursuit: Abraham Lincoln's Thirty-Year Struggle with Stephen Douglas for the Heart and Soul of America*. New York: HarperCollins, 2008.

Neely, Mark E., and R. Gerald McMurtry. *The Insanity File: The Case of Mary Lincoln*. Carbondale: Southern Illinois University Press, 1986.

Nicolay, John G., and John Hay. *Abraham Lincoln: A History*. 10 vols. New York: Century Co., 1890.

Noll, Mark A. *The Civil War as a Theological Crisis*. Chapel Hill: University of North Carolina Press, 2006.

Papers of Abraham Lincoln: Legal Documents and Cases. Edited by Daniel W. Stowell. 4 vols. Charlottesville: University of Virginia Press, 2008.

Phillips, David. *The Day Niagara Falls Ran Dry*. Toronto: Key Porter, 1993.

Potter, David M. *The Impending Crisis: 1848–1861*. Edited by Don E. Fehrenbacher. New York: Harper & Row, 1976.

Rable, George C. *The Confederate Republic: A Revolution Against Politics*. Chapel Hill: University of North Carolina Press, 1994.

Religion and the American Civil War. Edited by Randall M. Miller, Harry S. Stout, and Charles Reagan Wilson. New York: Oxford University Press, 1998.

Remini, Robert V. *At the Edge of the Precipice: Henry Clay and the Compromise That Saved the Union*. New York: Basic Books, 2010.

———. *Henry Clay: Statesman for the Union*. New York: W. W. Norton, 1991.

Revie, Linda L. *The Niagara Companion: Explorers, Artists, and Writers at the Falls, from Discovery Through the Twentieth Century*. Waterloo, Ontario: Wilfrid Laurier University Press, 2003.

Ross, Frederick Augustus. *Slavery Ordained of God*. Philadelphia: J. B. Lippincott, 1857.

Schott, Thomas Edwin. *Alexander H. Stephens of Georgia: A Biography*. Baton Rouge: Louisiana State University Press, 1988.

Searcher, Victor. *Lincoln's Journey to Greatness: A Factual Account of the Twelve-Day Inaugural Trip*. Philadelphia: John C. Winston, 1960.

Sears, John F. *Sacred Places: American Tourist Attractions in the Nineteenth Century*. New York: Oxford University Press, 1989.

Simon, James F. *Lincoln and Chief Justice Taney: Slavery, Secession, and the President's War Powers*. New York: Simon & Schuster, 2007.

Simon, Paul. *Freedom's Champion: Elijah Lovejoy*. Carbondale: Southern Illinois University Press, 1994.

Smith, James. *The Christian's Defence*. Cincinnati: J. A. James, 1843.

Souvenir of Niagara. Buffalo, NY: Sage Publishers, 1864.

Spiegel, Allen D. *A. Lincoln, Esquire: A Shrewd, Sophisticated Lawyer in His Time*. Macon, GA: Mercer University Press, 2002.

Stahr, Walter. *Seward: Lincoln's Indispensable Man*. New York: Simon & Schuster, 2012.

———. *Stanton: Lincoln's War Secretary*. New York: Simon & Schuster, 2017.

Steele, Oliver G. *Steele's Book of Niagara Falls*. 10th ed. Buffalo, NY: Oliver G. Steele, 1847.

Steiner, Mark E. *An Honest Calling: The Law Practice of Abraham Lincoln*. DeKalb: Northern Illinois University Press, 2006.

Stephens, Alexander H. *A Constitutional View of the Late War Between the States: Its Causes, Character, Conduct and Results, Presented in a Series of Colloquies at Liberty Hall*. 2 vols. Philadelphia: National Publishing Company, 1868–70.

Stoddard, William O. *Inside the White House in War Times: Memoirs and Reports of Lincoln's Secretary*. Edited by Michael Burlingame. Lincoln: University of Nebraska Press, 2000.

Strong, Douglas M. *Perfectionist Politics: Abolitionism and the Religious Tensions of American Democracy*. Syracuse, NY: Syracuse University Press, 1999.

Tackach, James. *Lincoln and the Natural Environment*. Carbondale: Southern Illinois University Press, 2019.

The Assertions of a Secessionist: From the Speech of A. H. Stephens of Georgia (November 14, 1860). New York: Loyal Publications Society, 1864.

Thomas, Benjamin P. *Abraham Lincoln: A Biography*. New York: Alfred A. Knopf, 1952.

Tise, Larry E. *Proslavery: A History of the Defense of Slavery in America, 1701–1840*. Athens: University of Georgia Press, 1987.

Tocqueville, Alexis de. *Democracy in America*. New York: George Dearborn & Co., 1838.

Townsend, William H. *Lincoln and the Bluegrass: Slavery and Civil War in Kentucky*. Lexington: University of Kentucky Press, 1955.

Van Deusen, Glyndon G. *William Henry Seward*. New York: Oxford University Press, 1967.

Washington, Joseph. *They Knew Lincoln*. With a new introduction by Kate Masur. New York: Oxford University Press, 2018. First published by E. P. Dutton, 1942.

Waugh, John C. *On the Brink of Civil War: The Compromise of 1850 and How It Changed the Course of American History*. New York: Rowman and Littlefield, 2003.

Weber, Jennifer L. *Copperheads: The Rise and Fall of Lincoln's Opponents in the North*. New York: Oxford University Press, 2006.

Weed, G. Morton. *School Days of Yesterday: Buffalo Public School History*. Buffalo, NY: Buffalo Board of Education, 2001.

Wharton, Francis. *A Treatise on Theism, and on the Modern Skeptical Theories*. Philadelphia: J. B. Lippincott, 1859.

White, Ronald C. *A. Lincoln: A Biography*. New York: Random House, 2009.

———. *The Eloquent President: A Portrait of Lincoln Through His Words*. New York: Random House, 2005.

———. *Lincoln's Greatest Speech: The Second Inaugural*. New York: Simon & Schuster, 2002.

Widmer, Ted. *Lincoln on the Verge: Thirteen Days to Washington*. New York: Simon & Schuster, 2020.

Wilentz, Sean. *The Rise of American Democracy: Jefferson to Lincoln*. New York: W. W. Norton, 2005.

Wilson, Douglas L. *Honor's Voice: The Transformation of Abraham Lincoln*. New York: Alfred A. Knopf, 1998.

———. *Lincoln's Sword: The Presidency and the Power of Words.* New York: Alfred A. Knopf, 2006.

Winkle, Kenneth J. *The Young Eagle: The Rise of Abraham Lincoln.* Dallas: Taylor Trade Publishing, 2001.

Wish, Harvey. *George Fitzhugh: Conservative of the Old South.* Southern Sketches 11. Charlottesville, VA: Green Bookman, 1938.

———. *George Fitzhugh: Propagandist of the Old South.* Baton Rouge: Louisiana State University Press, 1943.

Woldman, Albert A. Boston: Houghton Mifflin, 1936.

Zeitz, Joshua. *Lincoln's Boys: John Hay, John G. Nicolay, and the War for Lincoln's Image.* New York: Viking, 2014.

Essays, Journal Articles, and Chapters in Books

Barbee, David Ranking. "President Lincoln and Doctor Gurley." *Abraham Lincoln Quarterly* 5, no. 1 (March 1948): 5.

"The Divine Ordinance of Slavery" (review of Frederick Augustus Ross, *Slavery Ordained of God*). *Saturday Review* (London), July 4, 1857.

Guelzo, Allen C. "Apple of Gold in a Picture of Silver: The Constitution and Liberty." In *The Lincoln Enigma: The Changing Faces of an American Icon,* edited by Gabor Boritt, 86–107. New York: Oxford University Press, 2002.

Hawthorne, Nathaniel. "My Visit to Niagara." In *The Centenary Edition of the Works of Nathaniel Hawthorne,* 2:281–83. Columbus: Ohio State University Press, 1974.

O'Brien, John A. "Seeking God's Will: President Lincoln and Rev. Dr. Gurley." *Journal of the Abraham Lincoln Association* 39, no. 2 (Summer 2018): 29–54.

Parkinson, Robert Henry. "The Patent Case That Lifted Lincoln into a Presidential Candidate." *Abraham Lincoln Quarterly* 4, no. 3 (September 1946): 105–22.

White, Ronald C., Jr. "Abraham Lincoln's Minister: Phineas Densmore Gurley." In *Capital Witness: A History of the New York Avenue Presbyterian Church in Washington, D.C.,* edited by Dewey D. Wallace, Jr., Wilson Golden, and Edith Holmes Snyder, 112–26. Franklin, TN: Plumbline Media, 2011.

Wilson, Douglas L. "Lincoln's Rhetoric." *Journal of the Abraham Lincoln Association* 34, no. 1 (Winter 2013): 1–17.

———. "The Power of the Negative." *Wall Street Journal,* January 16, 2013.

Wilson, James F. "Some Memories of Lincoln." *North American Review* 163 (December 1896): 670–71.

Illustration Credits

Grateful acknowledgment is made to the following for permission to reprint photos and illustrations.

Prologue

xvi Lincoln and his secretaries, photograph by Alexander Gardner, 1863: LIBRARY OF CONGRESS, PRINTS AND PHOTOGRAPHS DIVISION, WASHINGTON, D.C.

Part One: Lawyer

4 Springfield, Illinois: LIBRARY OF CONGRESS, PRINTS AND PHOTOGRAPHS DIVISION, WASHINGTON, D.C.

5 Mary Lincoln, photograph by Nicholas H. Shepherd, 1846 or 1847: LIBRARY OF CONGRESS, PRINTS AND PHOTOGRAPHS DIVISION, WASHINGTON, D.C.

Chapter 1: The Lyrical Lincoln: The Transcendence of Niagara Falls

6 Abraham Lincoln, photograph by Nicholas H. Shepherd, 1846 or 1847: LIBRARY OF CONGRESS, PRINTS AND PHOTOGRAPHS DIVISION, WASHINGTON, D.C.

12 *Nathaniel Hawthorne,* painting by Charles Osgood, 1840: PEABODY ESSEX MUSEUM, SALEM, MASSACHUSETTS

13 *Charles Dickens,* painting by Francis Alexander, 1842: MUSEUM OF FINE ARTS, BOSTON, MASSACHUSETTS

14 John Bunyan, *Pilgrim's Progress:* HERITAGE AUCTION, DALLAS, TEXAS

15 *A General View of the Falls of Niagara,* painting by Alvan Fisher, 1820: SMITHSONIAN AMERICAN ART MUSEUM, WASHINGTON, D.C.

18 Robert Chambers: COURTESY OF THE NATIONAL LIBRARY OF SCOTLAND

Chapter 2: The Humble Lincoln: A Lawyer's Vocation

22 Lincoln and Herndon advertisement: *Illinois State Journal* (Springfield), November 27, 1858

22 Lincoln and Herndon law offices: *Frank Leslie's Illustrated,* December 1860

27 John Todd Stuart: Library of Congress, Prints and Photographs Division, Washington, D.C.

29 Abraham Lincoln's "spot" resolutions notes: National Archives and Records Administration, Legislative Records, RG 233

30 Carpetbag: Abraham Lincoln Presidential Library, Springfield, Illinois

32 Woodward County Courthouse, Metamora, Illinois: courthousehistory.com; courtesy of Keith Vincent

33 David Davis (1855–65): Brady-Handy Photographic Collection, Library of Congress, Prints and Photographs Division, Washington, D.C.

35 William H. Herndon, photograph by L. C. Handy, probably 1870s: Library of Congress, Prints and Photographs Division, Washington, D.C.

38 Stephen Trigg Logan: Abraham Lincoln Presidential Library, Springfield, Illinois

Chapter 3: The Fiery Lincoln: Slavery and a Reentry to Politics

46 Abraham Lincoln, photograph by Johan Polycarpus von Schneidau, 1854: Library of Congress, Prints and Photographs Division, Washington, D.C.

49 State Capitol, Springfield, Illinois, 1858: Abraham Lincoln Presidential Library, Springfield, Illinois

50 "Am I not a man and a brother": Library of Congress, Prints and Photographs Division, Washington, D.C.

54 America, illustration by Edward Williams Clay, 1841: Library of Congress, Prints and Photographs Division, Washington, D.C.

55 Slave auction, New Orleans, Louisiana: Library of Congress, Prints and Photographs Division, Washington, D.C.

56 George Fitzhugh, circa 1855: Library of Congress, Prints and Photographs Division, Washington, D.C.

Chapter 4: The Defeated Lincoln: Failure and Ambition

60 Abraham Lincoln, photograph by Alexander Hessler, February 28, 1857: Library of Congress, Prints and Photographs Division, Washington, D.C.

62 Stephen Arnold Douglas, photograph by Mathew Brady, 1850–52: Library of Congress, Prints and Photographs Division, Washington, D.C.

63 Vandalia State House: Vandalia Historical Society, Vandalia, Illinois

67 James Shields: Library of Congress, Prints and Photograph Division, Washington, D.C.
69 Lyman Trumbull, photograph by Mathew Brady: James Wadsworth Family Papers, Library of Congress, Prints and Photographs Division, Washington, D.C.
71 Edwin M. Stanton: Library of Congress, Prints and Photographs Division, Washington, D.C.

Chapter 5: The Republican Lincoln: The Birth of a Party

76 Abraham Lincoln, photograph by Amos T. Joslin, May 27, 1857: Library of Congress, Prints and Photographs Division, Washington, D.C.
81 "Uncle Sam's Youngest Son, Citizen Know Nothing," 1855: Library of Congress, Prints and Photographs Division, Washington, D.C.
83 Musical Fund Hall, Republican Convention, announcement of nominations, 1856: Free Library of Philadelphia, Philadelphia, Pennsylvania
84 John C. Frémont and William Dayton campaign, from photograph by Marcus Root: Library of Congress, Prints and Photographs Division, Washington, D.C.
85 Cartoon, "The Great Republican Reform Party," by Nathaniel Currier, 1856: Library of Congress, Prints and Photographs Division, Washington, D.C.
88 *Alexis de Tocqueville,* portrait by Théodore Chassériau, 1850: Yale Collection of American Literature, Beinecke Rare Book and Manuscript Library, Yale University, New Haven, Connecticut

Chapter 6: The Principled Lincoln: A Definition of Democracy

92 Abraham Lincoln, photograph by Alfred M. Byers, May 7, 1858: Archives & Special Collections of the University of Nebraska–Lincoln, Lincoln, Nebraska
94 Mary Lincoln in mourning attire, photograph by Joseph Ward, 1865–82: Library of Congress, Prints and Photographs Division, Washington, D.C.
95 "The Old Clothes Scandal": *Harper's Weekly,* October 26, 1867
96 Robert Todd Lincoln (1870–80): Brady-Handy Photograph Collection, Library of Congress, Prints and Photographs Division, Washington, D.C.
97 "Trial of Mrs. Abraham Lincoln for Insanity," *Chicago Daily Tribune:* Chronicling America: Historic American Newspapers, Library of Congress, Washington, D.C.
98 Bellevue Place sanatorium, Batavia, Illinois: Abraham Lincoln Presidential Library, Springfield, Illinois
99 Bellevue Place register: Frazier Museum, Louisville, Kentucky
100 Myra Bradwell: Library of Congress, Prints and Photographs Division, Washington, D.C.

Chapter 7: The Outraged Lincoln: Pro-Slavery Theology

104 Abraham Lincoln, photograph by Samuel G. Alschuler, May 25, 1858: LIBRARY OF CONGRESS, PRINTS AND PHOTOGRAPHS DIVISION, WASHINGTON, D.C.

110 Frederick Augustus Ross: LIBRARY OF CONGRESS, NEWSPAPER MICROFILM DIVISION, WASHINGTON, D.C.

112 Newspaper mastheads: *Daily National Intelligencer, National Anti-Slavery Standard, The National Era, Richmond Enquirer, Charleston Mercury:* KAREN NEEDLES, LINCOLN ARCHIVES DIGITAL PROJECT COLLECTION, COLLEGE PARK, MARYLAND

116 "Slavery as It Exists in America," illustration by John Haven, 1850: LIBRARY OF CONGRESS, PRINTS AND PHOTOGRAPHS DIVISION, WASHINGTON, D.C.

Chapter 8: The Unity Lincoln: Secession and the Constitution

122 Abraham Lincoln, photograph by Samuel G. Altschuler, November 25, 1860: LIBRARY OF CONGRESS, PRINTS AND PHOTOGRAPHS DIVISION, WASHINGTON, D.C.

125 Lincoln's transition office: *Frank Leslie's Illustrated,* NOVEMBER 24, 1860

127 Alexander Stephens, 1865–80: LIBRARY OF CONGRESS, PRINTS AND PHOTOGRAPHS DIVISION, WASHINGTON, D.C.

129 *Declaration of Independence,* painting by John Trumbull, 1817: YALE UNIVERSITY ART GALLERY, NEW HAVEN, CONNECTICUT

Chapter 9: The Kentuckian Lincoln: An Undelivered Speech to the South

134 Abraham Lincoln, photograph by Christopher S. German, February 9, 1861: LIBRARY OF CONGRESS, PRINTS AND PHOTOGRAPHS DIVISION, WASHINGTON, D.C.

139 Time card for special train, Monday February 11, 1861: THE ALFRED WHITAL STERN COLLECTION OF LINCOLNIANA, RARE BOOK ROOM, LIBRARY OF CONGRESS, WASHINGTON, D.C.

141 *The Boyhood of Lincoln,* painting by Eastman Johnson, 1868: LIBRARY OF CONGRESS, PRINTS AND PHOTOGRAPHS DIVISION, WASHINGTON, D.C.

144 Burnet House, Cincinnati, Ohio, by Adolphus Forbriger, lithographer, between 1850 and 1860: LIBRARY OF CONGRESS, PRINTS AND PHOTOGRAPHS DIVISION, WASHINGTON, D.C.

Chapter 10: The Theological Lincoln: A Meditation on the Divine Will

148 Abraham Lincoln, photograph by Mathew Brady, May 16, 1861: LIBRARY OF CONGRESS, PRINTS AND PHOTOGRAPHS DIVISION, WASHINGTON, D.C.

155 New York Avenue Presbyterian Church, Washington, D.C., photograph by

Titian Ramsay Peale: New York Avenue Presbyterian Church Archives, Washington, D.C.

156 Phineas Densmore Gurley: Presbyterian Historical Society, Philadelphia, Pennsylvania

158 Abraham Lincoln delivering his second inaugural address, March 4, 1865, Washington, D.C., photograph by Alexander Gardner: Library of Congress, Prints and Photographs Division, Washington, D.C.

Photo Insert: Images of Fragments and Notes

1–2 Chapter 1: Fragment on Niagara Falls (September 25–30, 1848): Library of Congress, Prints and Photographs Division, Washington, D.C.

3 Chapter 2: Fragment: Notes for a Law Lecture (July 1, 1850?): Library of Congress, Prints and Photographs Division, Washington, D.C.

4 Chapter 3: Fragment on Slavery (July 1, 1854?): Courtesy of Harlan Crow Library, Dallas, Texas

5 Chapter 3: Fragment on Slavery and American Government (1857–58): Courtesy of The Gilder Lehrman Institute of American History, New York, New York (GLC03251)

6 Chapter 4: Fragment on Stephen A. Douglas (December 1856?): Abraham Lincoln Presidential Library, Springfield, Illinois

7 Chapter 5: Fragment on Sectionalism (July 23, 1856): Courtesy of the Scheide Library, Special Collections, Princeton University Library, Princeton, New Jersey

8–9 Chapter 5: Fragment on the Formation of the Republican Party (February 28, 1857): Courtesy of The Rosenbach, Philadelphia, Pennsylvania

10 Chapter 6: A Definition of Democracy (August 1, 1858?): Abraham Lincoln Presidential Library, Springfield, Illinois

11 Chapter 7: Fragment on Pro-Slavery Theology (October 1, 1858?): Abraham Lincoln Presidential Library, Springfield, Illinois

12 Chapter 8: Fragment on the Constitution and the Union (circa January 1, 1861): Abraham Lincoln Presidential Library, Springfield, Illinois

13–15 Chapter 9: Fragment of Speech Intended for Kentuckians (February 12, 1861?): Library of Congress, Prints and Photographs Division, Washington, D.C.

16 Chapter 10: A Meditation on the Divine Will (September 2, 1862?): Courtesy of John Hay Library, Brown University, Providence, Rhode Island

Index

Note: Page numbers in italics refer to photographs or their captions.

C

D

E

M

N

X

Y

Z

ABOUT THE AUTHOR

RONALD C. WHITE is the *New York Times* bestselling author of the presidential biographies *A. Lincoln* and *American Ulysses,* and the *New York Times* Notable Book *Lincoln's Greatest Speech*. White earned his PhD at Princeton and has taught at UCLA, Colorado College, Whitworth University, and Princeton Theological Seminary. He has lectured at the White House, been interviewed on the *PBS NewsHour,* and spoken about Lincoln in England, France, Germany, Italy, Mexico, and New Zealand. He is a Reader at the Huntington Library and a Senior Fellow of the Trinity Forum in Washington, D.C. He lives with his wife, Cynthia, in Pasadena, California.

ronaldcwhite.com

ABOUT THE TYPE

This book was set in Bembo, a typeface based on an old-style Roman face that was used for Cardinal Pietro Bembo's tract *De Aetna* in 1495. Bembo was cut by Francesco Griffo (1450–1518) in the early sixteenth century for Italian Renaissance printer and publisher Aldus Manutius (1449–1515). The Lanston Monotype Company of Philadelphia brought the well-proportioned letterforms of Bembo to the United States in the 1930s.